STONEHENGE DECIPHERED

Astonishing Secrets of the Iconic Henge

ALUN G REES

Three Pools Publishing
Written by Humans, for Humans!
North Adams, Massachusetts

Three Pools Publishing

PO Box 74

North Adams, Massachusetts

www.ThreePoolsPublishing.com

Copyright © Alun G. Rees May 2024

First printing. 2025.

Library of Congress Cataloguing-in-Publication Data

Rees, Alun G

Stonehenge Deciphered: Astonishing Secrets of the Iconic Henge / Alun G Rees.

Includes bibliographical references and index.

ISBN: 978-1-968683-17-7 (Paperback)

ISBN: 978-1-968683-01-6 (E-Book)

The cunning and the craft of early people
That built alike small dwelling and great hall,
The well-wrought legends lost among the ages,
The gods of old gone now beyond recall.

Camp a chelfyddyd y cenhedloedd cynnar,
Aneddau bychain a neaddau mawr,
Y chewelau cain a chwalwyd ers canrifoedd,
Y duwiau na wyr neb andanynt 'nawr.

Cofio – 'Remembrance'
by
Waldo Williams. The Bard of Preseli.

I offer this book to the memory of Waldo Williams, poet champion of the sacred landscape of Preseli, and to the living inspiration of my partner Stephanie.

Contents

PLAN OF STONEHENGE

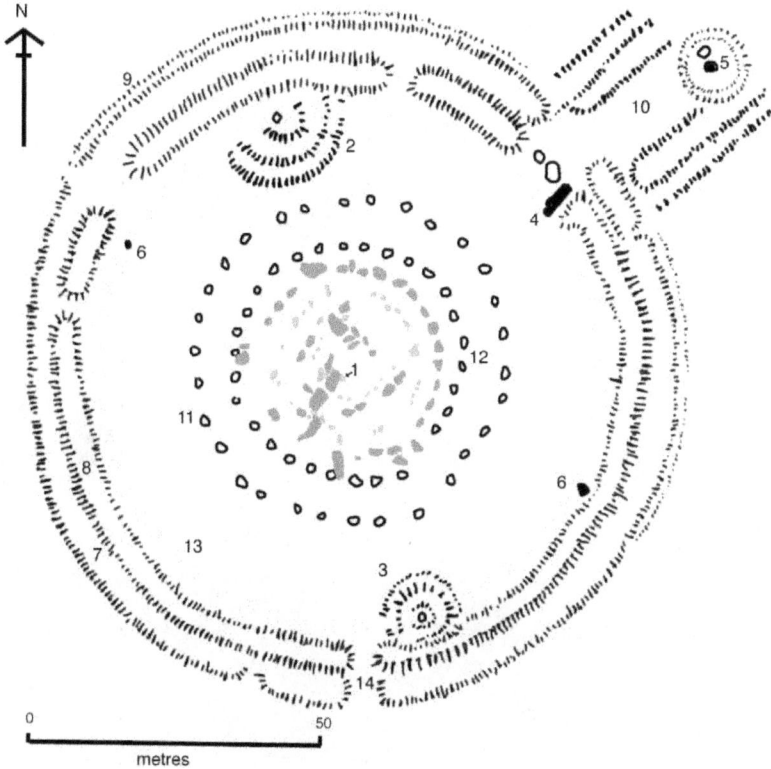

(After Cleal, Walker, & Montague, Stonehenge in its Landscape & Pitts, M, Hengeworld (London, Arrow 2001) published under a Creative Commons Share-Alike licence.)

A plan of Stonehenge today (excluding the Trilithon lintels for clarity) with the holes no longer containing stones shown as open circles, and existing stones shown grey for sarsens from the Marlborough Downs, and lighter grey for the smaller Bluestones from Preseli.

KEY TO PLAN:

1. The Altar Stone, a six-ton monolith of green micaceous sandstone from the Orcadian strata of Northern Scotland, at least five hundred miles from Stonehenge.

2. Barrow mound with a missing Station Stone

3. Two smaller mounds, also missing a single Station Stone.

4. The recumbent (fallen) 4.9 metre Slaughter Stone.

5. The outlier Heel Stone.

6. Two remaining Station Stones from the original four, which tracked the Solstice and the moon's Standstill phases.

7. Ditch

8. Inner bank

9. Outer bank

10. The main entrance to Stonehenge joining the Avenue with its parallel pair of ditches and banks leading 3 km to the River Avon, and the small Bluestone circle of 23 stones knowns as Bluehenge at West Amesbury.

11. A ring of 30 pits called the Y Holes.

12. A ring of 29 pits called the Z Holes. Both rings were dug in the final development of Stonehenge for a re-arrangement of the stones, but they were never used.

13. The ring of 56 empty sockets, called the Aubrey Holes where the first Bluestone circle of Stonehenge once stood.

14. The smaller southern entrance. Count seven, clockwise, from this entry and you locate Aubrey Hole VII, where a seminal excavation was made in 2008.

Introduction

The jackdaw calls used to echo like shots across Salisbury Plain. There was a squadron of starlings too, wheeling above the old Stonehenge visitor centre before parading for inspection, fearless along the fence-line, ready to glean any crumbs left over from tourist snacks. In the history of my life, I liked nothing better than to queue at the food kiosk in the old entrance to Stonehenge for a cup of tea and a warm pasty, consumed at a rickety aluminium table as I enjoyed a session of Stonehenge people watching. The daws have nested in the lintels of the megaliths for the best part of the monument's life, self-appointed custodians of the henge, and I often wondered how many generations of iridescent starlings had watched pilgrims come to pay homage at the stones.

People still come to Stonehenge to venerate our ancient ancestors, and I suppose they always will especially at the Solstice when devotees with a bewildering array of New Age beliefs, bound by fellowship, spirituality, and a love of the stones arrive to express gratitude as the year lengthens after winter's occlusion; joy when they bathe in the light of summer's longest day. It's a famously hypaethral temple Stonehenge, Siegfried Sassoon's 'roofless past,' a place open to the elements precisely so that the passage of the sun and moon can be observed from within the sanctuary of its megalithic rings.

Arguably the greatest centre of religion ever created in the long history of Britain, Stonehenge first cast its spell on me in the summers of 1985 and '86 when I was assigned by my newspaper to cover the running confrontation between the police and the so-called Hippy Convoy attempting to set-up camp at the henge. It was a game of cat and mouse to decide who would control Stonehenge during the Solstice when the 'hippies' wanted to hold another Free Festival amongst the stones. English Heritage, the government agency who manage historic monuments, got an injunction banning the take-over and an often-ugly struggle spanned those two years until Heritage got its way and ever since the sun has reached its zenith above a peaceful, more or less drug free, gathering of Neo-Druid and pagan worshipers.

Those two years of Solstice unrest allowed me to wander freely among the megaliths courtesy of a press pass, and for no particular reason I began to visit regularly in the weeks and months that followed, a habit that's continued over the decades since. Stonehenge had me hooked, and I looked forward to munching on a pasty and watching a tea bag struggle to give the milky brew some colour at the al fresco cafeteria. I loved the old, subterranean visitor centre with its hotchpotch of ugly concrete buildings and its intimate proximity to the megaliths, just a short stroll away through a tunnel under the road. There I would sit watching the turnstiles click, counting the stream of humanity that washes around the henge year in year out, a coach-carried tide, 'the tribes of Nike, Adidas and Reebok' as the playwright Alan Bennet has it.

I watched pregnant women waddle around the trilithons in a pre-natal pilgrimage, and newlyweds arrange themselves against the backdrop of the Stones for that special album photo. Once I saw a young man drop to his knee, offering an engagement ring skywards which, to his relief, his love eagerly accepted. Good for them. Another time, I was standing at the counter waiting for my usual tea and pasty, when I noticed a young couple in the queue, each from a different tour group, start to chat their eyes sparkling with obvious attraction. The young woman was American I'm sure, the man a Swede or maybe a Dane, probably students both of them, and I gazed, fascinated as they swapped numbers and promised to connect. I hope they did and if they ever recognise themselves in these words, perhaps they'd let me know how it all went.

A family group held my attention one day in the deathly grip of winter, as they covertly scattered some of a loved one's ashes just off the official path around the henge. I guess they were a widow and her three grown sons and, their reverences complete, they embraced in a sad huddle against the headstone-grey of the sky and the henge. Going by the rules perhaps they shouldn't have done it, but it touched me deeply to think that grieving men and women had performed similar rites with cremated remains in that same place five thousand years before. Nothing much new then, under the Stonehenge sky.

Inevitably, the old visitor centre was demolished in 2013, along with the intrusive A344 road, to be replaced by a new centre, a mile and a half away and out of sight. I dislike the new one, which has all the charm of a regional airport terminal, its ticket plaza open to the Plain's frequent, queue-drenching squalls. Worse still, the government plans to burrow a two-mile long tunnel under our World Heritage jewel to hide the A303 west country trunk road from sight except, of course, for the obligatory service road and life-preserving ventilation shafts on the surface above, rendering the old pedestrian subway an insignificant blight by comparison. Ah well, I still let the call of the daws take me back to a time when Stonehenge first exercised my curiosity.

The droves of visitors are unrelenting still, packed into air-conditioned coaches they roll along the Three-O-Three, driven by curiosity, bucket lists and the obligatory photo opportunity, turning Stonehenge into a modern Babel where a dozen languages can be heard at any given moment. For some it's simply a toilet stop but cynical tourists can't take the magic away and Stonehenge continues to create resonant memories, evoke powerful emotions, and magnify the soul. It's a place that opened my eyes to the wonders of prehistory and set me off on a journey through the pages of endless books and studies, and on the road to visit stone monuments from Wales to Cumbria, Scotland and the Cornish peninsula too. And I'm lucky enough to live near Marlborough in Wiltshire, a short drive from Stonehenge, and a bracing walk over the Ridgeway to wonderful Avebury with its outliers at Silbury Hill and the West Kennet Long Barrow.

Over the years, I've immersed myself in the prehistory of the island of Britain and the enigmas of Stonehenge and it wasn't long before I started filing stories on archaeology to my newspaper, mentored by my friend Mike Pitts, the UK's most successful archaeology writer. Along the way I was also present at one of the most important excavations ever undertaken at Stonehenge and helped a campaign to put precious golden artefacts from the orbit of the World Heritage Site on public display; appropriate I suppose as I was once UK Campaigning Journalist of the Year.

Time marched on and other books were written, some successful, others not so much, but I always had the ambition to draw the threads of the Stonehenge story together. And so, I've used my investigative skills and an ability to stand back and look at the wider picture unfettered by academic strictures, to reveal some of the henge's astonishing secrets, answer some of the big questions still debated over Stonehenge and offer some thrilling new ideas of my own.

Just how did the ancestors move the Bluestones, one hundred and fifty miles from the Preseli mountains of Wales to Salisbury Plain? Who were the people who pulled off such an astonishing logistic challenge? How did ancient astronomers use Stonehenge? The list is long and grows perennially but I've come up with credible answers, fresh insights, and new theories to answer the big Stonehenge questions.

I describe the secrets revealed in this book as 'astonishing' and three of them should indeed change the way we view Stonehenge forever. First, I pull together the strands of research from multiple universities to explain in unambiguous terms, just why the Bluestones of Preseli were considered indispensable for the Stonehenge project by our Neolithic ancestors; so special, so sacred, they were moved 150 miles from Pembrokeshire to Salisbury Plain.

I also highlight sensational, peer reviewed research into three golden artefacts from graves within the orbit of Stonehenge, which are inscribed with complex geometry making them the world's first, mathematical protractors, used to track the sun at the exact location of the monument and to precisely describe the measurement of every megalithic circle at Stonehenge.

And third, I record the electrifying links I've established between these three golden, artefacts, to the Nebra Sky Disc from Germany, the foundational astronomy of the first known civilisation of ancient Sumeria in the Fertile Crescent, and predictive astronomy used by NASA to this day.

I hope these revelations will change forever the popular perception of Stonehenge and confound the accepted wisdom the Neolithic and Early Bronze Age people of Britain had no writing and therefore couldn't leave a record of any geometry or mathematics they possessed. I also advance a convincing new theory from the leading authority on the waters of the Bristol Channel, proposing the Bluestones would have been conveyed by sea, not overland, to the River Avon at Bristol and inland to Stonehenge in a very short time span indeed, perhaps as little as nine or ten days depending on the weather.

A couple of momentous developments emerged at Stonehenge while I was researching and writing these pages. The first was the incredible geophysical survey data obtained by Prof. Vince Gaffney, revealing a vast new ritual landscape hidden beneath the turf of Salisbury Plain, not least the existence of a huge circle of giant pits seeming to swirl around the hub of Durrington Walls. More recently there's been the game-changing discovery of a Scottish provenance for the famous Altar Stone at the henge, involving as much as a six-hundred-mile, epic transportation of the six-tonne megalith. I'll give you my thoughts on both these discoveries as my story unfolds.

On these pages I'll describe some of the many dramas played out in the long story of Stonehenge with a list of characters ranging from the astronomer Edmond Halley, the architect Sir Christopher Wren and evolutionary scientist Charles Darwin to Bronze Age overlords and the Neolithic dynasty from Wales who gifted us Stonehenge in the first place. We'll meet our island's first architects, goldsmiths, shamans, and heroic navigators as the tale unfolds and there's a shocking prehistoric genocide, ritual executions and the Georgian melodrama of an unsung, lower-class hero who gave archaeology an icon recognised around the world. The heroes of modern archaeology and the 18th Century Antiquarians, who pioneered the science, populate these pages too, together with the high-tech advances in genomics and landscape telemetry transforming the science of the past.

Indeed, most of the material I've drawn on was already out there, buried in scholarly papers and academic publications, insulated from a mainstream audience, but wherever I've leant on the knowledge or published works of others I say so in the text and acknowledge it in the bibliography. When I interpret the facts, speculate or propose theories of my own I make that clear, and where I struggle with my own partialities and bias I admit that too, but essentially nothing here is invented, delusional, hippy hogwash or sci-fi fantasy.

Throughout this book, I attempt to conjure scenes from our deep past by putting a human face on the framework of archaeological evidence. I realise it's difficult to view such distant events through the prism of modern values, belief systems and responses, however I've tried my best to look at events through the ever-revealing lens of human nature.

For time beyond countenance Stonehenge has been the stone-cold nursery of legends. No question it's an iconic place, a symbol and an enigma, that too, but it's also a portal between the hard facts of prehistory and our dreams of a prelapsarian era; a beguiling utopian mystery. The reality for those ancient people may have been very different, doubtless harder and probably more prosaic, but the dreams and imaginations we've embroidered around the place bind Stonehenge tightly into the fabric of our Island's soul; a megalithic milestone, pointing back down a road we've already travelled, and onwards to a journey without end in sight.

I invite you to join me on this adventure, exploring quarries hewn into gorse clad mountains, along ancient ridgeways to smithies where stunning gold regalia were created, and onto the foaming seas off wild Wales. There's a popular phrase in archaeology these days, which speaks of the 'Unrecoverable Past,' that which has been lost through the many agencies of historical erosion. I'm not sure who coined the phrase but it's a good one and here, on these pages, I've endeavoured to show at least some of that lost past is indeed recoverable.

THE LIE OF THE LAND

Roll-up the tarmac ribbon of the Three-O-Three highway through Wiltshire, sweep aside modern housing developments and erase the military architecture of Salisbury Plain, then picture wide sweeps of chalk grassland fringed by woods of ash, alder, hazel and beech. Gin clear, chalk streams make detours to find a course around the chalk bulwark of the Plain, as we find ourselves in the pristine landscape where a hunter-gatherer clan first settled close to the place we know as Stonehenge.

Then, around 3000 BC Neolithic farmers arrived from the continent to displace the Mesolithic foragers, bringing with them technologically superior stone tools, smallholder farming skills and a passion for standing stones. It wasn't too long, perhaps five or six hundred years, before yet another wave of continental migrants arrived, following roughly the same trans-continental routes, but this time they brought metal and the Bronze Age with them possessed, as they were, of more sophisticated agricultural skills and the alchemical power of the forge. The metal-workers embraced the standing stone culture they found here, symbolised by Stonehenge, and embarked on their own feverish development of the monument. So, over a span of seven millennia beginning with that band of Mesolithic foragers around 8000BC, three very different cultures left their mark on this ritual canvas, imposing their particular legacy of sacred constructs on the human geography of Stonehenge. It's a complex picture and I've chosen to view it in three distinct dimensions.

First, we have the immediate space of the Stonehenge hinterland, largely delineated by the boundary of the World Heritage Site, including features like The Cursus, the ceremonial Causeway, Woodhenge, the Durrington Walls henge and village settlement, and the important grave at Bush Barrow. In total this immediate, Stonehenge orbit incorporates seven ceremonial monuments, eleven long barrow burials, four hundred and seventy-four round barrows, six hill forts and enclosures, and twenty-two kilometres of earthworks as well as the 'cradle' Mesolithic settlement at Blick Mead. Neither should we forget the World Heritage Site embraces part of the town of Amesbury, a slice of the military base at Larkhill, as well as the villages of West Amesbury, Normanton and the hamlet of Lake in the Woodford Valley.

Zooming out from the immediate topography of Stonehenge we have a wider view, illustrating the relationship between the henge and more distant places. Fifteen miles away is West Woods on the Marlborough Downs, where the huge sarsen stones used to build the Trilithons were sourced. Much further afield, there's the uniquely nascent relationship with the Preseli Mountains (Mynydd Preseli) one hundred and fifty miles away in Wales. The quarries that supplied the original Bluestones are located here at Carn Menyn, Carn Goedog and Craig-Rhos-y-Felin, as well as a doppelganger stone circle at Waun Mawn, thought to be a prototype for Stonehenge itself. Nearby are two contenders for an embarkation port should the Bluestones have been transported by sea, one at Milford Haven, the other further north, around the coast at Newport, Pembrokeshire. Further still, perhaps as far six hundred miles away, the famous Altar Stone was sourced north-east of the Great Glen in Scotland then carried south a very long way.

However, there are a couple of potentially confusing issues I need to clarify, beginning with the names of rivers as there are two called Avon directly related to the Stonehenge story (there are three others elsewhere in Britain.) It's a mix-up thought to have come about when Roman centurions stuck standard-issue gladius swords into the ribs of Celtic tribesmen, pointed at a river and asked what it was called. Thinking the Romans were too thick to know the word for river, the Celts replied 'afon', which is indeed the Welsh word, and the name stuck.

In the Stonehenge context, we have the Bristol Avon which rises in the Cotswolds and runs for nineteen miles through Bath, eventually reaching the sea four miles downstream from Bristol at Avonmouth. The other is the Wiltshire Avon, a longer river, which rises near Devizes in the Vale of Pewsey then runs south passing Durrington Walls and glides past Blick Mead at Amesbury, very close to Stonehenge. On through Salisbury, it's joined by the Wylye, Nadder, Bourne and Ebble, before flowing through the western edge of the New Forest in Hampshire to enter the English Channel near Christchurch, Dorset. Many, speculative accounts of the Bluestone journey include the Wiltshire Avon because the formalised, ceremonial causeway leading up to Stonehenge begins on its banks at West Amesbury.

Distances can be confusing in relation to Stonehenge and Pembrokeshire, relying on a small flurry of calculations depending on whether you want the 'crow flies' number, which is 134 miles, or the mileage relating to the various routes overland or by sea. The overland distance from Wales swings between 150 and 200 miles, depending on the itinerary. The so-called A40 Route for the Bluestones, advocated by many archaeologists, is around 220 miles and a seaward passage for the Stones might vary from 140 to nearly 240 miles depending again on the passage taken. I've decided to refer generally to a distance of 150 miles, unless specifying a particular theory about the transport of the Bluestones.

That's the obvious geography dealt with but there's another dimension to the immediate Stonehenge topography, one which has also been carefully mapped and deserves some explanation because it's invisible to our eyes, hidden under a cloak of soil draped over the 2,600 hectares of the Stonehenge World Heritage Site. Invisible to us maybe, but not to the latest technology and we have to turn to no less a scientific eminence than Charles Darwin, who was the first to explain the reason for the apparent sinking envelopment of our prehistory. Darwin's first major success wasn't his world-changing work on evolution, but a book dedicated to the doings of the humble earthworm with the indigestible title: *The Formation of Vegetable Mould Through the Action of Worms, With Observations on Their Habits.*

Published in 1881 it was the first insight into the importance of worms for the health of the soil and it had a huge impact on modern agriculture that echoes to this day and, even though it was later massively eclipsed by his famous '*On the Origin of Species*,' the earthworm textbook sold many more copies during the great man's lifetime. While he was pondering the relentless work rate of the humble earthworm, it occurred to the ever-inquisitive Darwin the churn of soil caused by their activity might explain why archaeological remains appear to vanish into the ground. He took a train to Salisbury with his wife Emma and their son Horace, and then a carriage to Stonehenge, where else, to put his theory to the test. Darwin dug around the two halves of a stone which had split on the outer edge of the monument and found both had nearly been enveloped by soil over time.

In line with the popular thinking of his day Darwin refers to them as 'Druidical stones,"' and after conducting his measurements, which young Horace helped 'protract on paper,' the great man concluded the action of millions of earthworms depositing their soil casts on the surface over millennia had been responsible for burying the stones. The stones hadn't sunk at all, they'd been buried in a vanishing trick performed by nature's relentlessly industrious magicians.

Darwin was on the money, and it's now generally accepted that in an average European soil setting, earthworms will deposit two inches of tillage over a site in ten years; two hundred inches in a thousand. An impressive burial party indeed and the action of earthworms, together with the effects of burrowing animals like badgers and rabbits, has implications for the dating of excavations, which archaeologists are fully aware of and factor into their work. Put simply, while earthworms are busy burying antiquities creatures like rabbits are upsetting the layers in the historical cake by burrowing into it, haphazardly flinging bits of flint, pottery and other dating material, back to the surface as they create their habitats leaving a jigsaw for archaeologists to puzzle over.

It's important then to realise, while we're able to observe the three-dimensional heritage of Stonehenge above the surface there's a fourth dimension buried below with inferences for our understanding of the geography of the area. For the best part of a couple of hundred years this world beneath the turf was the sole domain of the trowel wielding zealots, known as field archaeologists and needs must, it involved a lot of informed guesswork.

Then along came the all-seeing eye of a technology that goes under the general heading of 'geophysics,' allowing scientists over the past thirty years or so, to peer deep beneath the turf and discern all sorts of ancient human constructions. Suddenly, the remains of ditches, banks, walls, pits, and building foundations are revealed. The techniques available include GPR (Ground Penetrating Radar), OSL (Optically Stimulated Luminescence) and Lidar (Light Detection and Ranging) and I have no intention of attempting to explain how they work, except to say they involve pulses, beams, lasers, lots of digital technology and they're precisely mapped on the ground by GPS kit, not unlike the satnav on your phone.

The acknowledged, archaeological maestro of this high-tech dowsing is Prof. Vince Gaffney of Bradford University, who's undoubtedly done more than anyone over the past three decades to extend our knowledge of Britain's prehistoric geography, notably with his mapping of the underwater landscape of Doggerland, a vast, inundated Mesolithic landscape now under the waves of the North Sea. In 2020 Prof. Gaffney set out to investigate some buried anomalies close to Durrington Walls with his Stonehenge Hidden Landscape Project and caused a seismic shock when he produced a subterranean map of Greater Stonehenge, providing us with a thrilling new vision of a religious landscape, spreading across a vast area, packed with features, which haven't been seen by the human eye for over four thousand years.

Using the latest OSL technology his team revealed a geophysical world covering four square miles around the monument, including no fewer than seventeen, previously unknown, major ritual sites. Most notably they discovered a huge ring of pits over a mile in diameter, encircling the encampment and henge at Durrington Walls, just a couple of miles from Stonehenge itself. Taken as a whole these 4500-year-old indentations, which have been dubbed the Henge Pits, measuring some ten metres across and five deep, are the largest prehistoric structure in Britain, and may yet reveal some astronomical alignment.

Science is still feverishly assessing these discoveries, but they've provided us with another dimension to the geography of Stonehenge, which may be no easier for the man or woman in the street to decipher than Harry Beck's famous map of the London Underground, but still clear enough to describe a Stonehenge bustling with life, the great epicentre of religion in the Britain of its day, gifting us with a fascinating geography indeed.

MAJOR FEATURES ON THE STONEHENGE LANDSCAPE

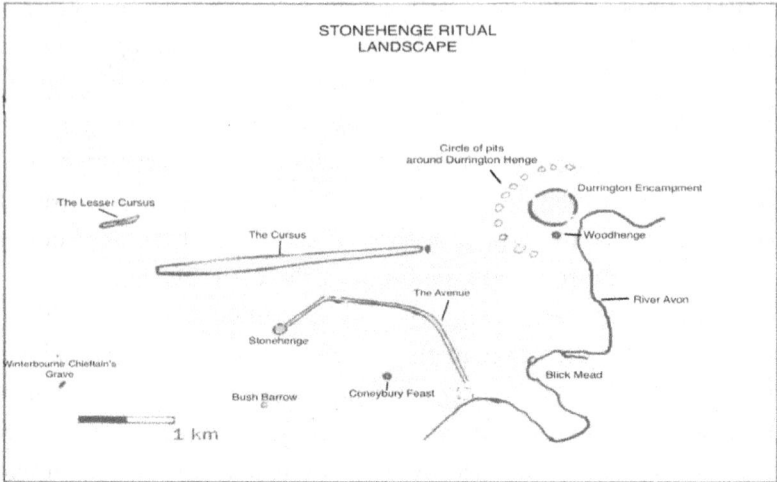

STONEHENGE RITUAL
LANDSCAPE

Circle of pits
around Durrington Henge

Durrington Encampment

The Lesser Cursus

The Cursus

Woodhenge

The Avenue

River Avon

Stonehenge

Winterbourne Chieftain's
Grave

Blick Mead

Bush Barrow

Coneybury Feast

1 km

Source: After Brigantes Nation

I've marked the sites and constructions I think are important in the immediate orbit of Stonehenge myself so forgive my crude cartographical skills. Only two burials are marked, those of the Winterbourne Chieftain and the Bush Barrow Giant, however the whole area is broadcast with round barrow burials, scattered across the landscape like frisbees abandoned in a park.

2

TALON MARKS
OF THE GODS

Ten thousand years ago a hunter-gatherer, whether man or woman
it matters not, washed the dust off a freshly knapped flint in a
pool the clan was camped beside. The translucent flint was left to dry
but when retrieved it had undergone an astonishing metamorphosis, and
was stained a vivid, luminescent pink. The details of this discovery are
obviously lost in the long ago, but the place is real enough, it's called
Blick Mead and it's less than a mile from Stonehenge.

Today Blick Mead stands in the grounds of an old Tudor abbey, close
to the River Avon but constantly assaulted by the roar of traffic on the
Three-O-Three, which whips by just ten meters away. Once the only
sound was the gurgle of the spring spouting from the chalk at a constant
11 degrees, to feed the languid pool, not hot but still a warm halo of
breath on the landscape. And that otherworldly magenta-pink stain in its
waters? It comes from the pigmentation of the rare algae *Hilldenbrandia
rivularis*, which thrives in the shallows of the spring.

I've no doubt the pink genie swimming in Blick Mead gave it a supernatural status among those Mesolithic people, marking it out as a place
of liminal magic inhabited by the spirits and water nymphs of the time;
whatever the names they gave them. But the clan would go on to
discover an even more auspicious sign nearby, an augury etched into the
chalk, and this second chance determination does indeed gift us the
foundation story of Stonehenge.

That's a thrilling legacy in itself, but the lineage of that hunter-gather group also gives us a heart-rending window into one of the most seismic events of British prehistory, which I'll describe soon. I may be giving Blick Mead a big billing, but I promise it lives up to the hype although it might be helpful to first paint a picture, as best I can, of the way Mesolithic hunter gatherers ordered their lives in the pristine, post-glacial landscape of our island around 8000 BC.

Those ancient people lived an eco-sympathetic lifestyle, which leant heavily on three topographies, the first being sheltered coastal locations, then river valleys and third sites close to springs. Coastal sanctuary encampments, with their relatively warmer weather and abundance of food resources, seem to have been their fall-back settlements providing a safe haven during winter and when times became tough. In southern Britain the Mesolithic camp on the small island at Goldcliff, not far from the Welsh side of the Second Severn Crossing, is a brilliant example of such a place. Studied for three decades by Prof. Martin Bell of Reading University, Goldcliff comes complete with the evocative footprint sets of a hunter gatherer group, preserved in the mud; adults leading, toddlers following behind. More recently the professor has found an ancient fish trap, woven from willow whips, within sight of Goldcliff island, not dissimilar to the traditional basket-shaped 'putcher' traps used to catch salmon on that very spot until about twenty years ago.

Plenty of good food on the coast then, with fish and a wide menu including edible seaweeds, sea herbs like samphire, shellfish, and the occasional big mammal such as a seal. My own favourite protein-packed tidal delicacies include mussels, cockles, and winkles, all of which would have been available to hunter-gatherers. Limpets, held fast on rocks in their own roundhouse villages were abundant and the ancients cooked them in the shell on flat griddle-stones set into fires. I've tried baked limpets, and they've got the usual shellfish 'taste of the sea' thing going on, however Special Forces mates tell me limpets are a nourishing survival food and, when eaten raw, an acceptable Mesolithic-style chewing gum; just be sure to pull the black sack off the flesh first they say. So far I've resisted the temptation.

Rivers were important too, as they offered bands a reasonably safe route to make hunting and foraging incursions into the interior, while avoiding the dangers of the forest. They could move quickly upstream and down on dugout canoes, choosing the best sites to camp whilst afforded reasonably good three-sixty views for security. Like coastal areas, river valleys have a food bounty waiting to be harvested. Hazel groves on the banks and peppery cress in the flow of the stream, fish and wildfowl were plentiful and beaver too which, I'm told, have a tasty, red meat. It's important to realise in Mesolithic times rivers were a different beast, generally wider and deeper and during his ambitious Stonehenge Riverside Project, Prof. Mike Parker-Pearson estimated the Wiltshire Avon at Amesbury was sixty meters wide back in the day, compared to the relatively dribbling ten metres of the stream today.

Piecing the detail together it seems Mesolithic hunting bands would have stuck, more or less, to one familiar river system retreating back to their coastal shoreline bases seasonally. Perhaps the two Avons featuring in the Stonehenge saga, the Bristol Avon running into the Severn Estuary and the Wiltshire Avon running close to the henge then on to the English Channel, would have supported different clans of foragers. The two rivers have a shared watershed at the western end of the Vale of Pewsey where clans may have met for marriage arrangements, barter, territorial affirmation and religious rites. The Native tribes of eastern North America were using river systems in just this way to travel through the huge blanket of forest of the region when European farmers first arrived in the 16th Century.

Springs have also exerted a particular pull throughout the history of mankind often related to the liminal nature of such places, considered to be intrinsically sacred, and there's every reason to believe the luminescent pink, staining power of Blick Mead would have magnified that belief. Importantly, springs were also a draw for animals like deer, wild boar and aurochsen and there's certainly evidence they were used in the Mesolithic to ambush quarry.

Along the course of the Bristol Avon, we have evidence of Mesolithic activity at a spring beneath the White Horse at Cherhill, about two miles from the large Mesolithic encampment at Windmill Hill. Following its tributary river, the Marden, from Cherhill we come to the Avon and eventually the famous hot springs at Bath and ten miles downstream Hotwells in the Avon Gorge, both with evidence of Mesolithic activity. In the valley of the Wiltshire Avon, so entwined with the Stonehenge story, we have the Blick Mead spring itself, and another Mesolithic encampment at a small spring in West Amesbury. There's more hunter-gatherer activity downstream at Downton, Lower Burgate and Bickton, although the last two sites are not directly related to springs. Finally, the Wiltshire Avon reaches the sea near Christchurch where the extensive Mesolithic encampment at Hengistbury Head probably represents the Blick Mead clan's safe place on the channel shore.

It seems hunter gatherers first came across Blick Mead in their pursuit of auroch, the giant, wild cattle of the post-Ice Age landscape. Aurochsen were up to three times the size of modern cattle, but not genetically related, sporting a huge span of deadly, lyre-shaped horns and were frequently red in colour; bulls with a white stripe down the length of their back, and fierce beasts by all accounts. Sadly, they were hunted to extinction, with the last recorded kill made in 17th Century Bulgaria but back in Mesolithic Britain they were plentiful on Salisbury Plain. A team led by Prof. David Jacques, found their hoofprints close to the springhead at Blick Mead, where they came to drink and perhaps seek winter shelter in the relative warmth of the spring, which has hollowed a cup into the chalk out of the prevailing wind.

The clan would have quickly identified Blick Mead as a place favoured by aurochsen, representing an abundance of meat on the hoof, with one beast capable of feeding two hundred people at a sitting, although bringing one down would only have followed a carefully calculated risk and reward balance. Too big to conveniently carry off, they'd have been butchered on the spot, some roast for a hunt feast, much of the rest wind dried for pemmican, once again similar to Native American practices. Ultimately, home is where the auroch carcass is processed, and they would have stayed at Blick Mead until the last sinew had been taken to make string. I suspect it would have been a camp in chime with the movements of the aurochsen, probably a winter place when the beasts moved off the Plain as the grazing became thin in autumn.

David Jacques' dogged detective work at Blick Mead reveals an encampment with remarkable dating evidence, showing it was used by hunter gatherers for four thousand years, from 8000 BC until around 4000 BC. His excavations at the site have revealed a great deal of human activity over a long span of time with nearly 100,000 discarded flint implements, used for butchering the large number of aurochsen eaten there, evidenced by their discarded bones. The team also found the tooth of a domesticated dog and scientists were able to say it fed well on its share of the quarry from the cooking fires of its human, hunting companions. Analysis of pollen samples show the site was set in an open meadow with light-loving plants surrounded by forest, in other words the perfect place to ambush an auroch, if you had the courage.

There's some debate over whether these finds are evidence of large, tribal gatherings for feasts, or smaller gatherings demonstrating continued use over many, many generations, or elements of both. It's an important differentiation but at the end of the day we can be reasonably sure the role of Blick Mead is pivotal in the story of Stonehenge and, indeed, the sweeping saga of human settlement on the island of Britain. Prof. Jacques' discoveries make a compelling case that Blick Mead was indeed the 'Cradle of Stonehenge,' and, it was the professor's own mother, volunteering at the dig in 2015, who discovered the first pink-stained flint in the excavation. Serendipitous indeed.

The story doesn't end there because those foraging people made a second discovery that led to the foundation of Stonehenge itself, and that seems to have happened soon after the clan familiarised itself with the Salisbury Plain landscape surrounding the spring. What they found was a powerful sign from the gods on the ground at the site of Stone-henge, just a fifteen-minute walk from their Blick Mead sanctuary. There, in plain sight, were sets of parallel glacial striations, grooves left in the surface of the chalk by the melting water of a retreating glacier forming corrugations about thirty metres wide, running one hundred and fifty meters west from the position of the Heel Stone. These V-shaped furrows cross the slope diagonally and fate decreed these periglacial stripes, as geologists call them, are precisely aligned with the setting sun of the Winter Solstice.

The Mesolithic foragers happened across these furrows, observed their Solstice alignment, and marked the place on the horizon with three huge, forty feet high, totem poles a few metres west of the glacial imprints, raising fresh, replacement timbers over hundreds of years. The last of the totems was dated to 7650 BC and their location eloquently marks them as signposts on the landscape, and probably the scene of

Solstice ceremonies to mark a time of year when little played on the Mesolithic mind so much as the need to see the days of winter lengthen again into the season of plenty. There's nothing else like those totems in the British Mesolithic and nearly five thousand years later the periglacial stripes would be incorporated into the ceremonial Avenue leading into the heart of Neolithic Stonehenge.

Over time soil filled the grooves, and turf grew over what we know today to be a geological coincidence, but when those Mesolithic people first encountered them the furrows were as clear as day in the bright, white chalk of Salisbury Plain. Imagine how the clan must have felt when they saw the last rays of the Solstice sun gleaming down those rake lines in the chalk. Surely, they must have believed these were a profound sign left on the ground to help them track the solar passage, surely they must have thought they'd found the Talon Marks of the Gods.

IF THE STORY OF THE BLICK MEAD PEOPLE WERE INDEED TO END HERE, it would still be one of the most thrilling in the epic history of Stonehenge, but it doesn't, and the sequel was played out when Neolithic farmers crossed from the continent to colonise Britain and began to impose an agricultural imprint on the landscape.

There's long been speculation about the fate of the hunter-gatherers who lived their arcadian lifestyle along the coasts and river valleys of these islands for nearly five thousand years until the advent of farming. Were they assimilated into the new farming culture? Did new diseases brought over by the Neolithic farmers decimate them or were they violently purged? Academics have labelled it the Neolithisation Debate, and for a long time it was characterised by a great deal of informed guesswork by some very knowledgeable people. However, the past decade has seen enormous advances in genome science, which have provided partial answers to some questions long buried in the landscape, revealing a dark passage of time, which would fundamentally transform the human fabric of Britain.

Genomic mapping here, and on the continent, tells us Neolithic farmers didn't interbreed with the Mesolithic hunter gatherers as they moved relentlessly west with their cereal crops and domesticated live-stock. In fact, hunter-gatherer gene markers largely vanished from the sequencing record following the arrival of the Neolithic colonisers in their westward advance.

It's important to realise the migrations and innovations of those times came to Britain's shores about a thousand years after they'd already played out on the other side of the channel, simply because of our island's isolated geography, off the northwestern edge of the continent. But arrive they did and a 2023 study by University College London and the Natural History Museum smelt a rat when they identified hunter gatherer genes vanished more rapidly here than on the continent, remarking: *"In contrast to other European regions, the transition to farming in Britain occurred with little introgression (interbreeding) from resident foragers, during initial colonization, or throughout the Neolithic."*

This could be put down to a smaller population of Mesolithic foraging bands on these islands or perhaps the new farmers didn't need any Mesolithic input because their farming practices and lifestyle had already been perfected before they crossed the English Channel. But that doesn't explain what actually happened to the Mesolithic Britons, while a 2024 study by Lund University in Sweden does. It describes nothing less than a prehistoric genocide around 5,900 years ago when Danish hunter-gatherers were simply eradicated within three or four generations, an event only explained by the slaughter of a probably naive and relatively tiny population of foragers.

The same thing obviously happened here in Britain and perhaps there are some parallels in the fate of Native American hunter-gatherers when the East Coast was first invaded by European farmers, with some limited intermarriage, a lot of death from introduced disease, and a lot of murder too with some Native clans fleeing to the margins to cling onto their way of life in remote habitats.

During the Neolithization of Britain, DNA evidence suggests the incomers subjected hunter-gatherers to the 'Danish Solution,' killing their Mesolithic forerunners wherever they found them and driving others into margins like the reed beds of the Somerset Levels. Disturbing stuff you may think, and you've probably worked out already that like the rest of the Mesolithic population, the Blick Mead clan eventually came to a bad end. They did, but their end gives us a remarkable and utterly unique insight into the dramas that unfolded when farmers met foragers. Across the plains of time, we can glimpse the ghosts from two cultures present at a banquet held six thousand years ago, just five minutes' walk away from Blick Mead where the fate of the clan was sealed.

That feast took place at a natural hollow in the Stonehenge chalkland known as the Coneybury Anomaly, and according to the Historic England Record the excavated pit contained *'a considerable assemblage of early Neolithic pottery representing a minimum of 41 vessels, plus flints...also a large assemblage of animal bones representing a minimum of 10 cattle, plus several roe deer, two red deer and a pig, A radiocarbon date of 3980 – 3708BC was obtained.'*

A hell of a banquet, representing the barbecuing of a large quantity and wide variety of animals on the menu, with other studies estimating fourteen roe deer were on the bill of fare, as well as a trout and a single beaver, probably from the Wiltshire Avon, just over the lip of the hill below Blick Mead. That date, around 3800 BC, puts us right at the start of the so-called Neolithisation of Britain but the thing that's raised archaeological eyebrows is the sheer diversity of the meat on offer, clearly delineated between domesticated animals and creatures hunted in the wild. Knapped flints found at Coneybury were also divided between Neolithic and Mesolithic styles, leading to the inevitable conclusion this was a meeting between two cultures: the farmers and the foragers.

The balance of the food offerings also suggests an effort to be equitable as a single deer provides far less meat than a cow, so that sixteen deer and a couple of baskets of fish, with a beaver thrown in the mix, would more or less match the meat from ten cattle. The single beaver is enigmatic because there's a long belief in traditional medicine that beaver have healing qualities and, interestingly, the castoreum gland found at the base of beaver's tail contains salicylic acid, the active ingredient of aspirin, found naturally in the willow bark that's a big part of their diet. Was the Coneybury Beaver a special, healing gift presented by the hunter-gatherer guests? We'll never know but having said that beaver offer decent eating as well a hangover cure.

In any event the evidence is clear, the Coneybury Feast was an extraordinary and important convocation of the two, distinct cultural groups as the picture painted by the 2018 study of this Stone Age Summit Meeting suggests: *"What took place at Coneybury, and who was involved? We argue on the basis of multiple lines of evidence that Coneybury represents the material remains of a gathering organised by a regional community, with participants coming from different areas. One group of attendees provided deer...we conclude the most likely scenario is that group comprised local hunter-gatherers who survived alongside local farmers."*

What then were they talking about at this elaborate barbecue, these two quite distinct groups? I'm going to hazard a guess and list some possibilities, emphasising we can never hope to know the reality of it. Were they, for instance, exploring the possibility of cooperating? Might they have chatted about marking out areas where farming would take place, and those where hunting would be allowed? Certainly, hunting across areas where domestic sheep and cattle graze would be disruptive. Did they explore the possibility of the hunter gatherer clans providing seasonal help at harvest time? Or were the farmers suffering herd predation by wolves and bears, a problem which they could sub-contract to skilled hunters? And wouldn't it be nice to think the banquet was actually held to celebrate a marriage between high status families from both communities, but sadly the DNA evidence would rule out such an alliance as a forlorn hope.

I confess, when I first learnt about the Coneybury Feast and the process of Neolithisation, my thoughts turned immediately to treachery. History is littered with examples of foul calumny at feasts, from the Romans, through to the poisoning Medicis of medieval Florence and so on. In Britain we have the infamous treachery at Glencoe in the Highlands when the Campbells broke bread with the McDonalds before slaying them as they digested their meal. And significantly, the oral history and legend of Stonehenge itself gives us the infamous Treason of the Long Knives, (Brad-y-Cyllyll in Welsh) which tells of the massacre of British chieftains by Saxon warriors at a feast held to organise a peace treaty in the 5th Century, soon after the Romans abandoned Britain. According to Geoffrey of Monmouth, in his Historia Regum Britanniae, the Saxons hid knives concealed in their shoes and fell upon the Celtic chiefs during a banquet held close to Stonehenge.

Certainly, there's no direct evidence of a massacre at the Coneybury Feast, no human bones at all in fact, and it's notoriously difficult to prove murder without a body. But I can't help feeling the farming folk had a hidden agenda and the feast was a good opportunity to pick the brains of the hunter-gatherers for their undoubted knowledge of the entire land-scape. My gut feeling is the Neolithic farmers were on a scoping exercise, smiling and chatting over roast venison as they downloaded the Mesolithic data base.

I'm going to speculate further and suggest the farming folk might have learnt of the significance of the special place an arrow shot from Coneybury, which had been puzzling them. It's where a glacier had scarred the chalk with lines that point to the Solstice sun. So then, was the Solstice secret first revealed at Coneybury, and the seed of Neolithic Stonehenge first planted at the feast?

Quite a thought and one I find credible. We'll never know the definitive answer of course, but 21st Century DNA science tells us no good came of it all. The Blick Mead folk may not have been murdered at the Coneybury Feast, but the broad-brush evidence of genome mapping tells us it couldn't have been too long afterwards that the Mesolithic heritage of Britain was abruptly shattered with only seven to nine per cent of their lineage present in our modern DNA. There's little doubt then, the hunter gatherer people who found the Talon Marks of the Gods were clawed down by the farmers and the first chapter of the Stonehenge saga was written in blood.

3
THE ADVANCE PARTY

The Blick Mead clan had long since gone when a toddler made the hazardous journey from Wales to Salisbury Plain, the first of a series he made back and forth, until he died in his thirties somewhere close to Stonehenge. His skeleton was found buried in a high-status long barrow on the Plain and the story of this man, who died between 3630 and 3660 BC, gifts us an extraordinary insight into the dynamics of Neolithic life and a great deal of prehistoric food for thought. Why did he make so many long hazardous journeys, and who were this man's evidently powerful family and clan connections?

I call him the Winterbourne Chieftain and when his time came he was buried with great reverence in the Winterbourne Stoke Longbarrow at a spot slap-bang on a junction where traffic bound for the Stonehenge Visitor Centre syphons off the west bound Three-O-Three highway. Today, the chieftain can be found a mile away from his original grave, suspended in a cabinet as one of the prize exhibits at the Visitor Centre Museum, although a few pagan types are not happy with the indignity of the Chieftain just hanging there. They may have a point, although I think it's a replica skeleton and, like it or not, what we know of his illuminating life story does make the Winterbourne Chieftain one of the stars of the Stonehenge firmament.

Historic England, the government agency, records the Chieftain's grave as: *'A long barrow at the end of the Winterbourne Stoke Crossroads, orientated north-east to south-west. Excavated in 1863 by John Thurnam who found a primary, flexed male skeleton with a bludgeon like flint implement, eight inches long, and six secondary burials, one man, one woman and four children, with a plain urn shaped food vessel, two feet from the top of the mound.'*

At first sight the presence of other burials in the mound might suggest a family 'vault' but the other internments took place a lot later, perhaps as long as a thousand years in the Early Bronze Age and can be put down to the obvious attraction of laying loved ones to rest in such a commanding position. However, there's no doubt our Chieftain was an important person, having owned single occupancy of a very large grave indeed, which was originally a turf burial before the massive chalk barrow we see today was piled above; a bit like adding an imposing head-stone to a new grave.

When 21st Century archaeo-osteologists looked at the Chieftain's skeleton, the nitrogen isotope levels in his teeth revealed most of his protein intake came from animals, deer, sheep, pigs etc, which is not unusual as Neolithic people seemed to have a cultural aversion to eating fish. Further examination found the Chieftain to be taller than the Neolithic average at just under five-feet-eight inches, and bone analysis suggests he would have been wiry of frame; probably weighing around twelve stone. There was no skeletal evidence of serious disease, and the Chieftain seems to have led a fairly trouble-free life with leg and back problems caused by torn ligaments, which would have sorted themselves out in weeks rather than years. It looks as though he passed away in his thirties or forties, which wasn't so young for the time, and though his cause of death is unknown it's reasonably certain it wasn't a traumatic or violent death.

However, to gauge the true significance of the Winterbourne Chieftain we need to ask what was going on at Stonehenge in the days of his life, and what does science have to tell us about his life's journey. The answers are truly revelatory because the Chieftain was active around Salisbury Plain at a time when the first great construction works were being undertaken in the Stonehenge landscape. In particular the ceremonial promenade of the Cursus was being etched onto the landscape by teams of Neolithic builders using only deer-antler pickaxes to dig out a ditch and bank, two miles long and over a hundred metres wide, and right inside the timeframe of the Chieftain's life. The Antiquarian William Stukeley, named this strange feature The Cursus, mistaking it for one of the elongated arenas the Romans used for horse and chariot racing. Forget the Roman name and the wildly off-target dating, and we have the first major, monument to be constructed on the Stonehenge landscape, about five hundred years before a stone circle was erected at the monument around 3000 BC.

What then does the Cursus represent? Well, for a start, it's not unique in the British Neolithic and although they are mysterious structures there's some evidence their primary function was for funeral rites. Others believe they are ceremonial walkways, parade grounds if you like, expressing the routes where cattle had been herded. Does this imply our Neolithic forebears were a cattle-honouring culture where possession of herds marked out status, and perhaps, just perhaps, these Cursi were laid out at places where cattle were 'shown off' at some forerunner of our modern agricultural shows. An attractive idea but who knows?

We do know a Cursus certainly represents a lot of hard work by significant numbers of the community, and my thoughts are that like most great Neolithic projects, it would have been a largely seasonal endeavour. These were agricultural folk, and even my friends on the tractor driven farms of today consider taking time-off from agriculture a serious decision. In winter bad weather and the need to provide extra forage makes the husbandry of livestock necessarily more intense, and anyway the weather's no good for digging. Late summer would be a bad time too because of the imperative of gathering the harvest, which leads me to suspect work on sacred constructs like the Cursus, and later Stonehenge itself, would have been a springtime and early summer activity.

The result of all that back-breaking work, only shows today as a relatively faint, turf-covered imprint on the landscape, more clearly visible from the air but then only as the weal of a scar that would have been a brilliant, chalk-white promenade across the Plain when freshly dug. That aerial view reveals the Cursus as a pair of almost parallel banks, with outer ditches, varying from a hundred to a hundred and fifty metres apart in a roughly east-west orientation about five hundred metres north of where Stonehenge would eventually be erected. In fact, it was in 2008 that Prof. Julian Thomas's team from Manchester University gave us an accurate dating for the Cursus, from an antler pick excavated in the ditch, of 3600 to 3300BC.

At its western end there's a substantial long barrow, which is aligned north to south and although it's impossible to know whether the cardinal alignments of the Cursus and the barrow were deliberate, common sense suggests it was. Again, if you were to take imaginary lines from the eastern end of the Cursus it would have struck through the totem forest of Woodhenge and down the incline to the Wiltshire Avon, but that too may be putting an entirely modern interpretation on it.

There does seem to be some sort of alignment with the Summer Solstice sun, shared with the avenue at the south-eastern entrance of the huge Durrington Walls henge, and that leads to a best guess the Cursus was also a processional route for Solstice rites, which may have been the propitious time for funerals too. Prof. Thomas, and his team from Manchester, also discovered an entrance pathway into the Cursus had been blocked-off at the time it was still in use, leading the professor to observe, *it may have been sanctified or cursed*. Who knows, perhaps a chieftain or high priest dropped dead with a heart attack at the spot during a ceremony, rendering that entry to the Cursus taboo.

Another intriguing theory, rests on the fact the Cursus marks the midsummer sunset at its western end and the midsummer sunrise at its eastern extremity, in other words it delineates the area of the sky where the sun never appears. Did the Cursus map the dark world of fear and uncertainty when the sun seems to be travelling through the underworld, a spine-tingling concept indeed. So then, was the Cursus an astronomically inspired representation of the underworld or a place to parade top class cattle seeking 'best in show' or perhaps it was both, as the Neolithic mind may have seen no need for such distinctions, especially if cattle were inextricably woven into their culture, rather like the Masai of East Africa today.

Twenty-first century, strontium isotope analysis of the Winterbourne Chieftain's teeth and bones have revealed his unique itinerary beginning when he was a two-year-old and first made the journey from Wales to Salisbury Plain, presumably with his parents and probably other members of his family and tribal society. Isotope signatures tell us he stayed on the chalk downlands for seven years and then, as a nine-year-old, made the long, potentially dangerous, and no doubt exciting journey back to Wales. He didn't stay long in his native land because he was off again on the return journey to Wiltshire at the age of eleven and then the tempo of his back-and-forth journeys upped considerably, as he made the passage three more times in his teens, at the ages of twelve, fourteen and fifteen.

Whatever was going on it seems the teenage Chieftain and his parents were people of great influence in both locations, and at this point I should say that, although the scientists believe Wales is the most likely western destination, there's an outside chance it may have been Devon. I'm going to apply that instrument of common sense called Occam's Razor and say the subsequent Bluestone link between the two landscapes makes it fairly obvious the young Chieftain was travelling between Preseli and the Stonehenge area.

But what was going on here? Why the toing-and-froing between the two locations? I think the answer lies in the Chieftain's family who must have been powerful people engaged in the early stages of conceptualising a big temple at Stonehenge. They were the ones forging bonds and social contracts between the two areas, brokering the deals that would make Stonehenge eventually happen. They represent the human link that brought together those two vital elements of the first Stonehenge circle, the Bluestones and the glacial striations I call the Talons Marks of the Gods. It's more than likely the young Chieftain and his family were the ancestral vanguard of Preseli people, the advance party of a 'Cambrian Dynasty' who five hundred years later would bring the Bluestones with them to build Stonehenge, an indomitable band of folk known as the Aubrey Hole VII people, and we'll meet them soon on these pages.

As far at the archaeological record shows nothing was constructed at the nearby site of Stonehenge itself for another five hundred years after the creation of the Cursus in the Chieftain's time, but of course that doesn't mean nothing was happening up there at the scene of those Talon Marks in the chalk. Not all ceremonies need a totem or an altar to validate them and it doesn't take a huge effort of imagination to see people dancing around the glacial striations or simply standing on them, holding their arms up in supplication towards the Solstice sun.

Personally, I don't believe it's credible the Stonehenge location would have been forgotten or ignored in the time between the demise of the Mesolithic tribes to the construction of the first circular ditch and bank at the site, around 3000BC. Prof. Thomas of Manchester agrees, and is quoted as saying, *"What's still so intriguing about the Cursus is that it's about five hundred years older than the Henge and that strongly suggests there was a link, and that it was very possibly a precursor."*

To understand the seemingly aeonian passages of time involved in Neolithic architectural projects it's my contention you have to understand and accept the Neolithic concept of time may have been very different from our own, western linear ideas. Their sacred projects weren't just community driven, they were driven by multiple generations too, so that the seed of an idea conceived generations earlier were passed on, in just the way they passed on their oral history for centuries, until the plan was eventually achieved. For sure, this is what happened at the famous monument of Callanish in the Outer Hebrides where observations of Major and Minor Lunar standstills were made over many generations before they eventually constructed a monument with a visually stunning aspect I'll be describing later in the book. Generational projects, pursued over hundreds of years, require a quantum view of life and time, incorporating the ancestors and the generations yet to be born into the plan, ensuring the previous and future generations were intellectually present in a very real sense at every stage of the project. Native American cultural traditions mirror this idea with any big, new ideas, religious or cultural, deliberately planned with the past seven generations and the next seven generations at the heart of all the tribal thinking. Those people, the ones in the past or yet to come, are all very much alive in the eyes of the tribe and a vibrant element of community thinking.

To my mind the Winterbourne Chieftain was immersed in the beginnings of a multi-generational, literally monumental effort, and his extraordinary life adds weight to Prof. Thomas' theory the Cursus was indeed a long-term precursor for Stonehenge. The positioning of those Talon Marks of the Gods were far from forgotten, and his family link with Preseli underscores and adds weight to the idea.

That's a wonderful heritage, which has been brought to life at the Stonehenge Visitor Centre with the facial reconstruction of the Winterbourne Chieftain, created by Swedish forensic artist Oscar

Nilsson who, in a nice touch, calls his sculpture 'Into the Light' and portrays the Chieftain blinking as he emerges from the burial barrow into the once-more as he comes to life again. The reconstruction reveals he was a handsome chap, incongruously likened by some to Walter White the Breaking Bad character, no doubt though he was one of the dominant powers in the pre-Stonehenge landscape, the man who probably helped forge the enduring clan links that eventually brought the Bluestones from Wales, and the man most likely to have overseen the first, landscape-scale construction at Stonehenge in the form of The Cursus.

Our Chieftain was buried in an auspicious setting, on the high point of the western ridge of the Stonehenge landscape and placed in the grave with him was a well-crafted piece of flint, described in the academic papers as a 'bludgeon'. One end is thinner, designed for grasping, and although it's characterised as some sort of blunt force weapon, I fancy it may have been held by the Chieftain as a badge of office not unlike the baton insignia of Roman legates, and those held later by medieval and modern field marshals. Perhaps most telling of all, is the fact that when our Neolithic ancestors built the Chieftain's huge, long barrow mausoleum they carefully positioned it in line with the rising sun on midsummer's day, a completely Solstitial orientation, which speaks volumes for his importance within that community.

And there's one last startling fact about the Winterbourne Chieftain that gives pause for thought too. He was buried 'apodis,' and laid to rest without his feet. The early archaeologists who uncovered his skeleton could find no sign of his feet bones at all, and he's still without them as he hangs in the Stonehenge museum gallery. Later on, in the Neolithic and the Bronze Age too, the robbing of the feet in death seems to have been the post-mortem punishment of a sacrificial victim. Why? Because this was a predominantly pedestrian society and people walked everywhere when they couldn't use a boat, so to deprive a man of his feet meant he wouldn't be able to walk through the afterlife, a terrifying punishment indeed.

Was the Chieftain being punished then? I don't think he was at all. I think the opposite is true, and his family and the clan took his feet away because they didn't want him to wander off and leave them on the grassy downland of Salisbury Plain as he walked through the afterlife, back to the windswept heather of Preseli where he was born.

It might have been the place he expressed undying love for when he told the story of his life's adventure in the circle of light around the clan fire. I like to think they loved him so much they didn't want him to leave them and wander back home to Wales and in the next chapter I'm going to explain why Preseli may indeed have been a captivating place for our Chieftain, a place which nurtured the folk who eventually arrived to build Stonehenge.

4

A NEOLITHIC HOLY LAND

F ar, far away in the land of the westering sun of Wales, the rocky
carns of Preseli scrape the sky like the serrated backs of dragons
basking in the heather and gifted Stonehenge the monoliths, which stand
at its heart. It's an ephemeral place Preseli, haunted by Neolithic shades
with stone monuments of every kind broadcast over its slopes as if by a
giant's hand. Generations of archaeologists and geologists have travelled
to Preseli with science on their minds and come away bewitched. I live
under its spell too, and I can only say if you haven't been you're long
overdue.

Naturally enough it's the eighty or so Bluestones taken from Wales to
Wiltshire, which exercise the best Stonehenge minds and a great deal of
that academic thought has focussed on how they travelled such a
distance to Salisbury Plain. The link between these wistful Welsh mountains and Stonehenge is potent indeed, and not just a stone-cold connection as there are tangible human links between the two locations,
manifest in dozens of Neolithic and Bronze Age human remains with
isotope markers showing a long dynastic link, not least that of the
Winterbourne Chieftain. I'm going to say a lot more about those
resilient people later in the book, but first I want to conjure some ideas
about the culture of Preseli itself, past and present, before moving on to
talk about the way the Bluestones were moved and their unique characteristics.

Mynydd Preseli, to give this tiny jewel of a range its proper name, is
located above the northern arm of the Pembrokeshire peninsula roughly

bounded by the settlements of Fishguard and Newport to the north, Milford Haven to the south, Crymych to the west and Rosebush to the east. The range is essentially a slab of Ordovician mudstone and slate strata, with volcanic intrusions of rhyolite and dolerite giving the area its distinctive carns, tearing romantic rents in the cloak of gorse and heather that covers the hills. Its pinnacle of Foel Cwmcerwyn, at 536 metres, just qualifies Preseli as a mountain range, and it's a wet place characterised by expanses of windswept moorland edged by wallowing bogs, making it seasonally schizophrenic so that in summer the air is bee-droned, sweet with the coconut scent of gorse flowers and the lanolin of sheep's fleece, while winter brings the peaty smell of rain-soaked soil and acrid farmhouse smoke.

Several burnished rivers rush off its slopes, notably the Gwaun, which runs into the sea at Fishguard, the silver Nevern (Nyfir) with its estuary at Newport, the Taf at Laugharne, and one arm of the Cleddau, which decants into the vast natural harbour of Milford Haven. All of them have links to the deep past of the Pembrokeshire landscape and are justly celebrated in Welsh culture, not least because they spring from Preseli. Without doubt it's a bewitching place, crackling with the electricity of the past, and little wonder researchers on the multi-discipline Landscape & Perception study of Preseli, gave it the entirely appropriate epithet, 'the Stone Age Holy Land,' an idea I've gratefully leant on.

This notion of Preseli as 'sacred' is as old as the hills, but it took on an entirely unexpected significance early in the 20th Century when the War Office, now the Ministry of Defence, threatened to take over most of the mountain range and turn it into a permanent training ground for the military. In the process some two hundred farmers and their families were to be booted-off their traditional holdings, effectively ripping-out Pembrokeshire's rural heart at the stroke of a pen.

Fear not, there was a pen mightier than the military sword, one wielded by the renowned Welsh poet and pacificist Waldo Williams, 'The Bard of Preseli.' Waldo had been raised there, and his poems are woven from the fabric of the upland communities under threat, so he wasn't going to take it lying down, and soon became the figurehead of the campaign to preserve Preseli from bombs and bullets, martialling a battalion of farmers, chapel congregations, quarrymen, and a shock troop of radical preachers from the deeply non-conformist community.

Pembrokeshire they argued, had already ceded a huge expanse of its beautiful coast at the Castlemartin Firing Range to the south, about six miles from Pembroke Castle, where my own maternal family lineage lived and worked in the hamlet of Warren until it was swallowed-up by the range in 1938. Unlike Waldo, I'm not a pacificist but I think it's fair to say Pembrokeshire, including my own ancestors, had already done its bit for the military training effort.

Things were looking bleak for Preseli's future when a couple of the top brass came down to mollify the locals at a public meeting held in the village of Brynberian, which sits pretty much at the geographical heart of the mountain range. They weren't to know the dragons of Neolithic Preseli were already rising from their slumber in the rocky tors ready to weave their magic on the army. As Preseli historian Hefin Wyn tells it, the two Generals were taken to the furze fringed Common at Mynachlogddu where they were roasted by a trio of the fiercest chapel ministers known to science, and forced to concede it was indeed from Preseli the Bluestones had been taken to construct the cradle of English civilisation at Stonehenge; a fact only established twenty-five years earlier by the geologist Herbert Thomas. Would they, as proud English-men, allow Stonehenge to be desecrated by artillery and machine guns asked the Preseli Preservation Committee's very own Special Forces chaplains?

Certainly not, the idea was unthinkable they confessed and with that admission the War Office was outflanked and sent into a confused retreat, metaphorically stamping Preseli with the official seal of 'Sacred' as they left. However, according to Hefin it was the local taxi driver who'd shuttled the Generals to and from the railway station at Narbeth, who was the deal breaker when he chauffeured the generals through a dense fog that cloaked Preseli like smoke from a dragon's breath, and the officers were frustrated they couldn't get a clear view of the mountains they coveted for their own.

'Where are these damn mountains?' they asked.

'All round you,' said the cabbie, 'But you can only see them for 'arf the year, the other 'arf it's like this. Nothin' to see.'

It was the last straw. No point putting a training area somewhere soldiers couldn't see their hands in front of their faces for six months of the year, and Preseli was saved to be incorporated into the Pembrokeshire Coast National Park five years later. Without that critical defence of its integrity with Waldo in the vanguard, a whole raft of archaeological explorations simply wouldn't have happened. Prof. Mike Parker-Pearson, for instance, would not have been allowed to wander unrestrained across the mountains, following inspired hunches that led to some fantastic discoveries including the proto-Stonehenge circle at Waun Mawn.

Today, the Ministry of Defence does allow targeted archaeology on their training grounds, energetically led by their in-house archaeologist Richard Osgood. I once spent a fascinating and humbling day with Richard at an excavation on ministry property where physically and mentally wounded veterans were engaged in Operation Nightingale, with archaeology deployed as a very successful therapy. But Richard is the first to point out that by the nature of the military their needs are pre-eminent, and archaeology comes some way down the list of priorities.

Sadly, I've yet to see Waldo Williams mentioned in the acknowledge-ments of any of the many archaeological papers and books I've read where Preseli is centre front, and that's a shame because without his intervention very little archaeology at all, would have happened there after World War II, and much of their success rests by implication on the shoulders of the Bard of Preseli. Following his death in 1971 a grateful community raised a memorial to Waldo on the common at Mynachlogddu, below the Neolithic quarry of Carn Menyn. It's a Blue-stone menhir just like the scores raised by our ancestors five millennia before, and perhaps one day the Waldo Monument will join the list of thirty-eight officially protected, ancient sites, and countless other prehis-toric remains on Preseli.

That list is long and includes hill forts, round barrows dolmen and menhirs, sacred springs, Neolithic Bluestone quarries and the remnants of the 'Golden Road' a five-mile-long ancient ridgeway, where prehistoric gold landed from Ireland was carried east into Britain. A special place then Preseli, and through the prism of 21st Century knowledge a great deal of that singular reputation rests on the presence of the Bluestones used to build the first elegant but simple stone circle at Stonehenge, long after our Mesolithic friends at Blick Mead had been 'cancelled.'

This exceptional link between the two landscapes, first divined by Herbert Thomas in 1923, has been thrown into sharp focus by the investigations carried out by Mike Parker-Pearson since 2017 at Waun Mawn. Convinced there was a big stone circle to be found somewhere out on the expanse of the mountains, the professor's eye eventually lighted on Waun Mawn, which translates rather prosaically as Peat Moor, and that's pretty much what it is. At first glance, it's a featureless slope covered in rank heather and bracken, rising to the brooding ridge of Cwnc-yr-Hydd, and certainly not the most picturesque area of Preseli when rain sweeps in. On closer examination however, the moorland camouflages a fine array of standing stones, some of which have toppled over time and lie recumbent, with the imposing, eight-foot-high menhir called the Waun Mawn Stone at their centre.

Geophysical surveys commissioned by the professor found the shadow of a long-dismantled stone circle measuring one hundred and ten metres in circumference, arcing away from the Waun Mawn Stone and its three recumbents. And sensationally, that exact circumference is mirrored almost to the inch by the measurement of the first Neolithic, Bluestone circle at Stonehenge, one hundred and fifty miles away. I can only imagine the thrill felt by Mike Parker-Pearson and his team and buoyed by this exceptional discovery they started digging. From 2017 to 2021 they found eight pits with evidence stones had been removed, rather like the sockets of lost teeth; six more had been dug to receive stones but never made use of.

All fourteen pits were on the arc of trajectory of that huge circle, and at its centre archaeologists found a hearth, which seems to have been positioned over a void where a tree had once stood. Who knows, the hearth fire may have been used to light-up rites that were held at night, maybe to cremate bodies, or perhaps both. But in my mind's eye I also see the fires that burnt there illuminating performances, and I see dancers, drummers, and story tellers beguiling audiences in mankind's most ancient mythic arena, the wonderful circle of light cast by a fire. Why not, I don't believe our stone monuments were all about death, a subject which, unsurprisingly, preoccupies many archaeologists. Surely, these special places were focal points for all sorts of shared gatherings, after all they'd taken massive community energy to construct in the first place. Why wouldn't they use the same setting for a funeral and a Solstice knees-up? My heart tells me they did, and my head seems to nod in agreement. For every funeral a wedding.

However, the two most salient Stonehenge-related facts emerging from Waun Mawn, are that the stones involved were all Bluestones, and the circumference of one hundred and ten metres is almost precisely mirrored on Salisbury Plain when the first phase of fifty-six Preseli stones were set in a simple and eloquent circle at the henge. The implication is obvious, Waun Mawn was the prototype for Stonehenge and its stones, together with other, freshly quarried slabs, were lifted and transported to recreate a doppelganger on Salisbury Plain. If Parker-Pearson's team are on the money, there hasn't been a more relevant discovery in the firmament of Stonehenge science since Preseli and Salisbury Plain were first linked by Herbert Thomas.

Archaeological equanimity is not always a given, and when the first papers were published on Waun Mawn in Antiquity (the peer reviewed archaeology journal of Cambridge University) they were met with scepticism, leading to a clash of trowels between Mike Parker-Pearson and that other Stonehenge big hitter Prof. Tim Darvill. It's fair to say the two men, who were undergraduates together at Southampton University, approach Stonehenge from different perspectives with Tim Darvill perhaps more 'organic' and fluid in his approach, with Mike Parker-Pearson a tad more pragmatic, although both are spectacularly intuitive archaeologists.

I won't go into the fine detail of their dispute, which played out through contrary articles published in Antiquity, but in essence Tim Darvill describes Waun Mawn as 'an imagined' stone circle and seems to think the Mike Parker-Pearson team were indulging in a dose of wishful thinking. In his own defence Parker-Pearson cites the evidence of the excavated stone holes set in that unique circumference, with a large hearth at the centre, as Quod Erat Demonstrandum.

The debate continues, and that's good for academic rigour but, as a keen observer of all things Stonehenge, I'm sure the answer centres on the circumference measurement of Waun Mawn as, if accurate, it's an almost perfectly matches that of Stonehenge, and represents compelling if not conclusive evidence that Waun Mawn was indeed the forerunner of Stonehenge. To put it another way, if I were to cast Mike Parker-Pearson as an archaeological Poirot, and Waun Mawn as a murder scene, I'd say the professor has found a very large fingerprint indeed.

Mike Parker-Pearson's investigations also focussed on the source of the Bluestones identifying two, possibly three, Neolithic quarries previously not in the mix. Two leading geologists on the team, Rob Ixer and Richard Bevins, singled out quarries at Carn Goedog, the source of five dolerites found at Stonehenge, and Craig-Rhos-y-Felin where an unspecified number of Stonehenge rhyolites were hewn. Recently, another possible quarry has been found at Garn Turne on the eastern edge of Preseli, near Fishguard and close to a Neolithic dolmen. It's also important to emphasise the first quarry to be identified at Carn Menyn, above the village of Mynachlogddu, is still very much part of the ancient Bluestone quarrying story.

The evidence marshalled at Menyn, Goedog and Rhos-y-Felin is fascinating and shows how the geological characteristics of the strata, with vertical lines of cleavage, make Bluestones relatively easy to split away from the quarry face. Using simple equipment like hammerstones, wooden limbers and wooden chocks, left to swell in the wet environment, almost ready-to-go menhirs could be prised off the outcrop and carried to where they were needed. The quarries also have ancient platforms, like loading bays, about a meter high, enabling the stones to be brought down safely from the face and carried off on sledges. Charcoal from fire hearths at the scene, eventually yielded dates of around 3400-3000BC, pretty much aligned with the start of the first phase of the Stonehenge build.

In 2008 Tim Darvill and his Pembrokeshire-born, archaeological sidekick Geoffrey Wainwright did a great deal of work on Stonehenge and the Bluestones, and identified a number of springs on Preseli, which had been enhanced by the creation of small pools at the springhead using the rocks as mini-dams. I'm going to say a lot more about these springs and their relationship when I come to discuss the notion of Stonehenge as a 'Place of Healing' and I'm sure more will emerge on the nature of

Parker-Pearson's Waun Mawn discovery, and ever more detail on the Bluestone quarries too.

I believe it all adds up to a specific culture focused on the Bluestones, one that emerged in Preseli when Neolithic people arrived there during the great western migration six thousand years ago. Those original farming settlers probably landed serendipitously on the shores of Pembrokeshire and found a pleasant land indeed, and here they developed a whole culture based on the unique stones they found on the land.

It's from this viewpoint of a unique Bluestone Culture that I'd like to consider the signature creations of Neolithic Preseli; the stone monuments known as dolmen. Like the term menhir for a standing stone, dolmen is a Breton word linked to the profusion of stone monuments in that western corner of France. The Irish who have some grand examples call them dolmen, but dolmen are also known by the Gaelic term cromlech and in Cornwall they're called quoits after a medieval game; a name echoed in the word 'coetan' sometimes used in Wales. Preseli and the nearby Strumble Head peninsula own some of the finest examples of these very special pieces of our stone-age heritage, defined as *'prehistoric monuments of two or more upright stones supporting a horizontal stone slab found especially in Britain and France and thought to be a tomb.'*

That definition doesn't do anywhere near justice to the truly miraculous way the capstones, some of which weigh sixteen tonnes or more, seem to float above the upright orthostats, balancing on them as if on fingertips. Nor does the bald description of their function as 'a tomb' cut it, as a lack of funereal remains in many dolmen leaves that up in the air, just like their monumental capstones. The intuitive explanation is that of a portal to other dimensions although a complete understanding of many Neolithic monuments, including their dolmen, is well-nigh impossible when we only have vague ideas how those people viewed life, or indeed death.

In any event, these masterpieces of equilibrium are found in Cornwall, Wales, Cumbria, Scotland, Ireland, and Brittany too where the tradition settled then bounced across the North-West Atlantic to Britain. Archaeological convention has it they are the exposed, stone frameworks of passage tombs that were once covered in rubble and soil, and this appears to be the case with some dolmen, but others are now being classified as freestanding courtyard tombs, where cremated remains may have been placed on a cobbled yard under the capstone to be sanctified and remembered for a while, but not permanently interred.

Some believe the dolmen architects competed to erect the most ambitious, precariously balanced and breath-taking pieces of landscape art, achieving extraordinary feats of equipoise. I agree with this idea and seeing is believing when I've viewed some of the finest examples, time and again, yet still find myself muttering, 'Just how in the hell did they do that!' Lanyon Quoit near Penzance, Chun Quoit on Pendeen and Trevethy Quoit on Bodmin Moor are the best of the Cornish dolmen with Spinsters Rock on the edge of Dartmoor a rare example still standing in Devon. I can recollect, with a large slice of awe, the tombs of St Lytham's and Tinkinswood near my childhood home on Barry Island, which are extraordinary examples of the manhandling of massive capstones.

THE SILOUHETTE STONES OF PRESELI

Carreg Coetan Arthur, one of three extraordinary dolmen with Llech-y-Tripedd and Pentre Ifan, each with a different view of Mynydd Carningli, each silhouetting that unique view of the mountain in the shape of their capstones.
(Author's photograph)

Like most British stone monuments, dolmen are to be found roughly, but by no means exclusively, along the western half of Britain; basically, the rugged half where hard rock is plentiful. Craggy Pembrokeshire has its fair share, but I particularly want to home-in on three Preseli dolmen, which represent a remarkable testament to the culture of the early pastoralists who first grazed their livestock on those hills thousands of years ago. They are Pentre Ifan, Carreg Coetan Arthur and Llech-y-

Tripedd and each represents a masterclass in the architecture of equipoise, involving gigantic slabs of rock and pinpoint balancing, requiring incredibly heavy and unwieldly capstones to be manoeuvred into place.

Pentre Ifan, visually stunning and internationally famous, overlooks the Nyfir valley not far from the estuary harbour of Newport, and I love its location beneath Carn Meibion Owen where a resident tribe of ravens always seem to be in attendance, coughing their calls, while they dance on the breeze. Pentre Ifan is often cited as an example of a denuded passage tomb and the archaeological evidence seems to bear that out. However, I wonder just how much-top cover of soil and rubble was actually laid over this trapezoid wonder, and there's good reason to suspect most of that backfill was laid along the sides of the tomb, leaving the capstone's outline still visible.

It may also be the case its architecture was altered during subsequent development phases, when the ancients decided to strip the tomb down to its stone skeleton and create the dolmen we see today; a sixteen feet long, eight-foot-high work of art. Whether or not it was a tomb is debatable because there were no mortuary remains found at Pentre Ifan, which isn't to say it wasn't used for funerals. Bodies might have been brought there for rites, then disposed of in some other way, perhaps left out for sky burials supervised by the ancestors of the ravens on the Carn or cremated elsewhere. It's impossible to know, and that's because prehistoric bones and ashes are comparatively rare in Wales, where wet weather and acidic soil combine to destroy human remains. Those that do survive are few and often found in relatively dry cave burials.

Moving west, the least known and smallest of these three dolmen is Llech-y-Tripedd, which stands in a field between Newport and the tiny haven of Moylegrove. It has glorious views of the sea and the mountain of Carn Ingli, which towers dramatically above the Nyfir estuary to its north-east. The capstone of Tripedd is triangular and there's no evidence it was ever covered with soil and rubble, while its position in such a commanding location suggests it may well have been raised as a free-standing place of worship and ritual. Time alone will ordain its fate, but the capstone is almost completely cracked through and one of the orthostats has also split. I only hope it's still standing when I next visit.

The last of this triptych of Preseli dolmen is Carreg Coetan Arthur, which stands in the heart of the little harbour town of Newport above the Nyfir estuary, which is definitely one of my happy places. Carreg Coetan stands about three hundred meters from the southern bank of the river and once had views over the estuary until the monument was crowded in by a modern housing development in the 1980's. Despite the mediocrity of the setting imposed on it, Carreg Coetan is a spectacular piece of Neolithic engineering, with its thirteen-tonne capstone appearing to be supported by four uprights, until closer inspection reveals it's exquisitely balanced, almost floating, on the tips of just two of its orthostats.

It isn't known whether Carreg Coetan was once covered to create a chambered tomb, nor indeed the extent to which it may have been enveloped by soil and rubble, but it could be the capstones of all three dolmen were left partially exposed and for a very good reason, which I'll explain soon. In 1980, well known Welsh archaeologist Sian Rees dug around Carreg Coetan and found four cremation remains with some Neolithic pottery shards, and concluded they were probably partial 'offerings' placed around the dolmen shortly before 3000BC, right around the time Stonehenge's first Bluestone circle was raised. Carreg Coetan is enigmatic indeed, but I believe it's closely connected to the departure of monolithic slabs of Bluestone bound for Stonehenge.

You may be wondering why I've chosen to focus on these three dolmen in particular and the explanation lies in the capstones, which allow us an astonishing glimpse into the intimate love of landscape and aesthetic perceptions of our Neolithic ancestors. All three of these dolmen face Carn Ingli mountain, which towers majestically above Newport, and they form an acute triangle, one with another, around the mountain landscape. These three vantage points reveal a different and unique aspect of the summit, but when Carn Ingli is viewed with any of the three capstones standing in the foreground, that unique horizon is mirrored in the silhouette of the capstone.

Incredibly, the capstones of Pentre Ifan, Llech-y-Tripedd and Carreg Coetan Arthur were carefully chosen to mimic the view of Carn Ingli from their particular locations, and I suspect any soil and rubble piled against them was sculpted and shaped to complete the 'model' of Carn

Ingli when seen from each of the three vantage points. I call these three capstones the Silhouette Stones of Preseli, and they are truly awe inspiring.

It's wonderful and at the same time humbling, to think of the care and art our ancestors put into such an endeavour, and it offers us a captivating insight into the soul of those indomitable people. Not only were they tough engineers capable of manhandling huge slabs of rock, not only did they balance them in gravity-defying ways, but they went to enormous efforts to place their stones perfectly, with an artistic eye, on the canvas of the landscape. It tells us they must have held Carn Ingli - the Angels' Mountain in English - as sacred, and it also tells us they were prepared to express themselves in a way that magnified their souls.

No surprise then the people who followed, the modern folk of Preseli seem to have drawn down on the sanctity of Preseli by some process of spiritual osmosis, and it's no surprise either those hard-bitten Generals left that meeting in Mynachlogddu and returned to the War Office in London beguiled, probably pinching themselves and wondering what the hell had just happened to their best laid plans.

Whenever I've visited the wonderful dolmen of western Britain, I've thought the difference between a capstone and a lintel, a dolmen and a trilithon, is practically and architecturally inconsequential, resting alone on the fact the lintels at Stonehenge are spectacularly worked into uniform shapes. Certainly, the skills and techniques needed to raise and set either a dolmen or a lintel into place at significant heights, would have been similar and already mastered in the tradition of the Neolithic dolmen builders before work ever began on the Stonehenge trilithons.

It occurs to me the Stonehenge Trilithons might have been inspired by dolmen or even be an homage to the dolmens scattered across Britain and, when required, perhaps experienced dolmen builders turned their skills to the challenge of building a trilithon and gave us the Stonehenge we see today. Just a thought, but one worth considering, even if there will never be anyone to give us the definitive answer to an inspiring riddle.

Many people believe Preseli is endowed with some ephemeral power expressed by variations in the magnetometry of the landscape and I'm quite happy to acknowledge this may indeed be the case and eagerly anticipate the results of research I know is going on at the moment. Be that as it may, we only have to gaze across the sea to Ireland where Neolithic people were creating peerless wonders like Newgrange and Bru-na-Bhoine with their fantastic, infinitely spiralling rock art, while far to the north the Orkney Isles were buzzing with sophisticated trade networks and emerging as a brand leader in culture and fashion, whilst supporting a profusion of religious sites rivalling those of Stonehenge itself. What then made Preseli stand out in the Neolithic world?

The unique distinction possessed by the people of Preseli was, of course, their ownership and control of Bluestones. I'm sure those precious slabs of rock triggered people like the Winterbourne Chieftain to travel back and forth between Preseli and Stonehenge forging bonds and social contracts, planning and organising the big day when they'd start transporting hundreds of tons of stone a couple of hundred miles to erect the temple on Salisbury Plain. That momentous day finally came five hundred years after the Winterbourne Chieftain was laid to rest and was the culmination of a remarkable, multi-generational ambition. I'm about to introduce you to the inspired people from Preseli who pulled it off.

5

THE STONEHENGE
DYNASTY

O n a breezy, slightly overcast day in August 2008 I found myself
standing at the edge of a very carefully excavated pit, on the
outer edge of the great circle surrounding Stonehenge. Reaching into the
dig below me were two familiar faces of television archaeology, Julian
Richards, and Jacqui McKinley. Mike Parker-Pearson, overseeing the
project, was anxiously peering into the pit too, while another Stonehenge
authority, Mike Pitts took a break from digging to record events on his
camera.

Jacqui McKinley is Britain's best known osteoarchaeologist, a woman
who's made very old bones her business, while Julian Richards is familiar
to British television viewers presenting his hit archaeological series 'Meet
the Ancestors." On the other hand, I was only present as an archaeological voyeur thanks to an invitation from Mike Pitts, who's a neighbour in
Wiltshire, a family friend and fellow journalist, albeit an archaeological
specialist rather than a newshound. We were at a spot on the outer rim
of the henge known as Aubrey Hole VII, where the team were recov-
ering a large parcel of discarded human cremation remains and the mood
was intense because those experts knew this was a hugely significant dig.
In the end, it was going to take another eight years before the results of
their work came in but, in a nutshell, they'd reveal another stunning link
to Preseli.

Perhaps, I'd best start by outlining the background to Aubrey Hole
VII, which is a tortuous tale indeed. It began with the extraordinary

dedication of William Hawley, best described as an archaeological anchorite, who spent countless lonely hours excavating at Stonehenge from 1919 to 1926, often living alone for extended periods in a shed erected nearby. A retired Royal Engineers colonel, Hawley has come in for some justified criticism, but he did bring a certain military rigour to his work and quite successfully so, as he was first to identify antler picks as the primary building tools of the Neolithic era and first to excavate many of the fifty-six Aubrey Holes, representing the original Stonehenge circle. Named after the antiquarian John Aubrey, the holes are essentially empty sockets in the ground where the Bluestones were first erected around 3000BC (the earliest radiocarbon date for them is 2919BC) after they were carried to Stonehenge from Preseli.

In those long redundant pits, Hawley found a deal of human cremation material including ash and partly incinerated bone, together with the remnants of the wood used to fuel many funeral pyres. Scientific analysis at the time could do little with these remains and they were simply put into storage, until they became inconvenient. We may find it hard to fathom today, but no institution wanted to give the cremations shelf-space at a time when strontium and DNA analysis weren't even on the horizon and so in 1935 Aubrey Hole VII was dug-up again and the ashes of at least fifty-nine of our ancestors, were scooped into four hessian sandbags, and re-interred in the pit. A lead plate describing the circumstances of this unfortunate reburial was popped into the pit for good measure.

Those four, precious sacks of Neolithic humanity were the target of the Stonehenge Riverside Project excavation I was watching unfold that summer's day. The broad aim of the Project was to investigate and confirm the ceremonial route from the huge encampment at Durrington Walls, along the banks of the Avon for three miles to West Amesbury then up the processional Avenue to Stonehenge. During the planning stage, however, someone had the inspired idea that maybe, just maybe, modern scientific analyses could be applied to the remains they knew lay in Aubrey Hole VII. If only they could be safely retrieved.

What they found at the bottom of the pit was a chaotic jumble where the hessian sacks had rotted away, and the cremations had melded into the soil and chalk surround. Hence the concentration etched on the faces of the two diggers and, as if their nerves weren't taught enough, the cremation remains of a totally unknown female burial had fallen in from the wall of the pit. Incredibly she'd been missed in two previous excavations at Aubrey Hole VII.

I didn't know at the time, but the team were also discreetly working on another spectacular dig, close to the river in a meadow at West Amesbury at the foot of The Avenue, where they found the remnants of another Bluestone temple, which has since been variously named The West Amesbury Henge, Bluestonehenge or sometimes Bluehenge. It had been an oval of twenty-three Preseli stones, which were erected around the same time as those slotted into the Aubrey Holes on the Plain above. A lot was going on during this phase of the Riverside Project, and a lot was at stake.

Back at Aubrey Hole VII that August morning I was watching trowels scraping carefully around the last few pieces of the conglomeration of human and funeral pyre material one moment, and the next it was over, job done. The cremation remains had been successfully retrieved and the excavation was complete. I stood there aware I'd just seen something significant happen, it's just that I wasn't quite sure what it was! Fortunately, the Riverside Project people knew exactly what had to be done and the pot pourri of human remains and funeral pyre ash were taken to a laboratory in Oxford, where an international team collaborated on the fiendishly difficult job of separating this organic jigsaw and identifying the human material from the grave before they could even begin to analyse it.

You can't just dig-up human remains willy-nilly, and a licence had been obtained from the UK Justice Department giving the team two years to analyse the cremations, before they had to be buried again. As it turned out this nightmare of a three-dimensional jigsaw was so complicated the work dragged-on, and the team successfully applied for a five-year extension to that licence. Modern archaeology is sensitive to the sanctity of human burials, and I can testify to the care and respect shown when the remains of the people were recovered from Aubrey Hole VII that day. All those present were respectful and, I'm certain, immersed in their own thoughts about those ancient individuals; a stark contrast to the 1930's idea of shovelling them into sandbags.

It took another eight years for the story to actually break, published in the scholarly journal Antiquity in 2016, and the results were a sensation. Most of the remains were of adults, and of those adults the split between male and female was roughly half and half, but only twenty-four of the individuals isolated from the jumbled remains of the fifty-eight, had provided enough viable material to be analysed in the laboratory. None yielded any DNA material for coding because their teeth enamel had been destroyed in the furnace of the cremation, but crucially the strontium signatures laid into the bones by the diet at their places of nurture were recoverable and allowed the scientists to tell where those individuals came from.

Remove the science-speak, the complex chemical tabulations and the caveats always attached to such academic reports, and we're left with an absolutely breathtaking window into the drama that unfolded when our ancestors decided to undertake the daunting task of moving their precious Bluestones to Salisbury Plain. Incredibly, the strontium signatures, tell us that ten of those twenty-four individuals, forty per cent of the total, did indeed come from Wales. Preseli! Surely, they must have been natives of Preseli. Just think of it, those audacious, unstoppable people had been buried among the very Bluestones they'd carried with such monumental effort, across land and sea to Stonehenge.

There was more. Specialists also examined the charcoal from the pyres, mixed-in with the fragments of bone, which gave another glimpse into the humanity of these ancient souls. Through some alchemy beyond my grasp, specialist researchers were able to say the tree species on some of the cremation pyres, were typical of West Wales and not Salisbury Plain. In other words, when those people left Preseli to transport the Bluestones more than one hundred and fifty miles to their new home on Salisbury Plain, they brought the cremated remains of their loved ones with them to bury them again among the Stones they held so sacred.

It's an inspiring parable of the passion and loyalty of those people. No doubt they were responsible for bringing the Bluestones on their long journey from Wales but surely, they did so willingly for the sake of their religion, rather than under duress, in a war with the Irish, as suggested by the Merlin legend recounted by Geoffrey of Monmouth. They were buried at the feet of the Bluestones in the heart of the temple, an obviously prestigious setting, and that doesn't seem to fit the narrative of a conquered people, at least not to me. These were obviously some of the architects of Stonehenge, that much I think is clear and they were the people who organised the great transportation of some eighty or more stones from Preseli to Salisbury Plain.

There's one more seemingly impossible question that needs to be answered, and that's who ordered this gigantic logistical operation, who signed off on the metaphorical docket ordering the shipment of the Bluestones? Was it a paramount ruler or a high priest with enough influence throughout our island to requisition the Bluestones? I've thought about this a great deal since the startling results of the chemical analysis from Aubrey Hole VII were published in 2016 and here I'm going to at least attempt to recover some of that seemingly Unrecoverable Past by sifting through what is already known to make some reasonable deductions and then take a couple of stabs in the dark too.

What was going on when Stonehenge was first erected? What was the nature of society in Neolithic Britain and who held the power? If you like, what were the politics of Neolithic Britain? I've often wondered if there were several autonomous leaders centred around significant temples of worship, rather like the counts who ran medieval Italian city states, clustered around cathedrals on hill tops, staring suspiciously across deep valleys at each other.

Did the great stone circles of Avebury and Stanton Drew have different chieftains to Stonehenge or was there one paramount ruler centred on Stonehenge itself, or indeed some form of coalition between all the monolithic centres of worship. Maybe there were autonomous, regional chieftains who ruled over the temporal lives of the people, while an all-powerful priestly class ruled over them spiritually, not an unusual model for many societies. That might indeed make the most sense, with a high priest directing the worldly chieftains to put aside any rivalries for a while so as to focus on the work of the gods and bring the Bluestones to Stonehenge. That way things would have been made to happen.

Important work by Prof. Parker-Pearson has shown animals for these Winter Solstice feasts came from all over Britain, including the dominion of whoever ruled the area north of the Great Glen, six hundred miles away, where the Altar Stone is now known to have been sourced. That Altar Stone provenance demonstrates these islands weren't a series of insular social bubbles, but interlinked communities in obvious communication one with the other and able to come together for shared religious aims, if only temporarily and seasonally. Important people must have been calling the shots, and an informed guess would suggest the big cheese of Neolithic Britain was probably based at Stonehenge. Whoever it was, or they were, it seems clear that an all-powerful writ ran across these islands.

That had to be the case for cattle to be moved on the hoof across the length and breadth of Britain, from as far away as Scotland, and for the Bluestones to be moved overland, passing through a whole procession of territories. Logically that couldn't have happened without some overarching power willing it, and similarly a seaward passage for either the Bluestones or the Altar Stone from Scotland might have relied on a series of sanctioned landfalls on different clan coastlines.

And what of the original 'owners' of the Bluestones up on the salt-sprayed Preseli range, doubtless some of The Twenty-Four from Aubrey Hole VII among their number. What say did they have in the process? Were they the springhead of some priestly class whose great influence came from their possession of the Bluestones? Did they order their removal to Stonehenge? Did they donate the Bluestones to the great Stonehenge project, did they trade them or were the Stones seized as the spoils of war by an invading army as suggested by the 'Arthurian' legend in Geoffrey of Monmouth's famous book, a story cited by Parker-Pearson?

For me, the coincidence of a series of seemingly preternatural factors, suggests a priestly, rather than a temporal power, might have held sway in Neolithic Britain. Perhaps there was a high priest or priestess, who ruled the roost or maybe the position of high priest was incorporated with the role of king or queen, similar to the early Pharaohs of Egypt?

It surely can't be the case the Bluestones and the Altar Stone were moved such distances, across the disparate territories of various clans, without a command from a paramount chief or an elite priestly class and I believe the leading contenders are the folk buried in the Aubrey Holes where the Bluestones were raised in the first circle at Stonehenge around 3000BC. It's also fascinating to realise that with the preponderance of female cremations identified from Aubrey Hole VII it's an evens bet the people calling the shots may have been women.

Many of those people came from Preseli, while the rest were local to the chalk downlands, and it's reasonable to speculate they may represent a coalition of related tribes from the two areas, bound by ancient blood ties or treaty, who cooperated to create Stonehenge. I also believe the evidence suggests this project was a long held Neolithic aspiration planned over centuries by a people who measured communal projects in terms of generations rather than years. It's fair to submit the Winterbourne Chieftain, who voyaged many times between the two places, was one of the early links in the great Stonehenge task, which clearly hinged on the transfer of the Bluestones from Preseli to be plugged into the earth at the sacred spot marked out by the gods with their Talon Marks on the chalk.

It's difficult to avoid thinking of the ancients in anything but abstract terms, after all the only glimpses of those people are informed by their bones, the artefacts they left behind and the iconic Stone temples they bequeathed our landscape as their waymarks through eternity. However, it's not difficult at all to imagine them as a resilient and adventurous branch of the first Neolithic settlers on these islands, men and women who'd braved the Atlantic seaboard to be swept onto the shores of Pembrokeshire, where they'd settled on the moors and valleys of Mynydd Preseli.

Over time they forged alliances with another equally resolute branch of their people, who'd settled Salisbury Plain and, as I say, it's quite feasible they already had pre-existing blood ties with each other, explaining the multiple journeys of the Winterbourne Chieftain, who symbolises the generational nature of the Stonehenge build.

Mike Parker-Pearson characterises these folk as a high status 'Cambrian Dynasty,' who travelled from Preseli to Stonehenge with the eighty-plus slabs of stone and were eventually buried at the foot of the Bluestones, a funereal tradition which continued until the cusp of the Bronze Age. It's an empowering, human connection only discovered through a remarkable piece of archaeology within the ceremonial perimeter of the monument on that fateful August day. I feel privileged to have witnessed it and we should all be grateful to the Stonehenge Riverside Project team for revealing this thrilling saga to the world.

I'm going to suggest the people who signed off on the great Stonehenge project were the descendants of the Winterbourne Chieftain, and the early ambitions and plans had been in the making during his lifetime. It's just that they took four or five hundred years to come to fruition, and that may not have been of any concern at all in the Neolithic grasp of the nature of time.

Most of all though, I'm left with visions of our inspired ancestors gazing east towards Stonehenge as the sun rose on the day of departure, not knowing what fate held for them but grasping it all the same. Their stones, their decision, and their notional requisition note too. I suspect they may have been umbilically attached by religious devotion to the fate of the Bluestones and understood the stark reality they were unlikely ever to return to the heather-draped slopes of Mynydd Preseli. And so, they did what would have been the natural thing and took the remains of some of their loved ones with them, held securely in leather bags, until they could be buried under the cloisters of the new temple they would eventually erect.

When I think of those people, my eyes mist with a sense of the loss they must have felt, their longing for the landscape that was once beneath their feet; the indescribable human yearning for place, encapsulated for me in the Welsh word 'hiraeth.'

Committed to the Stonehenge vision, they were determined to take their dead ancestors with them for reminiscence, reverence and for continuity too, but essentially I think they took them along for love. It's obvious those Preseli folk were motivated by their spiritual adoration of the Bluestones and in the next two chapters I'm going to look at theories about how the megaliths were transported and explain what I think really happened before I turn to the thrilling reasons why the Bluestones were so important they were moved at all.

6

THE LONG MARCH

I believe the most likely candidates for arranging the movement of the Bluestones to Stonehenge are that Cambrian Dynasty who held sway over the quarries of Preseli, but how did they move the megaliths so many miles to the rolling downland of Salisbury Plain? It's been one of the most hotly debated riddles in the long saga of Stonehenge study, a mystery that's teased and often exasperated archaeologists, historians, and Stonehenge sleuths like me ever since their Welsh provenance was first confirmed by geologist Herbert Thomas a century ago. Over the next couple of chapters, I'm going to unpick the theories and propose some brand new, expert ideas on the way the Bluestones were conveyed.

First, let's consider the proposed overland routes and track them across the rugged terrain of Neolithic Britain. Even if a sea voyage ate-up most of the miles, the Stones still had to be hauled at least some of the way, over challenging topography, and I'll also consider the mechanics of how that overland carriage was achieved.

What's plain to see is eighty of these petrologically unique objects averaging two tonnes in weight, the heaviest being four and a third tonnes, were conveyed in a major Neolithic engineering and logistical exercise, one hundred and thirty-four miles as the crow flies, from Preseli to Salisbury Plain. We know too the subsequent tenants of Stone-henge, the metal working Beaker Folk who brought the Bronze Age to these islands, repurposed the Bluestones at least three times, dragging huge Sarsen megaliths from the Marlborough Downs to incorporate them into the architecture of their new, improved stone temple at the sacred site.

There are three main theories as to how the Bluestones were conveyed from Pembrokeshire, two of them involve human agency and come down to dragging overland or floating by boat or raft, over the sea. This is complicated by hybrid variations, which include lots of dragging and some floating, or lots of floating and some dragging. It's complicated.

The third proposition suggests the Bluestones were gouged out of the Preseli Mountains by a huge glacier then carried within the body of ice to be dropped around Salisbury Plain in the big melt at the end of the Ice Age. I'm going to say straight away, I don't buy it. Where are the rest of these glacial erratics, supposedly scattered randomly across the Wiltshire landscape by the agency of ice, the ones which weren't considered suitable, or even big enough, for the Stonehenge build? Well, there aren't any and surely we're not being asked to believe a glacier delivered just the right number of eighty or so Bluestones, conveniently close to where they were needed, with all but a delivery note? The truth is the entirety of large slabs and chunks of Bluestone in Southern England are, in some way or other, associated with human placements and for me that absolutely freezes out the ice cap theory.

What about the question of human agency? It's a vexatious one with the majority of those who reject the glacier theory still metaphorically squaring-up with each other to dispute whether it was 'By Land', or 'By Sea.' Both theories go in and out of fashion with the heralding of any new information supporting either proposition, all of which is entirely circumstantial. For a long while after confirmation of Preseli as the source of the Bluestones in the 1920's, the sea route was in vogue and discussed in articles replete with illustrations of our near-savage, skin-clad ancestors clinging precariously to a storm-tossed raft, with a bloody big stone resting on it.

Then in December 2015, Stonehenge expert Mike Parker-Pearson published a paper in Antiquity, which put the land-route cat amongst the sea-voyage pigeons. Following his revelations about the newly identified northern Preseli quarries of Carn Goedog and Craig Rhos-y-Felin, Prof. Parker-Pearson surprised everyone when he declared, *"The only logical direction for the Bluestones to go was to the north and then either by sea around St David's Head or eastwards overland, through the valleys along the route that is now the A40. Personally, I think that overland route is more likely."* The concept of the A40 Route for the Bluestones was born and, whilst not unchallenged, that hare's been running since and has become accepted wisdom by a large body of the archaeological hierarchy. I've driven the A40 Route many times and if you're not in a race it takes a good five hours with breaks to follow the wandering, 220-mile route from Whitland to Amesbury on well-maintained 21st Century tarmac. We can assume that would translate into multiple weeks, an estimate of forty-five days has been suggested, if you're manhandling a Bluestone along unmetalled pathways and tracks, across terrain of varying difficulty, with no protection from the vagaries of the British weather let alone wolves, bears and brigands.

Mike Pitts, the well-known Stonehenge luminary, intervened in the debate to suggest the last half of the A40 Route, the bit from Gloucester to Salisbury Plain, contains so many challenging escarpments it would have made no sense at all to the ancients. Why struggle up hills when you don't have too, asks Mike? Good point. Instead, he proposes an alternative, hybrid route, with lots of land and some water, which I characterise as A40 Lite.

Mike has an impressive CV as an archaeologist, journalist, author and broadcaster, and as I write he's about to relinquish his long and distinguished role as editor of British Archaeology magazine. He's also written two critically acclaimed, bestsellers on Stonehenge, first *Hengeworld* and subsequently *How to Build Stonehenge*. I heartily recommend them both, but for my money *'How to Build'* is far and away the best of a whole pile of books I've read on the subject over the years. Crucially, Mike is also one of the privileged few to have been granted much-coveted permission to excavate within the boundaries of Stonehenge twice, endowing him with a feel for the subject that's evident in his writing. Importantly, his A40 Lite journey was given some weight by the British Museum in the season of their wonderful 2022 exhibition - The World of Stonehenge - and with that in mind I'll describe A40 Lite in more detail and say from the start it's not easy terrain.

Where the journey begins at Preseli there are many humps, dips, screes and some difficult marshland topography on the way to present-day Whitland, where the route meets the modern A40 road it's named after. Whitland had to be the start-line for the remainder of the journey as the direct route to Brecon from Preseli is impassable because of an intervening roller-coaster of deep-cut gorges and fast flowing streams. From Whitland the track heads to Carmarthen, then skirts along the western bank of the River Tywi through a pleasant valley to Llandeilo, and then on to Llandovery where the river must be crossed to make progress eastwards.

It's here the Bluestone transport teams would be confronted with their first scary obstacle at the six mile long, steep-sided gorge of the Upper Tywi enroute to Pontsenni or, as generations of British soldiers know it, Sennybridge. In more recent times cattle drovers moving their herds at grazing pace towards the butchers of London at Smithfield Market, gave the gorge a wide berth as it was too easy to lose beasts into the void. Even when a turnpike road had been cut into the southern bank of the ravine in the 18th Century the Gloucester to Carmarthen stagecoach managed to drop off the edge, thankfully without loss of life.

Half-way along the gorge lies a hamlet, predictably named Halfway, where stagecoach horses were given a breather after the long haul from Llandovery. It's close to a watershed, where the Tywi has its source, while the Usk runs in the opposite direction, east through Pontsenni towards Brecon cutting through the steep-sided mountains of the Bannau Brycheiniog (Brecon Beacons). I think the Bluestone teams would have taken the northern bank of the Usk and continued through Brecon, on to Crickhowell and from there four or five miles further to Abergavenny. It's here Mike Pitts' A40 Lite option sensibly avoids the arduous drag through the Forest of Dean, across the Cotswolds and then the Marlborough Downs, by heading due south from Abergavenny down the Usk valley to its tidal reach somewhere near Caerleon. There, Mike suggests, the stones would have embarked on vessels to be ferried across the dangerous confluence of the channel and the Severn Estuary up to the mouth of the Bristol Avon.

The stones would have been paddled and poled up the Avon, through the Clifton Gorge and on to Bath, then along the Wylye Valley to Heytesbury, where they would have been disembarked to continue the rest of the journey either overland across Salisbury Plain or further along the Wylye to the Wiltshire Avon at Salisbury, then upstream for some fifteen miles to West Amesbury.

Here, some twenty-four stones were erected on the bank of the river, in a meadow opposite the beginning of The Avenue leading up to Stonehenge, while another fifty-six Bluestones were hauled onto the Plain and erected at the site of the henge. Looking at the topography, it seems to me the strange, boomerang shape of the Avenue's route is nothing less than an expression of the most convenient path along the natural contours up to Stonehenge. Perhaps, the ancients decided to formalise that heritage into the processional Avenue to honour the auspicious passage of the sacred stones to the temple site and incorporate it into a sacred pilgrimage from Durrington Walls.

To be fair to both Parker-Pearson and Pitts, neither rely entirely on the analysis of the northern situation of Preseli Bluestones quarries, to cast doubt on a sea voyage in favour of the landward routes. Both cited an anomaly (there seem to be plenty of those in the Stonehenge story) and it's one that until fairly recently could indeed have been interpreted as giving credibility to the A40 Route. It's the riddle of the Stonehenge Altar Stone, which happens to be the largest of the stones imported to Wiltshire, and although it's a very different species of rock, it's long been classified as of Welsh origin and classified as a 'Bluestone.'

The Altar Stone lies recumbent at the heart of the monument, in a bit of a jumble with two other stones laid over it, and the experts have been unable to tell from the evidence at the scene, whether it fell or was originally intended to be laid flat as an altar would. It's about two meters long and weighs six tonnes, against four tonnes for the heaviest of the Bluestones. The Altar Stone is a type of Old Red Sandstone (ORS) strata abundant in Wales, but in August 2024 the Stonehenge world was turned upside down when a new, definitive source for this sparkling, greenish/purple rock, was found in a geological formation known as the Orcadian Basin which stretches from Orkney across to Caithness and the Moray Firth on the mainland.

Incredibly, this serendipitous discovery was made by Anthony Clarke, a Welsh researcher working in Australia who was born and raised in the Preseli Mountains, where the Bluestones were quarried and remembers visiting Stonehenge as a child. He rightly points out his discovery demonstrates, *"Stonehenge seems to be this great British endeavour involving all the different people from all over the island."* Anthony's results were published in Nature and his research confederates couldn't have been more prestigious, including Rob Ixer and Richard Bevins, the two distinguished geologists who worked alongside Mike Parker-Pearson to identify new Bluestone quarries on Preseli.

I'll take the six-hundred-mile detour to Scotland in the final chapter of the book when I'll discuss the transportation options for the Altar Stone separately, and I'll also explain why it might have been carried so far in the first place. For now, I'll set the Tartan Altar Stone to one side, as one less argument in the overland theory for the Bluestones, and return to the passage of the 'genuine' articles transported to Stonehenge from Preseli.

Along his A40 Lite route, Mike Pitts mentions four tall, standing stones or menhirs between Brecon and Crickhowell, which he suggests might have been erected as waymarks for the A40 Route. That may indeed be the case and I'm familiar with one of these stones, the impressive Growing Stone at Cwrt-y-Gollen, a disused military estate on the outskirts of Crickhowell. I know it well from my years collaborating as a writer on book projects with ex Special Air Service soldiers. The BBC were filming an SAS documentary at Cwrt-y-Gollen, and I'd been asked to write the 'book of the film' requiring me to spend time there on location. I found the Growing Stone on my first visit and thereafter I'd wander across to wonder at it every time I returned. It's truly impressive.

However, you don't have to go far in that area to find equally impressive menhirs, standing as signposts and sentinels. There are two, just a few miles away on the steep pass between the River Senni and the River Hepste, with a view north to the A40 Route. They're called Maen Llia, part of my life since I was a kid, and Maen Madoc. Three thousand years later, the Romans built Sarn Helen, their strategic road across the roof of Wales, right alongside the waymarks of Llia and Madoc, which still bears a Legionary petroglyph. Do Mike Pitts' marker stones, necessarily relate to the movement of the Bluestones? They may well, but on the other hand they could be pointing towards something else entirely, the Stone Circles at Mynydd Bach or Cerrig Duon for instance, which are nearby at Trecastell and right on the A40 Route too. Or are they signposts for the courtyard tomb and large stone circle discovered at Arthur's Stone in the Golden Valley, on the Welsh border nearby? The fact is the whole of the area in a triangle between Brecon, Hereford and the Neath Valley has a complex network of menhirs, stone circles and chambered tombs, and the significance of their careful placing and distribution can only be a mystery to us.

The charting of these notional overland routes followed by our ancestors from Preseli to the Plain, is fascinating, and let's be honest, it's fun too for a Stonehenge enthusiast. But it's also a serious business because this story is the saga of a formative time of human progress on these islands. It's a time when sophisticated agriculture arrived to displace the old ways, a time when metal was about to change the world we live in forever and glister Britain with the gold of mesmerising artefacts. But surely there's little point in poring over maps or head scratching about the possible routes of the Bluestones without addressing a fundamental question. What were the mechanics of it? How did our Neolithic ancestors physically move them?

WHEN I'D CHECKED IN AT THE RECEPTION OF MY HOTEL IN THE ancient Inca capital of Cuzco, the receptionist gave me my room key and some well-rehearsed and very sound advice, "We recommend sir, that you go straight to your room, where the porter will bring you a refreshing cup of tea. Drink it, then sleep for an hour or two, or just doze on your bed. You'll find it very beneficial."

That cup of mate-de-coca did indeed prove to be of great benefit in a city that sits just over 11,000 feet above sea level, as the herbal infusion of fresh cocaine leaves provides an effective prophylactic against altitude sickness. It was 1992, the time of a largely bloodless political coup in Peru, and I was a staff correspondent for the Daily Express, and in that wonderful country at a time when visitors were thin on the ground due to the activities of the Marxist guerrilla group Sendero Luminoso and a serious contagion of cholera. Peru, of course, is a country groaning under the sheer weight of vast, stone-built temples and fortresses erected by the Incas in the ascendancy of their spectacularly successful Empire of the Andes until 1572 when Spanish Conquistadores finally snuffed-out its unique Bronze Age civilisation.

A depressing end, except that in Peru the huge, black volcanic stones manhandled over valleys, across rivers and thousands of feet up the precipitous sides of mountains, still stand in silent but eloquent testimony to their past triumphs and peerless construction skills. Inca architecture is nothing less than epic sculpture, displayed at the gigantic fortifications of Sacsayhuaman above Cuzco and the mega-stone constructions at Ollanta Tambo in the Sacred Valley nearby. Machu Piccu, the world's motif for all things Inca, is another nearly incomprehensible example of what the 'low tech' Inca people were able to achieve through imagination and cosmic inspiration, together with ropes, timbers, and endless muscle.

Over the years, I've increasingly reflected on the similarities between the two megalithic cultures of the Inca and the Stonehenge people. What could they possibly have in common? Quite a bit, despite a time gap of around four thousand years, and a distance of six thousand miles across the Atlantic Ocean and the thick end of the South American continent. For a start, both cultures morphed into a Bronze Age and had no iron tools or weapons, neither had the wheel and both built their stone constructs without mortar.

However, both the Incas and the Henge people had mastered the technique of 'puddling' or waterproofing the bottoms of their constructions with clay, to prevent water leakage. In the case of the Incas this was evident on their spectacular stone aqueducts and here, on our islands, the most commonly occurring archaeological feature of all are 'burnt mounds' consisting of large oak-built coffers for communal cooking, brewing and maybe for sacred sweat lodges too, but crucially waterproofed with a lining of clay.

Again, both the Incas and the megalithic masons of Britain and Ireland, used hammer stones to dress and fit their handiwork, with endless hours of flaking and picking to achieve the results they desired. Research has shown the Inca stonemasons, working with extremely hard granite and basalt, struck the surface of the rock at an angle of fifteen to twenty degrees, to achieve maximum efficiency with their Neolithic implements. I think the masons who worked the Trilithons at Stonehenge, may have arrived at the same, skilled modus operandi too, through trial and error.

There are differences of course. For a start it's certain the Incas could not have achieved stonework on such an epic scale without the aid of herbal cocaine, which was vital to sustain human activity at such high altitudes and still is. Again, the Incas never, ever tried to move stone material the twenty miles our ancestors moved the Sarsen Stones from the Marlborough Downs to Stonehenge let alone the one hundred and fifty miles they shifted the Bluestones from Wales. Instead, they moved most of their stone a maximum of two or three miles, albeit across dizzying precipices and unbelievably punishing terrain.

Interestingly, we do have a Spanish, eyewitness account of the way Incas moved leviathan rocks and, observing one of the last of their monumental achievements, Garcilaso de la Vega reported, *"They moved them, dragging them with muscle power using thick ropes, neither were the paths which they hauled them along level, but very rough mountains with steep slopes over which they were moved up and down with sheer human strength."*

It must have been quite a spectacle with around two thousand men, according to de la Vega, using rope cables made from the immensely strong fourcroya vine, to drag boulders weighing up to one hundred tonnes, five or six kilometres across a valley to where they were needed. It's all very well then, to propose an overland itinerary for the Bluestones, with the A40 Lite route currently favourite, but it still begs the question as to how the Stonehenge people successfully moved eighty Bluestones the best part of two hundred miles?

Personally, I don't think we can look to the Inca model of sheer muscle power, for a couple of reasons. First, it's unlikely the priests and paramount chiefs of Neolithic Britain, had a pool of manpower large enough to recruit on the scale of the Incas who, we're told, had thousands of labourers at their disposal to haul their megaliths, as I say, usually no more than a couple of miles. Secondly, the Incas moved lots of stones that were many times larger even than the Stonehenge Trilithons, and I suspect Inca megaliths had no intrinsic, spiritual value until they were incorporated into a sacred structure. This being the case they could afford to write off any breakages caused by rough handling across such punishing terrain and with rocks so huge that wouldn't have been the end of the world for the Inca architects; there were plenty more where they came from.

It was a different deal altogether for our Neolithic forebears, who had a smaller labour force drawn from a significantly smaller population and it's evident their cargo of Bluestones were also possessed of an innately sacred nature from the moment they were quarried. On top of that they had a lot further to go, so I suggest the epic journey to Stonehenge would have required more ingenuity and a far gentler touch than the Incas applied to the movement of their megaliths. Not for a moment, do I suggest those South American geniuses were short on ingenuity, they had it in spades; they just applied it to other problems more relevant to their reality.

For a hundred years or more the favourite theory for the movement of all the megaliths to Stonehenge, and other stone temples like Avebury and Stanton Drew, was the roller method. Most of us are familiar with this idea, where round timbers are placed in front of the stone, reducing the friction of the ground, which is then hauled by ropes to roll over them. Other labourers would then collect the timbers left behind during this process, to plonk them in front of the stone again, and so on.

I've never believed the roller method was credible, largely because whenever I consider it visions of crushed appendages, snapped joints and lacerated limbs are conjured. I can only believe it would have crippled so many people; the number of life-changing injuries would have become society-changing and quite unsustainable. Still, I had no better ideas of my own and I hadn't heard of any others until I read about an experiment carried out at a park in London in 2016, a year after the A40 Route was first mooted; an experiment inspired by Prof. Parker-Pearson's ideas.

A group of students had entered a project into the University College of London's Festival of Culture, in which they aimed to show how Neolithic people, using Stone Age technology, might have efficiently moved a Bluestone overland. To do this they constructed a twelve-feet long sledge with a pointed and upturned prow, then loaded it with a one tonne concrete block to replicate a half-scale Bluestone. In front of the sledge, they laid out a solid timber track, which crucially did not move but provided a semi-permanent roadway to ease the passage of the sledge. The results were remarkable. Doctoral student Barnabas Harris, who designed the experiment, had calculated fifteen individuals would be needed to move the loaded sledge along the trackway, but the team managed quite adequately with ten individuals pulling the sledge with ropes.

All forty-five of the players in this experiment, appropriately called *Moving Stonehenge*, were first given a background briefing by Mike Parker-Pearson, before they hauled the sledge up-and-down the park, using twenty-two permutations of numbers and differing roles for the crew. Major modern concerns, which wouldn't have burdened our ancestors, were health and safety of course, and the need to minimise damage to the perfectly manicured lawns of Gordon Square Park in Bloomsbury, owned by UCL itself.

Nevertheless, the sledge method proved infinitely safer than the dodgy, and now largely discredited 'rolling log' idea. It doesn't take a leap of the imagination to realise that on solid ground or on downhill slopes, particularly on well-drained land in summer, the sledge would likely have worked perfectly well without the need for a trackway and that's an important point. There's little doubt in my mind, Bluestone moving would have been an early summer, pre-harvest time undertaking and given dry, stable conditions underfoot, a reasonably small team could have hurried the loaded sledge along until they came to softer terrain where they could lay a prefabricated, semi-permanent trackway.

Mike Parker-Pearson was probably delighted with the Barnabas Experiment, at least I hope so, but it doesn't airbrush away the serious problems built into his A40 Route. I know the countryside it runs through well, and as I've already suggested, there are some serious obstacles along the way. For me, it's important when considering the A40 Route to rid our minds of the image of the present day, tarmac road from Preseli to the edge of Salisbury Plain. This may seem obvious, but I believe the simple act of naming the route after a well-maintained, modern road makes it subliminally more feasible and lends it a baseline of credibility it may not deserve. But is a seaward passage for the Bluestones any more credible? Time to look at the evidence and the options.

7

THE ESCALATOR

I spent much of my childhood and teens on the shores of the Bristol Channel, much of it as a kid growing up on Barry Island, and it's a seascape close to my heart. Stained by silt washed down from Wales and the Midlands by the mighty River Severn, the Channel is not the most inviting of waters until the current loses its grip on the sediment around the Gower coast and the sea becomes crystal clear.

I've always had a hunch the Bluestones made their way around the coast of Wales to the Bristol Avon, and then across to Stonehenge, and I've even had dreams of a dolerite rock somehow transmogrified into a boat, cruising up the channel with a sparkling bow wave, my partner Stephanie helming it through my imagination. That's not to say I'm blindly attached to the sea-borne theory of the Bluestone passage to Stonehenge, I'm not, and later I'll make the case for the Altar Stone being transported from Scotland overland rather than by sea, an altogether much longer cross-country journey.

When it comes down to it there are no facts to back-up either theory in the epic story of the Bluestones, but in the absence of firm archaeological evidence to the contrary I hope to prove a sea passage from Preseli would have been the natural one for our ancestors to have chosen and offer compelling reasons to back up that assertion.

We first need to ask whether those Neolithic people had the skills, and the vessels, needed to pull-off such a famous feat of seamanship no fewer than eighty times? Just how would they navigate the Bristol Channel, notorious for the second highest tidal range in the world, with ship-wrecking squalls that seem to come out of nowhere.

The truth is that more than five thousand years ago, men and women of extraordinary mettle were sailing the cold, exhilarating, often wild and always unforgiving seas around Northern Europe, to satisfy their burning impulses to explore, migrate to new territories, and follow the age-old pursuit of trade. We know this happened because the evidence is abundant and speaks for itself; it's called settlement.

Quite simply, many of those folk colonised islands and coastal margins, which could only be reached by seaworthy vessels across challenging and dangerous waters. Indeed, the islands of Britain and Ireland were settled by farming people who sailed or paddled here in craft that were buoyant enough to carry their families, their seeds for planting and even their superior breeds of domestic livestock. The tide rushed them in, and the song of the sea was surely in their veins.

These weren't skin-clad savages we've seen depicted, swept hither and thither like flotsam on crude boats no better than scooped out logs. Those ideas are nothing less than expressions of hindsight condescension by historians, as is the notion the ancients may not have had the skills to navigate the Bristol Channel. In my view it's patronising and flies in the face of overwhelming evidence to the contrary. There's certainly enough geographical evidence of maritime movement in the Neolithic, to fill several books.

First our ancient forebears colonised the Channel Islands of Jersey and Guernsey, which form an island bridge with the continental shores of France. Hugging the coast around Devon and Cornwall they settled sheltered coves to exploit the rich fishing, and they reached the Isles of Scilly, twenty-five miles off Lands' End, founding a vibrant community half of which was inundated in a later, Bronze Age climate event.

Others took a direct route from Iberia to negotiate the daunting, open waters of the Atlantic and colonise Ireland, some of them made landfall on the opposite shores of the Celtic Sea beneath Preseli, where they discovered the extraordinary Bluestones and made them the focus of a cult. Sailing on through the Celtic Sea we eventually come to the Isle of Man, where once again Neolithic people settled to farm and fish, leaving the ghost of their booming society in villages, cliff forts, cairns, and standing stones.

Northwards to Scotland and the famous archipelago of the Western Isles, where there's abundant evidence of Neolithic activity; not least the sophisticated moon temple of Calanais on the Isle of Lewis. No surprise really because Mesolithic hunter gatherers had managed to voyage there first, and I can't imagine for a moment these disparate communities just sat there, never voyaging to visit their neighbours or to fish and take flocks to graze on uninhabited off-islands.

At the very apex of Scotland, where the Atlantic meets the North Sea, are the Orkney Islands, and here we find one of the most momentous Neolithic landscapes in Europe where a World Heritage Site encompassing the Ness of Brodgar, the Stones of Stenness, Maes Howe and Skara Brae, rivals that of Stonehenge itself. Great trading folk, the Orcadian sailors brought continental cuisine home in the form of Common Voles, found impaled on cooking spits in the archaeological record with DNA showing the voles were imported from Belgium; a species, twice the size of our native British field voles and found nowhere else on the Islands of Britain and Ireland. Even further north, a hundred and sixty miles across open ocean and just four hundred miles below the Arctic Circle, Neolithic seamen colonised the Shetland Isles and founded a thriving whale hunting community.

In the North Sea there's evidence of a rich, Neolithic trade in amber beads from the Baltic shores of Estonia and Denmark to grace the jewellery of our Neolithic elite, in life and in death. Exquisite jadeite axes were brought from the distant Italian Alps, to be traded as status symbols and surely crossed the English Channel on some form of Neolithic ferry service to Dover. I may be labouring the point a little, but you can see what I'm getting at. These were consummate navigators and given their epic seagoing achievements, I'd say those Neolithic navigators could handle the seas around Wales, no problem.

The question of the vessels they used is more difficult and immediately comes up against a simple reality, wood rots. Consequently, the number of boats surviving from the Neolithic and Early Bronze Age is tiny, with only twenty or so examples in the whole of Britain, most of which are fragmentary. The finest example is the Dover Boat, which was found during work on a pedestrian underpass in 1992 and is a well-preserved example of a so-called sewn plank boat. This is pre-nail technology, as bronze nails just buckle when you bash them. Instead, overlapping boat planks were drilled, tied together with yew strips, then caulked with moss and pitch to make them waterproof, and nearly ten meters of the Dover hull were successfully salvaged from what had been a creek on the River Dour, leading to the English Channel.

Neolithic, sewn plank vessels have also been found on the Humber estuary at Ferriby and judged capable of carrying cargo of up to five tonnes, with the latest dating putting them in the same time frame as Stonehenge, so maybe something similar carried the Bluestones. Another ocean-going craft from those time is the currach, still used Ireland and built with waterproofed skins stretched tight over a wooden frame. Lightweight and up to thirty feet long, they could have operated with a small lug sail, according to the National Museum of Ireland. Somehow I don't see them carrying four tonne slabs of stone but, if you fancy a go there's a busy summer programme of currach racing on the west coast of Ireland, with fibre glass versions on sale at around 3000 euros a pop.

More importantly for the case I'm making, remnants of prehistoric boats have been found in the upper reaches of the Severn Estuary around Caldicot and Goldcliff, just below the Second Severn Crossing, where remains of sewn plank hulls have been found. I've no doubt channel crossings were made regularly between Wales and Bristol, and to reinforce this point the remains of a prehistoric 'hard,' a well-constructed jetty built of oak, have been found at Caldicott.

This is hugely significant in terms of Bluestone theories, as you don't build a hard for fun, it's done to tie-up boats out of reach of tide and storm so that cargoes and passengers can embark and disembark safely. They are formalised structures with a trading purpose, requiring a great community investment and a glance at a map, or indeed a maritime chart, will instantly reveal the significance of Caldicot and Goldcliff, with both in perfect locations for a cross-channel voyage, roughly opposite the mouth of the Bristol Avon. Moreover, Goldcliff is just a couple of miles upstream from the mouth of the Usk and, if Mike Pitts' A40 Lite theory is correct, the Bluestones might have been navigated out of the mouth of the river up to Goldcliff or Caldicot, then steered across to Avonmouth.

Goldcliff may also have played another key maritime role in any Bluestone voyage, providing a powerful, navigational aide for ancient Bristol Channel mariners. Originally, an island on the edge of a large salt marsh, today you'll find a well-constructed sea wall of limestone blocks cladding the forty-foot-high, cliff but that conceals a seven-foot-wide seam of Fools' Gold, once visible for miles down the channel as the iron pyrites glittered in the sunlight. About fifteen years ago, I visited Goldcliff and spoke to older locals, who could remember that wonderful sight before the cliff had been walled by the limestone blocks of a sea defence, and I'm sure those Cliffs of Gold would have been an awe-inspiring landmark and important navigational aid to the sea captains of the Neolithic and Early Bronze Age, as well as a source of pyrites firelighters.

So, our ancestors had the skills, and they seem to have had the vessels too, but which route would they have taken? Essentially, there are two credible seaward passages for the Bluestones. The first crosses from Wales to round Lands' End and then hug the south coast to enter the mouth of the Wiltshire Avon at Mudeford, before following the river's course north to Amesbury and Stonehenge. The other passage sees the Bluestones sailed from the natural harbour of Milford Haven in Pembrokeshire, then past the Gower Penninsula and along the South Wales coast to Caldicott on the Severn Estuary, opposite the mouth of the Bristol Avon.

This last section, across the neck of the channel then overland, fits the Mike Pitts A40 Lite narrative with the stones arriving at the mouth of the Usk to cross the estuary, but for me the complete Bristol Channel route seems the more convenient and obvious option, and the one I intuitively believe the ancients took. Then a chance conversation with an old friend opened my eyes to the inbuilt advantages of the Bristol Channel. I've known Captain Peter Binding for most of my life and while I pursued a career in journalism he, like his father and grandfather before him, made his living on the Channel as a Master Mariner who skippers a prestigious Trinity House Vessel sailing out of the port of Barry.

For those of you who aren't aware, Trinity House is the authority which has been responsible for the safe navigation of the seas around

England and Wales since its Royal Charter in 1513. The Captain's duties include the servicing of buoys and lighthouses, and the mapping of wrecks and sandbanks in the Channel (both of which can and do move under the relentless power of the tide) for the updating of the charts and navigational apps, relied on by commercial and recreational sailors alike.

He is without doubt the leading, living expert on the Bristol Channel and in September 2019, four years after Mike Parker-Pearson's A40 Route was first mooted, he was writing a magazine article about the important Roman harbour facilities at Barry, something I was only vaguely aware of despite years of living in the town. He explained there'd been three Roman harbours at Barry, two of them to the west of the town at Porthkerry and Cold Knap and one in a place called the Old Harbour, where the stonework of the original Roman quay can still be seen, supporting a more recent lime kiln above. I was fascinated as he talked me through the Roman naval complex, and then I asked the obvious question. Why Barry?

"The tide," said Captain Binding, "Barry is just one tide away from the mouth of the River Usk where the Romans had big military garrisons at Caerleon and Caerwent, which they re-supplied from the sea. Roman vessels would sail around Land's End, then up the channel to Barry, then wait for the tide to carry them up to the Usk as there's absolutely no point trying to go against the tide in the Bristol Channel. Wait and it would carry them effortlessly up to the Usk like a natural escalator."

As soon as he said it the penny dropped. I had memories of that great wall of Atlantic water surging into the restrictive funnel of the Bristol Channel, then lifting itself to an astounding height of forty-four feet, the second highest in the world after the Bay of Fundy in Canada. The tide dictated where and when we played as kids on the Island, and everything had to accommodate it, including the harbour architecture and the extra-long Lifeboat slipway needed to reach the water to launch at the lowest tides. I made an immediate link to the Bluestones and asked whether they could have been moved using the tide as a natural conveyor belt.

At the time Captain Binding knew nothing about Neolithic seamanship, but in theory he saw no reason why not, as long as they had suitable vessels. I was surprised to hear him dismiss Milford Haven as the port of embarkation for the Bluestones in favour of Newport, Pembrokeshire, which is indeed very close to the main quarry sources. And then I was taken aback when he offered this, "The Bluestones could have been floated from Newport to the mouth of the Bristol Avon on perhaps six tides in nine days, providing the weather and sea states were favourable."

Captain Binding had breathed new life into the Bluestone debate for the simple reason that in everything I'd previously read or heard from historians and archaeologists barely mentioned the tide except in a negative way. For them, the Bristol Channel tide was something that had to be overcome and, as if to prove them correct and reinforce this view, the power of the tide had been a factor in confounding at least two experimental voyages in replica, sewn-plank boats. Certainly, the tide has never been portrayed as a massive positive, and never as a natural escalator with an entirely predictable timetable, there to be ridden up the Channel by those in the know.

It's a game changer in the 'By Land' or 'By Sea' debate, and when I drove back over the Second Severn Crossing, the idea for this book was beginning to coalesce. Then along came Covid and together with the rest of the world I was distracted until early in 2022 when my conviction the powerful element of the tide and the Bluestones needed to be championed, set me to writing.

During this process I've had several conversations with Captain Binding, and I'll crystallise his opinions below although he insists I reiterate his opinions are based entirely on his knowledge of the vagaries of the Bristol Channel and freely admits they may be wrong when applied to the Neolithic world of Britain.

First, Captain Binding recognizes Neolithic sailors were absolute masters of their element and believes their skills, in terms of innate seamanship, knowledge of tides and currents, and awareness of coming weather, would easily eclipse modern, small boat sailors equipped with digital, navigation aids. Having said that, he doesn't believe any of the known models of Neolithic boats could safely carry the dead weight of a large slab of stone on the challenging Bristol Channel. At first this led him to side with the argument they'd been carried by land, aligning his opinion with the leading archaeologists proposing the A40 and A40 Lite routes. Not exactly what I was hoping for, as it didn't neatly fit my own speculative narrative of a seaward passage for the stones.

Working on the premise only rafts could have successfully carried the Bluestones, the Captain believes they would have had to coast-hop using the powerful tide of the Bristol Channel (Mor Hafren in Welsh) to carry them along, aided by the prevailing south westerly winds. Trying to paddle or sail against the tide is absolutely impossible and they would have worked with it, possibly with sewn plank or curragh-style boats lashed to either side of a raft, manned simply to steer the stones up the Channel. They would have anticipated when the tide was about to turn and then steered the raft close to shore to secure it with stone anchors below the tide line, then rest and wait until it turned to flow up the channel again, when they'd hitch another lift.

The ancient sailors would have paid close attention to the weather as the perfect combination would have been a strong tide and moderate, prevailing south westerly winds. Easterly winds, blowing onto the Bristol Channel would spell big problems as they are a well-known recipe for very rough and unpredictable seas, jeopardising both crew and cargo. At the first sign of an easterly, Captain Binding believes they would have anchored close to shore, perhaps even beached, and waited out the weather.

He surprised me when he dismissed Milford Haven as the port of embarkation out-of-hand and insisted Newport, Pembrokeshire, a matter of a few miles from all the main quarry sources of Bluestone, would be a master mariner's obvious choice; 'a no-brainer', in his words. With this in mind, they would have used the south running tide to expedite the thirty-five-mile passage from Newport around St David's Head and St Annes Head and past the mouth of Milford Haven. The flow through Ramsey Sound and Jack Sound at St David's, can reach up to nine knots but with a favourable wind the Captain says this would be a relatively simple passage for experienced Neolithic seamen.

Archaeologists have red flagged this passage as too dangerous for Neolithic mariners, but Captain Binding absolutely dismisses these arguments as misguided and plain wrong. He believes the voyage around the St David's peninsula would be routine for experienced Neolithic sailors. In his view the really dangerous part of a Bristol Channel passage would be the steep Liassic cliffs of the Glamorgan coast, with its boulder strewn beaches, with only two or three notched bays along the line of cliffs, and they would be difficult anchorages to accommodate the tide or escape easterly storms. The captain thinks the Bluestone crews would have timed their voyage to slide past this dangerous stretch on a single tide to Barry, while keeping a weather eye open for any hint of an easterly wind.

The crews would have paid particular attention to any chafing of the ropes, lashing the Bluestones into the frame of a raft. They would have frequently checked the state of the ropes against the sharper edges of the stones and would have carried a lot of spare rope in support vessels; rope being one of the most successful technologies of the Neolithic era.

MAP OF THE NOTIONAL ROUTES OF THE BLUESTONES

These are the three main routes proposed for the transport of the Bluestones from the cluster of quarries on Preseli. One is by land north of the Brecon Beacons, crossing the River Severn near Gloucester and on to Stonehenge, and is known as the A40 Route. The second, proposed by Mike Pitts, I call the A40 Lite because it takes a shortcut from the A40 route by heading for the sea at Uskmouth to cross the Bristol Channel and head for Stonehenge via the Bristol Avon. The third is by sea around the coast of South Wales, using the tide as a powerful natural escalator,

crossing the channel to Bristol then along the Rivers Avon, Frome and Wylye to Salisbury Plain and Stonehenge. Again, this is my hand drawn offering so pardon my cartographical skills.

It would have been common sense for a sea voyage of the Bluestones to be made with several stones at the same time in a flotilla of vessels, according to the captain. He imagines a scene where accompanying support boats would be in attendance, while back-up parties on land would be monitoring the progress of the stones from vantage points, ready to assist if needed. Captain Binding paints an inspiring picture of cheering communities gathered on significant headlands, waving the Bluestones on their way.

He surprised me with another impressive nugget of navigational knowledge when he mentioned the extra sailing time the ancients might have gained from the natural phenomenon of 'reverse tides' in the sweep of large bays. When the tide ebbs or flows in the general surge of the channel a relatively small contra-flow, develops in the opposite direction inside the shelter of a bay. He believes the Neolithic sailing masters, would have known all about this effect, and over the course of the voyage could have gained nearly a day's sailing by utilising it.

In perfect conditions, the Captain thought it would take around six tides and a matter of only nine days for a raft to reach the mouth of the Bristol Avon from Newport, Pembrokeshire, simply by using the power of the tide, with favourable prevailing winds, anchoring the vessel in step with its ebb and flow. Think of it. Six tides. Nine days!

For me the predictable, metronomic power of the Bristol Channel tide combined with the evident expertise of Neolithic seamen, and their ingrained knowledge of the seas around our coast, make the most persuasive argument for the transport of the Bluestones. I also believe it might explain the frequency of journey's to and from Preseli by people like the Winterbourne Chieftain as we come to view the Bristol Channel as a rapid, seaborne, Neolithic super-highway.

There was still one piece of the theory missing because Captain Binding still doubted the Neolithic craft we are aware of would be up to the job of carrying the Bluestones, again refusing to neatly validate my theory. Then, in October 2022 events took a slightly surreal turn when

Captain Binding called and, without any preamble, announced, "Stones weigh less in water."

I didn't get it immediately, until he sent me a link to an illustration he'd found, which portrayed a Bluestone underslung beneath a raft, so the water lapped above the stone and covered it. Eureka! Of course! Archimedes Theory of Displacement put into practice, all that stuff about buoyant force and fluid density we learn at school. It means the slabs of Bluestone would weigh approximately a third less in water, with the log assemblage of the raft providing the buoyancy necessary to carry it on the tide.

Once the Bluestone had been dragged on a sledge, most likely housed in a wooden cradle, from Preseli to the sheltered estuary of the Nyfri at Newport, it could be placed below the high tide line and the raft floated into position above it when the tide rose again. Bluestone and raft lashed together, with a sewn-plank boat roped to each side for steerage, and there you have it, a viable vessel to contend with the challenge of the Bristol Channel and a perfect vehicle to ride the tide.

The diagram he sent me, came from a book called *Stonehenge Solved by Len Saunders*, published in 2009. Intriguing, and that underslung cargo model certainly provides a solution for the Captain's doubts about the stability of Neolithic boats. Sadly, Len passed away in 2018 so there's no opportunity to speak to him about it and unfortunately, whilst Len's book has the diagram and a description of how he thought the ancients would have slung Bluestones under rafts, he doesn't spell out why they would have done so. There's no mention of Displacement Theory in the text, but then Len Saunders was a professional engineer and I'm guessing he thought the reason would be obvious to anyone but an idiot. Well, it's not of course, and there are lots of impractical idiots like me out there who need the obvious link to Archimedes spelt out.

Peter Binding had seen it immediately and believes it would be the only practical way to set the Bluestones on the water, before letting the tide do the heavy lifting. No surprise really, as he has long practical experience of this phenomenon on the Channel, with the huge navigation buoys he regularly deals with held on station by steel chains attached to large weights called sinkers. The preferred material for a sinker is cast iron as concrete sinkers, in line with Archimedes, would need to be of a much greater volume.

It's fair to ask whether our ancestors would have understood Archimedes' Theory. Well, probably not in the formal sense although, as we'll discover, they certainly understood complex geometry thousands of years before Pythagoras. However, I'm a great believer in discovery through experience, and there's no reason why Neolithic people shouldn't have had the wit to come to their own practical understanding of displacement theory through trial and error.

Captain Binding's view that Newport not Milford Haven would have been the natural choice for a port of embarkation is an important idea too. For decades, historians and archaeologists alike, have ruled out any passage around St David's Head as far too dangerous, and they often cite disastrous experimental archaeology, where replicas of a Dover Boat-style of sewn plank vessel, have been swamped or sunk on Bluestone re-enactment voyages; mostly with inexperienced crews of archaeology students trying to paddle against the tide.

More recently, however, Prof. Parker-Pearson seems to have softened his position and, if I understand him correctly, allows for the possibility the stones might indeed have been taken to the sea at Newport for passage up the channel, and Peter Binding's dismissal of the dangers of St David's Head puts Newport firmly in focus. Not only does Newport have a sheltered haven, but it's convenient for all the main sources of Bluestones.

Newport, as I've mentioned before, is a beguiling place squeezed between the imposing Preseli peak of Carn Ingli and the sea at the mouth of the Afon Nyfir - the River Nevern. Newport is no more than four and a half miles from Waun Mawn, about three from the newly identified quarry sites at Carn Goedog and Craig Rhos-y-Felin, suggested by Parker-Pearson; six from Carn Menyn. There's a harbour at Newport called The Parrog, which was established in the 18th Century to replace a far more ancient landing, apparently left high and dry by a change in the estuary's looping course. As far as I'm aware there's never been a detailed geophysical survey or excavation of any of the area surrounding the estuary of the Nyfir, leaving big questions to be answered by archaeology, the most important being, is there a Neolithic hard at Newport? What we do know is the wonderful dolmen of Carreg Coetan Arthur stands a bowshot from the estuary, and it's constructed with very large Bluestones.

A SUGGESTED BLUESTONE RAFT

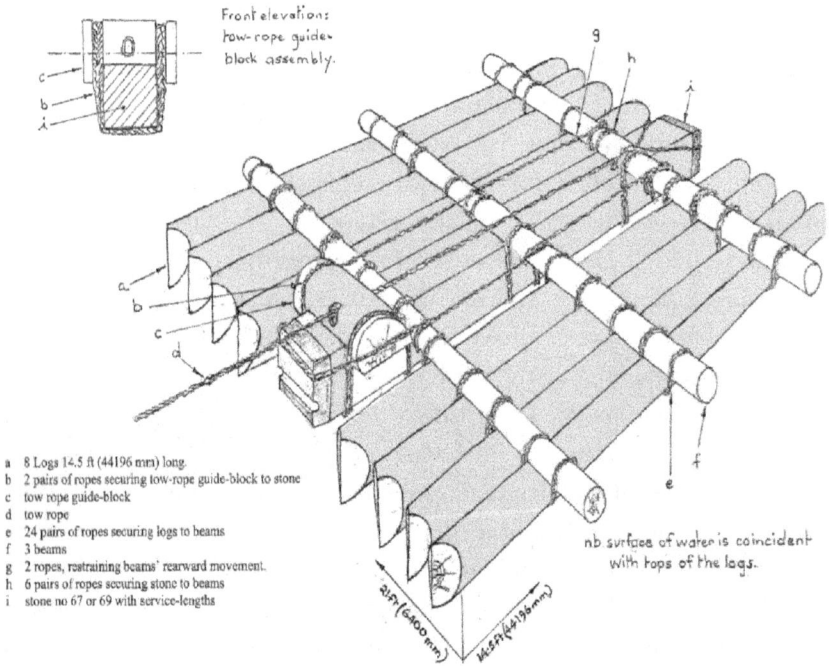

Front elevation: tow-rope guide-block assembly.

a   8 Logs 14.5 ft (44196 mm) long.
b   2 pairs of ropes securing tow-rope guide-block to stone
c   tow rope guide-block
d   tow rope
e   24 pairs of ropes securing logs to beams
f   3 beams
g   2 ropes, restraining beams' rearward movement.
h   6 pairs of ropes securing stone to beams
i   stone no 67 or 69 with service-lengths

nb. surface of water is coincident with tops of the logs.

21 Ft (6400 mm)

14.5 Ft (44196 mm)

Courtesy of Ian Tresman, Computer Knowledge.

This illustration shows Len Saunders' concept of a raft carrying an underslung Bluestone, covered by the channel water, to take advantage of Archimedes' Principle, and reduce the effective weight of the stone by roughly a third. The annotation on the diagram is in Len's own hand and includes figure d) a tow rope, but Captain Binding says a raft wouldn't need to be towed as the tide would simply carry it up the channel. Instead, it might have had Neolithic boats (curraghs or sewn plank vessels) lashed to each side, with a crew paddling solely for the purpose of steering the raft, which would be moored close to shore between rising tides.

My partner Dr. Stephanie Shelburne and I know Newport well, but we decided to have a closer look in the autumn of 2023 and found some interesting clues to back-up the assertion it was indeed the Bluestone embarkation port. We stayed with our friends Ed and Lou Sykes at their wonderful hotel and restaurant Llys Meddyg, just a five-minute stroll from the estuary. Llys Meddyg is a great place but it's also the best landmark to guide you into the Neolithic heart of Newport, the dolmen of Carreg Coetan Arthur, one of the three wonderful guardians of Carn Ingli mountain I've already mentioned. If you're driving from Fishguard to Cardigan on the main A487 road, you can't miss Llys Meddyg on your left-hand side as you're about to leave town, then turn directly left alongside it. You'll find Carreg Coetan about a hundred yards down the lane, again on your left.

Carreg Coetan is 5000 years old, placing it right at the same time-frame as the movement of Bluestones from Preseli to Stonehenge, but was there a Neolithic hard nearby? Stephanie and I went to pay our regards to Carreg Coetan then continued our exploration, walking over the river bridge to get a better view of the southern shore from the other side of the estuary. Stephanie sensibly pointed out any Bluestone harbour facilities would likely have been on that southern side, nearest the quarries, and we soon spotted a small, but significant creek cut in a neat square into the marshy bank, evidently man-made and notable enough to be clearly marked on maps of the area.

Back on the southern side to investigate this creek we realised it's adjacent to the remains of the first castle to be built in the area by the Normans, a rudimentary palisade and ditch fortification hastily thrown up by the invaders and known as Hen Castell, the Old Castle, a feature I'd long forgotten about. It was later superseded by a more substantial and defendable, stone fortification higher up the valley. In recent times Hen Castell has had a tennis court built over its south-western corner, however, its location is adjacent to the square-cut creek we'd spotted, which was obviously a Norman harbour for ease of seaborne supply during open warfare with the locals. It'd known the Norman stockade of Hen Castell had been built over a previous Iron Age structure and, who knows, it may have been a centre of activity in the Bronze Age and

Neolithic eras too, but no extensive archaeology has been done to comprehensively age the site.

Stephanie and I engaged in a bit of head scratching and map poring, which revealed the cromlech at Carreg Coetan Arthur lines-up with the Hen Castell and its adjacent harbour creek, in a straight alignment with the North Star. No surprise then, if I were looking for a Bluestone loading wharf, in other words a Neolithic hard, I think I'd start right there at Hen Castell, and I'd dearly love to see a geophysics drone buzzing over the estuary site any time soon.

My theory maintains the Bluestones were moved in a startlingly rapid time of under a fortnight, through the powerful natural escalator of the Bristol Channel tide and I've identified a strong contender for the port of embarkation as Newport, Pembrokeshire. But here's one more esoteric piece of evidence for a seaward conveyance of the Bluestones, which links Newport to Stonehenge.

One of the imponderables of any voyage is the danger of being lost at sea through sudden storms and squalls, and that's where the enigmatic role of Lundy Island comes into play. Lundy is a stark, granite outcrop with dizzying cliffs, lying ten miles off the Devon coast, at the point where the Atlantic Ocean meets the Bristol Channel. If a vessel is driven by a storm or loses steering in those waters it's more than likely to pass close to Lundy before being swept out to the open ocean, offering a last chance for a landfall and safety.

On the three-mile-long island, there are nine standing stones from the time of Stonehenge, and studies show they were arranged to form a celestial clock. There's also a small cairn of rocks, piled around another standing stone, as if to hide it from sight. It's three hundred and ten meters north of an old lighthouse building on windswept, open ground called Acklands Moor, at a point which forms a right angle, with a high degree of accuracy, between Newport and Stonehenge itself.

And if that's not spine tingling enough there are two Welsh names for the island. Ynys Wair is a twelfth century 'Arthurian' name referencing Merlin, while the more ancient Brythonic name is Ynys Fenelin, which translates as 'island of the elbow, bend or right angle.' Maybe then, Lundy was an ancient Neolithic, navigational aide pointing shipwrecked sailors and lost Bluestone rafts in the direction of Stonehenge. Who knows, but I'm quite prepared to believe it's true as we know those Stonehenge people had more than enough knowledge of geometry, astronomy and the whole earth science of geodesy to have arrived at this complex triangulation.

It's my belief the awesome, metronomic power of the Bristol Channel tide makes the strongest, logical case for the shipment of the Bluestones. Do I believe our Neolithic forebears could have dragged the stones around the long and exhausting A40 Route? Of course, I do they were a resourceful, motivated, and indefatigable people, obviously capable of gigantic feats. The truth is the argument for either route is purely circumstantial. Unless and until a Bluestone remnant, perhaps a lump broken off a slab, is found somewhere along the A40 Route it will remain an unproven theory, but wouldn't it be great if a Bluestone was found lying on the remains of an ancient log trackway over boggy ground, somewhere near Brecon?

On the other hand, there have been at least two claims of the discovery of sunken Bluestones, lending credence to the sea passage argument until they proved to be unfounded. If a Bluestone, covered in silt, were discovered on the remains of a sunken raft, somewhere near the Hen Castell in Newport my joy would be unalloyed, but until such a discovery is made, needs must, the debate will rumble on. However, I'm going to apply Occam's Razor to the alternatives and suggest the short haul off Preseli to Newport then, in good conditions, a nine-day ride on the tide would be the itinerary of choice for the ancestors, especially as they were steeped in a maritime culture.

I think my last word on this subject should be an acknowledgment of the logistical mastery possessed by those long-dead, Pembrokeshire folk who made that pioneering journey, whether they moved the Bluestones by land or by sea. A band of intrepid, determined individuals, they would have been the heroes of their day, cheered on their way, feted and celebrated by their communities long into their old age. Their names would have been recited and stories of their exploits told and retold for generations in the fireside circle of light, and they would have been esteemed as the founders of a great temple.

More than that, it's clear some of them were cremated and buried with reverence in the Bluestone sockets of the Aubrey Holes at Stonehenge, and it's my settled opinion, that chief amongst them would have been the Lithonauts, the Stone Navigators of the Bristol Channel, possessed of a faraway gaze, with the song of the sea surging in their veins. I imagine the thrilling sight of a flotilla of vessels carrying the Bluestones around the Worms Head on passage for the Avon; it's a heart pounding vision that won't easily fade.

Now the time has come to reveal the innate, and absolutely stunning geological characteristics of the Bluestones, which made them sacred to our Neolithic ancestors and absolutely indispensable for their great temple project at Stonehenge. The unique combination of characteristics endowed in the Bluestones are surely the reason they were moved in the first place.

8

STAR STONES

On the face of it, the only thing the two distinct geographical areas of Preseli and Salisbury Plain had in common during the Neolithic may have been grazing sheep and that's pretty much true to this day, so what were the overarching reasons for carrying the Bluestones such a distance?

Surely, those slabs of dolerite and rhyolite had to be very special indeed. Certainly, their alignment with the Solstice at Stonehenge was a function that could have been achieved by using other rocks, and indeed that eventually happened when the Sarsen trilithons from the neighbouring Marlborough Downs were incorporated into the henge.

Many other geologically different stones, in hundreds of other locations all over the islands of Britain and Ireland, were also deliberately aligned in some solar or lunar aspect. However, no other temple on these islands has comprised stones moved more than ten miles, let alone the 150 miles the eighty Bluestones travelled, marking them out as very special indeed and the question remains, why?

In Pembrokeshire people still believe Bluestones have the power of healing and that ancient narrative of seemingly magical, curative properties has also persisted down many centuries one hundred and fifty miles away in the Salisbury area. Was that it? Did the Neolithic people consider the stones to be therapeutic? I'm certain they must have, and I'll discuss this healing theory in more detail later, but would that be a compelling enough motive for moving the Bluestones such a distance? It may well have been part of the story, but there is an altogether more jaw-dropping inspiration as Bluestones uniquely possess natural, almost supernatural characteristics that endow them with an aura of the sacred and celestial. They are characteristics so powerful they inspired our ancestors to invest the enormous communal energy needed to transport those precious slabs from Preseli to the Plain, where they stand impervious to the elements to this day.

Despite first appearances, the Bluestones are not just dark lumps of rock like any other, albeit in a special setting, because that obvious grey surface is nothing more than an oxidised layer and the result of exposure to air and light. It's rock-rust if you like, hiding the inner beauty of the stone beneath but chip away at that oxidised layer and you'll find a different beast altogether as you expose a deep blue or green rock, which comes alive with the speckles and pins of sparkling quartz and feldspar-like minerals.

In short, raw Bluestone mimics the night sky and to the ancients it must have seemed like the stars above had been captured in the very essence of the mountain, a wonderfully sacred thing indeed, making the Bluestones of Preseli stand out in the Neolithic imagination. These days the word awesome is bandied about until its currency has little value, but I'm sure the sight of the constellations seemingly transfixed in stone, would have been truly awe-inspiring to our Neolithic forebears.

To the ancients they would look like nothing less than millions of twinkling stars captured in rock and it's fair to speculate, perhaps only the passage of the sun and the moon would have held more powerful symbolism for those people. No wonder they first used them for stone circles, menhirs and dolmen, in their original landscape of Pembrokeshire, no wonder they wanted them for their big temple project at Stonehenge, and no wonder either that the Winterbourne Chieftain's, Pembrokeshire family were so involved in making Stonehenge happen.

How did this innately, cosmic quality of the stones impact the way the Neolithic people may have viewed them and ultimately, how they displayed them in their assemblages on Preseli, at Bluestone Henge or at Stonehenge itself? I think the answer might lie in a layer of Bluestone flakes, chippings, and mulched dust, discovered under the turf at Stonehenge, referred to by archaeologists as the Stonehenge Layer or the Bluestone Debitage, a posh word for a spoil heap. I sometimes call it the Bluestone Crumble.

It's extremely difficult to quantify the components of this layer, which contains elements of all the rock types found at Stonehenge, including the giant Sarsens brought from the Marlborough Downs, as well as rhyolitic and spotted dolerite from Preseli. As much as half of it is rhyolite, and about twenty per cent spotted dolerite. Various experts have sampled this Bluestone Crumble over the decades, including Mike Pitts some forty years ago in an emergency excavation when Post Office engineers over-extended their own cable trench on the old road, and opened a seam of the layer at the base of the Heel Stone. More recently Bevins and Ixer of Craig Rhos-y-Felin fame, have tasted the crumble too as they searched for samples to match against quarry sources in Preseli.

In 2008, during their notable work at Stonehenge, another duo of leading experts on the monument, Prof. Tim Darvill of Bournemouth University, and his friend, the late Geoffrey Wainwright, a Pembrokeshire born archaeologist, also studied the layer. Their book, *The Stones of Stonehenge* is well worth reading, not least because it gives a shout out for the established, south Preseli quarry of Carn Menyn, as a source of many of the Stones and emphasises the importance of Stonehenge as a place of healing.

In 2011, they laid out their conclusions on the debitage in an article in Current Archaeology magazine: *"Our excavations confirmed what earlier excavations had hinted at: namely that the Bluestones started to be broken up and chipped away more or less from the time they were set up in each successive arrangement.*

"The great spread of flakes and debris, usually referred to as the Stonehenge Layer, is not as once thought the debris from a one-off act of dressing the stones prior to their erection. Instead, these flakes have accumulated over millennia and include evidence for the use of Bluestone to fashion axes."

These are important conclusions acknowledging the Stonehenge Layer was not the result of a one-off shaping exercise, but deposited inch-by-inch over millennia prompting the question, why were the ancients nibbling, slowly away at the Bluestones? It's suggested this accretion of the Layer was left-over from a destruction process, basically lumps knocked off for axes, sacred relics and healing keepsakes, and I suppose that's a reasonable inference, accounting for at least some of the layer.

But once again I'm going to apply Occam's Razor and suggest the ancient custodians of Stonehenge would not have sourced and transported slabs of stone with the utterly special quality of imitating the sky at night, then simply allow the weathering process to hide that magic. Wouldn't you or I want to invest time and energy into preserving such a stunning visual impact too, by periodically chipping and polishing off successive layers of the oxidised surface, by getting rid of that rock-rust to reveal the Bluestone night sky in all its glory. It's my belief the Bluestone Layer is nothing less than evidence of an ongoing, Neolithic and Early Bronze Age conservation programme, with relics and healing talismans perhaps a by-product of the process.

I once chipped away at a Bluestone myself, at Carn Menyn when I was a kid on a family trip to Pembrokeshire, where we have family roots. The effect was thrilling as the rock seemed to ignite with life in my hand and I remember it to this day, although my recollections are somewhat tinged with the guilt of hindsight as I had, in effect vandalised a special place, albeit long before the Carn was designated a protected Site of Special Scientific Interest. On another visit pre-Covid, with my partner Dr. Stephanie Shelburne, we heard the dull smash of hammers in a cleft out of sight on the crag. Sure enough, a couple of blokes were smashing at the stones and packing them into a rucksack, obviously to sell them on the black market. My days of confrontation were sadly behind me, but when we returned to our car there was only one other vehicle nearby so, setting aside my own juvenile culpability, I took the registration to pass on to the authorities, guessing the car might belong to the rock-looters.

The remarkable visually aesthetic property of Bluestone has indeed led to a thriving, international trade in the sacred stone of Preseli, both legal and illicit. It's a 21st Century demand undoubtedly fuelled by talk of Druids and Stonehenge, a link that's been debunked by science but won't go away. It's a demand that spans the spectrum from the tasteful with Bluestone chips mounted in lovely, legally sourced jewellery, to garish, awful stuff such as Bluestone skulls sculpted in China to supply the questionable, so-called pagan market. Shame on people who buy such tasteless junk, offensively consuming a piece of Preseli, but sadly there have always been unexceptional people who want to clothe themselves in the exceptional in order to appear mystical and 'special.' They're only kidding themselves of course, they don't fool me.

Legally sourced Bluestone jewellery is on sale at the official Stonehenge gift shop, where the English Heritage marketing blurb completely backs up the notion of the night-sky iconography of the stones with this statement, *"Embrace the magic of Stonehenge with our range of mystical Bluestone jewellery. The flecked quartz crystals within the hard granite, recall the night sky when polished."*

This vital characteristic of the visual power of the Bluestones was first fitted into the speculative jigsaw by the intuition of an early 20th Century geologist, called Prof. William Judd in June 1903. Back then Judd had no idea the Bluestones originated in Mynydd Preseli, something first proposed two decades later by another eminent geologist, Prof. Herbert Thomas. But Judd realised these stones had unique qualities and outlined his conclusions that year in The Wiltshire Magazine, suggesting they'd been shaped and polished at Stonehenge, forming the so-called 'Bluestone Layer' of dust and chippings at the base of the stones.

Judd's proposal, nearly 120 years ago, that the stones were 'shaped' in situ at Stonehenge, is a perfectly reasonable assumption for the time, although only two of the Bluestones were formally 'shaped' as they were grooved to conjoin one with the other. Apart from this erroneous assumption, Judd's article is spectacularly perceptive, and I will come back to it at in the final chapter when I consider the important and ephemeral role of oral history and legend in the world of Stonehenge.

More up-to-the moment research, commissioned by English Heritage, the custodians of Stonehenge, has shown there was another polishing exercise on the megaliths, carried out during the last, Bronze Age phase of the Temple. When Heritage scientists examined the large Sarsen Stones, dragged thirty miles from the Marlborough Downs, with the most up to date scientific equipment they were found to have been completely pick-dressed to remove their brown/grey oxidised outer layer to expose the brighter, white rock beneath.

This process was carried out by the ancients on all the faces of the megaliths, which could be viewed from the northeast aspect of the local topography and the sides of the stones along the Solstitial Axis were found to have been the most carefully worked. This strongly suggests the architects of Stonehenge made a special effort to highlight those Sarsens standing along the north-east, south-west axis to reflect the rays of the sun the moment it shone through the Temple on both the midsummer and midwinter Solstices. What a stupendous sight it must have been, with the flashing white of the giant megaliths, set against the heavenly crescent of Preseli star stones, creating a moment of pure religious theatre. A compelling reason indeed, for the ancients to move the Blue-stones over that challenging distance, in the greatest engineering and logistical project of the era.

In the last iteration of Stonehenge, the Bluestones were set like a pristine, petrological tiara within the horseshoe ring of polished Trilithons at the temple. Why wouldn't they want to keep their precious stones as mirrors of the Milky Way; heaven petrified on earth? Of course, they would! But there was something else, another compelling and lyrical quality within the Bluestones, that also made calls upon their souls and inspired the ancients to such herculean effort, because the Bluestones of Preseli own another, unique and quite mind-blowing attribute. They are lithophones...

It was the summer of 2006 when a group of scientists first walked out onto the dramatic landscape of Mynydd Preseli, climbing amongst the jagged outcrops, so reminiscent of the serrated backs of dragons slumbering in the gorse. The team was about as diverse as it gets comprising archaeologists, neurologists, aerospace engineers and, importantly, percussionists. They came from the Royal College of Art, Bournemouth and Bristol Universities, English Heritage, the University of Wales, and even prestigious Princeton USA.

The study was headed by Jon Wozencroft, a senior tutor at the Royal College of Art and Paul Devereux, an expert on archaeo-acoustics; the echoes of prehistory to you and me. Professor Tim Darvill was co-opted as advisor and consultant to a project with the stated aim of immersing themselves in that special place Preseli. It was called the Landscape & Perception Project and posed the question, *"What might Stone Age eyes and ears have perceived in this landscape and what aspects of it made it become important to the builders of Stonehenge?"*

What a great question, with the provenance, destination and ultimately the purpose of the Bluestones at the heart of it and the team spent successive summers among those dragons' backs, with family members frequently arriving to help with their work among the outcrops around Carn Menyn. I like that idea very much, as it suggests they approached the task in what I imagine might be a Neolithic fashion, with a fusion of different skills including dynamic young people under the focussed leadership of a wise old head, we'll call him a professor, to mentor the work. All the while they were cradled by the affection and input of the wider clan represented by their families. Wonderful stuff.

I believe the group spent six summers wandering around Preseli, using small rocks to bash Bluestones lying in the landscape, as they set out to prove the stones are lithophones, musical megaliths that can be played like a xylophone or a set of tubular bells. They acoustically tested over one thousand Bluestones, mostly on the Carn Menyn quarry ridge and found an average of ten per cent were lithophones, rising to twenty per cent in certain locations, forty percent or more near quarry sites and in some 'hot spot' locations, such as the Carn Menyn quarry investigated by Prof. Darvill, nearly a hundred per cent. Surely, this suggests our Neolithic forebears knew precisely the dolerites they needed to quarry; the ones that rang.

The team didn't quite leave no stone unturned but found one of the three guardian dolmen of Carn Ingli at Pentre Ifan has *'no remarkable acoustic properties,'* whilst expressing delight that Carreg Coetan Arthur in Newport... *'has a fine ringing capstone. The supporting orthostats (uprights) allow for excellent resonance because they make only point contact with the underside of the capstone".*

These findings are an absolutely game-changing perspective of the value and purpose of the Bluestones to the ancients, and I'll paraphrase a report on their work from the Journal of Time and Mind, which observed folk in Preseli had long been familiar with lithophones, and the ringing Bluestones made the landscape sacred to Stone Age people. In layman-speak, the acoustic quality of the Bluestones meant they could be 'played' making the stones magical and super-important to the architecture of Neolithic temples. I've no doubt the ancients thought of them as the work of the gods, so why wouldn't they choose their temple stones on the purity of the sound they emitted?

English Heritage researchers were already on board with this project and in July 2013 unprecedented permission was granted to allow researchers from Bournemouth and Bristol University to go into the hallowed precincts of Stonehenge and bash the Bluestones with small rocks, albeit in a musical way! The team didn't expect great results as lithophones need 'resonant space,' that is sufficient room to vibrate and produce *"the pure sounds that can be experienced on Carn Menyn."* An inhibiting factor, they noted, is the Bluestones at the henge are set deep into the ground and some have modern concrete underpinning, which can also dampen their acoustic potential. However, according to the Journal of Time and Mind... *"To the researchers' surprise, having tested all the Bluestones at the monument, several were found to make distinctive (if muted) sounds. This was a sure indication they would have been fully lithophonic if they'd had sufficient resonant space. Furthermore, a number of Bluestones at Stonehenge show evidence of having been struck...this may have been in order to create an acoustic environment according to Wozencroft. The Landscape & Perception team believes the bluestones came from a mysterious soundscape, imbued with special magic and sanctity in the eyes of the megalith builders. This may have been the prime reason behind the otherwise inexplicable transport of these stones nearly 200 miles from Preseli to Salisbury Plain. There were plentiful local rocks from which Stonehenge could have been built, yet the bluestones were clearly considered special."*

Special indeed and crucially the Landscape & Perception group also addressed the puzzling provenance of the debitage layer around Stonehenge, the Bluestone Crumble as I like to call it, and had this to say: *"Many of the bluestones at Stonehenge have been struck at some point in the past. These markings could be due to people centuries ago hacking off pieces for healing or good luck, or they could be the result of attempts to dress the stones, or some might be because the stones were struck to elicit their sonic qualities."*

There we have it, a clear conclusion the Bluestones were chimed at

Stonehenge, explaining the layer of rock dust and chippings that had built up over a long period of time. I find that to be a thrilling idea, casting the great stone temple on Salisbury Plain in a completely new light as a theatre of religion, a spectacular of sound and vision.

There's nothing new about ancient civilisations using rocks as musical instruments and plenty of people still play them to this day in Mexico, the USA, Vietnam, India and Africa. In America, archaeologists puzzled for years over a set of deliberately shaped, 5000-year-old stones, long and angular with rounded edges, found at the Great Sand Dunes National Park in southern Colorado. That is, until local consultant archaeologist Marilyn Martorano, based at Longmont tapped one of these strange discoveries and realised, they were the component keys of a prehistoric xylophone.

Perhaps the most bizarre example of a lithophone can be found at Skiddaw in the Lake District where Victorian musical entrepreneurs made a huge and complex xylophone from sonorous rocks sourced in the slate deposits. The Richardson's, father and son, played Handel and Mozart on their instrument and there was a command performance for Queen Victoria in the 1800's. Believe it or not they marketed themselves as the 'Rock Band' and their xylophone is still intact and playable in the Keswick Museum and Art Gallery.

Generally, these stone instruments sound truly musical with different notes emitted by different stones, rather like water in bottles, but if you don't believe me there are plenty of YouTube videos of people playing them, and they sound rather melodious and soothing.

Through time and space, sound and temples have been inextricably linked, with singing and chanting as a baseline requirement for praising deities. There are some religious persuasions who prefer to internalise their exaltations with elements of silent worship; Quakers and Trappists among them. But they're exceptions as the vast majority of supplicants prefer their god or gods to clearly hear their prayers and praise; you only have to think of the turbo-decibel power of cathedral organs with pipes like mortar tubes, filling every crevice of a consecrated space with sound. Around the globe there's a long list of extraordinary sounds, musical and tonal, offered to the heavens. Think of the Mormon Tabernacle Choir, or the constant, repetitive nasal notes of a Buddhist temple. Reverberations seem to have been important too since the dawn of human time, possibly inspired by the echo of thunderclaps, perceived as an omnipotent voice.

Again, there's a growing body of thought the astonishing images of Palaeolithic cave art were part of a religious devotion where 'movement' was created by a sophisticated use of flickering torches and the amplified cave echoes of drums and voices were part of the show too; the original sound and vision if you like, with stalactites and stalagmites the obvious lithophones of choice. A drama like this may have unfolded in the remarkable caves of Nerja in the Spanish province of Andalusia, home to the world's largest stalagmite standing at an astonishing thirty-two metres high. The cave is also home to Palaeolithic cave paintings and in 2022 an international team of archaeo-acoustic experts from the Artsoundscapes group, found lithophones in the cave demonstrating clear notes, providing circumstantial evidence for the notion they were played. When all's said and done echoes in a cavern or the vaulted ceiling above a church choir, are fundamentally similar in acoustic quality and sacred mood.

Cultures around the planet and throughout time, including the Mayan and the Pre-Inca Chavin people of Peru, have created structures which emulate the reverberative qualities of caves and rainforests. The Inca temple of Viejo Sangayaico is dedicated to the gods of lightning and thunder, said to live on a nearby mountain, and features an acoustically designed platform built above a hollow soundbox so that when it's danced on, the footfall creates the sound of thunder.

In the Mediterranean, the famous underground burial chamber and temple of the Hypogeum on Malta has a 6000-year-old Oblong Room where sounds are deliberately echoed from alcoves in the stonework. The Hypogeum is reminiscent of the famous Whispering Gallery of St Pauls in London, designed by Christopher Wren, coincidentally a Wiltshire lad who grew up at East Knoyle, not far from Stonehenge, and skilfully chiselled his initials onto one of the giant megaliths at the monument. I wonder if he had some strands of the Bluestone people chiming in his DNA?

However, the temple which resonates most closely with my idea of the days of living worship at Stonehenge, are the Musical Pillars of

Hampi in Central India, albeit a relatively recent 500-year-old temple, on a bend in the Tunghabandra River. Despite its relative youth it has fifty-six lithophones in twelve feet high, limestone pillars incorporated architecturally into the temple and played by the priests. They're still played today by tour guides, and there are videos online of the columns being flicked and pinged with fingers, to create clear musical notes. What a wonderful thing, and Hampi is on my ever-growing and over-ambitious, bucket list.

Meanwhile, as the Landscape & Perception Project were establishing the sonorous qualities of the Bluestones on Preseli and at Stonehenge itself, the University of Salford were contemporaneously examining a different proposition, one that the architects of Stonehenge had designed their temple acoustically, particularly in its later and most familiar Early Bronze Age phase. The Salford researchers conducted complex experiments at Stonehenge and at a full-sized concrete reconstruction of the famous British temple in Maryhill, Washington State, USA. This highly technical study, carried out in collaboration with Huddersfield and Bristol Universities, found a sound quality which prompted them to conclude, *"This type of reverberation is typical, for example, in a lecture hall where good speech intelligibility is required."*

The researchers were so comfortable with their findings they set up an immersive experience at the Museum of Science and Industry in Manchester, where visitors could experience a recreation of sounds within the Stonehenge circle. In other words, in layman speak, Stonehenge was designed to maximise the impact of sound on those who worshipped and celebrated there, and it seems the outer ring of Sarsen trilithons were designed to harbour and usher the sound created within. In my book the lithophonic Bluestones would have played a central role in that soundscape.

I've had a couple of thoughts arising from the conclusions of these two, distinct research projects. The first is to ponder whether there's a link between the 'playing' of the Bluestones and the debitage of the Stonehenge Layer, found at the foot of the megaliths. Is it possible the process of ringing the stones might also have been an opportunity to keep them pristine and shining? Did they polish as they played, leaving the detritus behind in the form of the Stonehenge Layer? I pose the question believing the answer is yes.

The Landscape and Perception research mentions the Bluestones are set so deep in the ground, that probably affects their 'resonant space' and mutes the chimes they make. I wonder whether they were set so deep in the soil originally and turn once more to that giant of natural science Charles Darwin for a possible explanation. Have earthworm deposits, built up at the base of the Bluestones, affected their acoustic quality in their modern context? Were the Bluestones originally set more acutely in the ground with a smaller footprint, minimising the sound-baffling effect of soil and making their bell-like quality pristine? I'm not qualified to make that judgment, but I suspect the answer may lie in the shape of the Aubrey Holes, the footprints marking where the Bluestones were first set in a circle. I simply pose the question and hope that someone with the relevant expertise might take it up.

Again, we have the Salford led research, showing the great Trilithon arrangement at Stonehenge was constructed acoustically, but let's not forget the Bluestones were re-arranged within that gigantic horseshoe of megaliths, and it's not unreasonable to speculate they were placed in this new setting so that they could be played to better effect with the Sarsens acting as a sound-system, a set of stone speakers, to resonate their chimes across the landscape around the henge.

Before I close this chapter, there's one more spine-tingling strand to the story of the musical stones of Preseli. On the southern slopes of Mynydd Preseli, east of the rocky pinnacles of the Neolithic quarry at Carn Menyn, lies a village called Maenclochog. It's a place with a colourful history where, no doubt, some of the Neolithic quarrymen of Preseli and their families made homes in the lee of the mountains.

It's quintessentially a place of Bluestones, and two of them once stood like ancient, eight-foot-high twins just outside the village boundary near a manor house called Temple Druid built by the celebrated London architect John Nash. Local tradition says these Neolithic menhirs were often played, that is until a couple of 18th Century quarrymen used gunpowder charges to blow them up. These idiots were searching for a hoard of treasure, by legend buried under the standing stones, but there was no treasure of course, and now no Bluestone chimes at Temple Druid either.

However, there had been other significant pieces of Bluestone in Maenclochog as slabs were hung in the belfry of the parish church of St Mary's which, with ultimate irony, were chimed to call Christian worshippers to their prayers, that is until the whole church was mysteriously demolished in 1790. According to the Dyfed Archaeological Trust the church was, *'entirely rebuilt in the same location as its predecessor but retaining none of the earlier fabric.'* Unusual indeed, possibly unprecedented, and there seems to be no record of the predecessor church at all, which smacks to me of a purging or cleansing operation. I suspect the ringing of a Bluestone in a church belfry, with all its Druidical connotations, must have come to the attention of the Diocese at St David's, who decided to erase this pagan symbolism and start their church again from the ground up, this time without a Neolithic lithophone to call the congregation to evensong. More wisps of smoke curling from the fire of history clearly showing a five-thousand-year-long, living connection between those Neolithic quarrymen and Preseli's recent history. And to underscore that unbreakable thread, the ancient Welsh name Maenclochog, translates as Bell Stone or Ringing Stone. Oh, and the two delinquents who blew up the Druids Lodge lithophones made their living hewing stone at a quarry called Bellstone! A thrilling provenance indeed, and I'm reminded of the wonderful lyric written by Welsh poet Gwyneth Jones, inscribed on the facade of the Wales Millennium Centre in Cardiff, which perfectly expresses the idea... 'In These Stones Horizons Sing.'

At the start of this exploration of the secrets of the Bluestones I posed the question why? What is so unique and desirable about Bluestones that the ancients felt compelled to move them nearly two hundred miles to their great new, religious building project at Stonehenge?

For me the answer is clear, and I believe I've made a compelling case for the visual and musical qualities of the Bluestones to have been at the heart of that compulsion. Those startling visual attributes, with sparkling mineral pins and cauda broadcast over a background of deep blues and greens, evoked the great wheel of the universe petrified into the rock of

Preseli. When revealed it transforms the Bluestones into Star Stones, and if that weren't inspiration enough for the ancients, you can play chimes on them too, sending celestial notes to the heavens. Our fore-bears surely revered such a wonderful, petrographic miracle and it would have been a matter of critical importance for them to convey those stones to the place they believed their power would be most manifest, and that place was Stonehenge. How the Bluestones were conveyed to Stonehenge is still a matter of conjecture as we wait for some definitive evidence, but I believe the why of it is as clear as day.

The Bluestones were too special to be left behind on the sea-kissed slopes of Preseli because they gifted the ancients a portal to the heavens, which could also play stellar music as an homage to their gods. Too sublime to be ignored, too sacred to leave behind, they had to move the Bluestones at any cost so that's what they did, and through all its phases the Star Stones of Preseli kept their place at Stonehenge's ceremonial heart.

9

THINK BIG!

That first, eloquently simple, stone circle consisting of fifty-six Bluestones stood alone as the epicentre of religious devotion in southern Britain for some five hundred years or so. In my interpretation of the altogether exceptionally magnetic pull of Stonehenge, the Preseli stones were kept polished to reveal images of the Milky Way and chimed to honour the gods at great rites and ceremonies like the Solstice. It couldn't last though, nothing is set in stone, not even at Stonehenge, and the inexorable trapdoor of change opened to allow another group of people, powerful and audacious, to cross the channel and bring their fantastic new ideas with them. They arrived around 2500 BC and their effect on the whole of Britain was nothing less than momentous, positioning the island on the cusp of a new era.

Properly called the Bell Beaker People, I've known them as the Beaker Folk since my school days, so I'll stick with that name for the vibrant people who left Asia Minor and the hills of modern Turkey then, mimicking the previous Neolithic migration, moved to all points west around the Mediterranean, north through Europe and eventually across to Britain. They brought with them a more sophisticated agriculture with potent cereals and better-bred livestock, but they also brought an alchemical magic in the great game changer of metal technology and the Bronze Age had arrived in Britain. Metal working began with the crude, open-fire casting of copper giving rise to a relatively short archaeological era known as the Chalcolithic, which lasted hardly any time at all here in

Britain, largely because the harder, easier to cast alloy of Bronze arrived here at on its heels.

Funeral rites changed too, as the long barrow tombs of the Neolithic were abandoned in favour of a variety of Round Barrows constructs. Some of these newer burials contain the distinctive Beaker pottery, associated with the metal-working migration, yet have no bronze but lots of stone age technology, while one famous grave has no bronze, some flint and copper artefacts and an abundance of Beaker pottery. To coin a Latin phrase, it seems this was a time of *lapis et metallum*, the era of stone and metal technology, and the debate between various experts centring on interpretations of this period of adjustment, has been vigorous with Oxford archaeologist Dr. Neil Brodie cleverly characterising it as '*a theoretical storm raging around a blind eye.*'

That debate continues, but when metal working arrived here the effect it had on the settled society must have been profound, creating a foundation-shaking uncertainty as the transition unfolded. Witnessing the creation of metal can have a deeply transformative effect on the human psyche as the sight of molten metal emerging, sparks flying, from the glowing foundry before solidifying into a perfectly shaped cast is hypnotic and must have seemed like wizardry to the ancients. Little wonder so many of the most powerful gods from the later Iron Age are associated with the casting and forging of metal and are still potent deities to this day.

In my own experience, my youngest son Morgan qualified as a traditional blacksmith under the renowned tutelage of Chris Blythman and Pete Smith at the National School of Blacksmithing in Holme Lacey near Hereford. I never saw Morgan work metal until he'd qualified, but when I first watched him forging I confess I had a moist eye and was awestruck by the sight and sound of my son hammering out glowing metal on an anvil. It's a process nothing short of magical so I can well understand the absolute air of confidence and social authority emanating from those early Beaker Folk who were privy to the secrets of the crucible and the anvil, and I've no doubt those metalworkers had a bit of a swagger in their step when they arrived on these shores.

It's likely that a fusion of the old Neolithic ideas of stone monuments with the big, bold concepts of the metalworkers, led to the megalithic development of Stonehenge at this time. The Beaker Folk were already familiar with Neolithic standing stone temples, which abound in places like Brittany, but I wonder what they must have thought when they arrived at Stonehenge to find an array of stones that sparkled with a cosmos of 'stars' like the night sky, while priests were able to play celestial peals on them. They must have found the Bluestones every bit as otherworldly as the incumbent, Neolithic tenants of Britain found the fiery metallurgy the Beaker Folk had brought with them.

Everything that happened from that moment onwards at Stonehenge may well have sparked from that first meeting and a fusion of the two cultures on Salisbury Plain when, I believe, the Beaker Folk fell under the spell of the Bluestones' chimes and felt compelled to develop the temple and take it to new, dizzying heights. To use the vernacular, I think they decided to 'think big and go large' and it wouldn't have been too long before they found the means to do just that, a couple of miles west of the ancient borough of Marlborough where 'streams' of the huge boulders we call sarsens, run down two or three valleys in the chalk, across the river Kennet and into West Woods; home to the most spectacular bluebell forest in Europe.

This cascade of extremely hard stone begins above the ancient Ridgeway track overlooking Avebury, then flows through the chalk coombes of Fyfield Down and Pickle Dene over the river Kennet, into Lockeridge Dene and then into West Woods itself. In Wiltshire the sarsens are known as grey wethers because, from a distance, they fool the eye into seeing a flock of grazing sheep; a wether being the Old English word for a sheep. I know these places very well, having walked them regularly most weeks for the past forty-five years, and there's never a time when I don't thrill to the thought the architects of Avebury and Stonehenge once wandered amongst the wethers, casting a critical eye over the sarsens as they made choices of undoubted architectural, aesthetic and spiritual importance.

Sarsens were formed about 55 million years ago in the Palaeocene, post dinosaur period when a thick layer of sand and gravel was laid in some locations on top of the existing chalk in a shallow sea. When the ocean bed was lifted above sea level, a long process of hardening began through the percolation of ground water, rich in dissolved quartz, and the silcrete rock we know as sarsen stone was formed.

The best examples are in Wiltshire, but sarsens are to be found in a broad sweep of Southern England from Essex in the east, through the North Downs of Kent and South Downs of Sussex, parts of Hampshire and Dorset and as far west as Devon. They are a very hard rock indeed and the Wiltshire sarsen array on the Marlborough Downs are important to the world of Neolithic history, representing the open 'quarries' where huge rocks, scattered randomly on the surface, were sourced for use in the construction of a variety of monuments from stone circles to long barrows.

Our ancestors used sarsens copiously, taking scores of them for the great stone circle and avenues just over the hill at Avebury, and to construct the wonderful long barrow, passage tombs at East and West Kennet as well as the huge dolmen known as the Devil's Den right in the middle of a whole flock of grey wethers on Fyfield Down.

Perhaps the most evocative of all the sarsens engaged for human activity is the Polissoir or Polishing Stone on Overton Down, a mile from Avebury where, over countless generations, first stone then bronze axes were sharpened on the rock, until the 'edging' bowls and grooves on the Polissoir, were turned vitreous and glassy through perpetual use. Many of these Neolithic monuments, clustered to the north of Stonehenge, preceded the time when the high-status priests of Stonehenge decided to build the Trilithons we see today, but there's little doubt the availability of huge sarsens at West Woods just thirty miles to the north of Stonehenge was an important factor in the decision to think big.

There'd always been a feeling amongst archaeologists that the megaliths for Stonehenge were sourced on the Marlborough Downs, it just made sense. But it wasn't until 2020 that some scientific detective work by geomorphologist Professor David Nash of Brighton University homed in on West Woods in particular, rather than the other streams of sarsens near Marlborough. And then a core drilled out of Stone 58 at Stonehenge in the 1950's, suddenly emerged from the unlikely setting of a home in Florida USA, where it had been kept safely for decades, and returned to English Heritage who were delighted to have a sample to work on.

Prof. David Nash and his team then analysed the chemical signatures of the remaining fifty-two sarsens at Stonehenge, including Stone 58, using minimum damage techniques but crucially they were able to crush test the core sample returned from Florida. This gave them the hallmark minerology that was finally matched against a sample in West Woods, a place with a gloomy modern history blighted by the wholesale destruction of hundreds of sarsen stones in the 1950's when a quarrying company chewed them up in giant grinding machines to produce gravel for road surfaces and high-quality setts for driveways and courtyards. There are still some sarsens left in the woods, but many more depressions on the forest floor where others were extracted for the crusher.

Thankfully, West Woods is now held under the stewardship of Forest England and, despite the ravages of commercial stone breaking, it's a place full of history and prehistory with round barrows and a well-preserved length of the Wansdyke, an Iron Age boundary separating Saxons from Celts, not unlike Offa's Dyke. In April, West Woods dazzles with acre after luminescent acre of bluebells, and I can only hope the architects of Stonehenge enjoyed them too as they wandered about selecting their megaliths.

More recent research on fragments found at Stonehenge, led by Jake Ciborowski of Galway University in Ireland, suggests a couple more sources of stones within the Marlborough sarsen streams, adding Totterdown Wood, and Monkton Down to West Woods. Sensationally, 3D laser technology, showed one of the Monkton Down pieces had been taken off an existing megalith during the work to dress the stones on site, four and a half thousand years ago.

Other, small sarsens seem to have come from much further afield with three fragments sourced at Bramdean in Hampshire, about thirty miles away, and Stoney Wish, East Sussex, a sizeable seventy-seven miles from Stonehenge. One theory is these much smaller and more portable Hampshire and East Sussex stones may have been symbolic offerings, brought in a spirit of unanimity to join like-with-like from different tribes at the great megalithic temple. At least that wouldn't have required dragging a huge Sussex sarsen across the South Downs to Stonehenge.

Which brings us to the idea of the daunting task of moving eighty of those huge megaliths, average weight twenty tonnes, from the Marlborough Downs to Stonehenge, although their success tells us the ancients had it covered. I'm going to suggest they already had the proven technology available in sledges of the type road-tested by Barney Harris at University College London and it's my belief they'd already used this model to move Bluestones across various stretches of land, as well as sarsens and other stone types used in many of the other sacred constructions across the island of Britain.

The accepted route for the Stonehenge sarsens is pretty direct as they would have headed due west towards Milk Hill, where the Alton Barnes White Horse is a major landmark today, then down into the Vale of Pewsey to a half-way point at Marden Henge. Marden is an extraordinary site, which has been sadly destroyed by agriculture since the Antiquarians first probed its thirty-five acres, held within an arm of the Wiltshire Avon. Inside the outer bank and ditch the ancients built a mini-Silbury hill and an inner henge, with the socket holes of standing stones, around 2400BC, the same timeframe as the megalithic redevelopment of Stonehenge.

Some believe the West Woods sarsens were 'rested and recharged' here before they were taken onwards to Stonehenge, but in any event the megaliths were probably moved a mile or two from Marden to the stark escarpment of Salisbury Plain and up onto the plateau through the funnel of a re-entrant in the contours at the quaintly named Marden Cowbag. From there they'd have been dragged across the Plain, over Black Heath and Orcheston Down and then into the orbit of Stonehenge itself.

A mighty endeavour indeed and one I'm sure would best be undertaken after winter's slippery rains and before the all-important, labour-intensive harvest. The muscle burning method of transportation is just one element of this spectacular, almost frantic, re-imagining of Stonehenge around 2500BC and the explosion of projects around the sacred landscape was epic. We have the wholly ambitious construction of the workers'/pilgrims' village at Durrington Walls close to the banks of the Wiltshire Avon and, a couple of miles downstream of Durrington the boomerang-shaped processional route from the riverbank at West Amesbury up to Stonehenge was being formalised into The Avenue. Around this time, work also began on the enormous circle of pits around

Durrington henge only recently discovered by Prof. Vince Gaffney, which will hopefully offer fresh insights into this period.

THE SARSEN STONES OF THE MARLBOROUGH DOWNS

My partner, Dr. Stephanie Shelburne, with Brig the Spaniel, sitting on Fyfield Down in one of several 'streams' of sarsen stones, known as Grey Wethers, that run

through the area west of Marlborough where the Stonehenge Trilithons were
sourced. Two miles ahead is the giant stone circle of Avebury, also built of sarsens
from the Grey Wethers. Two miles behind the camera is West Woods, linked by
chemical analysis to one of the megaliths at Stonehenge.

WHOEVER WAS STEERING THE GREAT STONEHENGE PROJECT, WHETHER Neolithic farmers or Bronze Age Beaker Folk, probably a fusion of both, the fact is Stonehenge was reconfigured three times, with the use of sarsen megaliths to create what seems to be a protective arm around an inner horseshoe of re-positioned Bluestones. I have no doubt the Bluestones were kept at the heart of this 'New Stonehenge' because of their evocative audio-visual properties and were polished and played to celebrate the deities of the sun and moon.

Eventually, the erection of the awe-inspiring Trilithons marked out Stonehenge as the truly great World Heritage construction we see today, with the lintels and the uprights supporting them fitted together by mortise and tenons joints, carefully hewn into the stone like ancient Lego bricks. Only six of those lintels remain in place on the outer sarsen circle but on completion of the work there would have been an enclosed ring, some thirty metres in diameter, creating a marvellous spectacle as the crowning glory of the Stonehenge concept.

I've already expressed my own ideas on the superbly crafted Trilithons, and those thoughts take me back to the sea-kissed hills of Wales, Cornwall and Ireland where exquisitely balanced Dolmens stand out on the horizon. Were the Neolithic dolmen the original inspiration for the Trilithons? After all, when you boil it down, a Trilithon is a large beam supported by two uprights: not so different to the giant capstones and orthostats of a dolmen. It also occurs to me that the skills required to lift a twenty-tonne capstone onto the orthostats of a dolmen are precisely those needed to raise the lintel of a Trilithon onto its megalithic uprights. Were the Trilithons a highly stylised and sophisticated homage to the courtyard dolmens? I wouldn't be surprised and once again, who can tell, but I don't think the raising of the massive dolmen called the Devil's Den, right at the portal to a stream of sarsens on Fyfield Down near West Woods, is coincidental.

One thing is certain, the building activity at Stonehenge was accompanied by an explosion of round barrows, littering the surrounding ritual landscape in every direction, like frisbees abandoned in a park. There are scores of them, but the barrow assemblage of Winterbourne Stoke, with nine Bronze Age round barrows cluster, symmetrically around the massive, Neolithic long barrow burial of the Winterbourne Chieftain stands out. The Winterbourne Stoke assemblage, reinforces my own thoughts the megalithic renaissance in the sacred landscape, marks a synergy between the two cultures until Stonehenge eventually emerges from the Neolithic to become an exclusively Bronze Age temple.

So far, I've talked about stone implements, superseded by copper and bronze, but another metal, elementally pure and incorruptible, signs-off this particular evolution and marks the crowning zenith of the Stonehenge epoch in splendour. That metal is gold of course, and it's time to meet the people from burials who were there to witness the wonder of it all when Stonehenge began its explosive expansion; one of them is the famous Amesbury Archer.

10

THE PATHS OF LONG AGO

A round 2300BC, a man in his mid-forties must have breathed a sigh of relief when he limped painfully to the shores of the English Channel and saw the thin, white line of Britain on the horizon. It had been a long, seven-hundred-mile passage on foot and by riverboat across France from his home in the Alps, and I imagine he finished his journey on a cross-channel ferry, maybe even the Dover Boat, before walking over the South Downs to reach Stonehenge.

We first heard of this pilgrim in 2002 when groundwork on a new school in the town of Amesbury was dramatically halted after a contractor's digger exposed an ancient grave. There was a glint of gold and the on-site archaeologist, always present at any build close to Stonehenge, called in a team from Wessex Archaeology. The Wessex team excavated through the night, illuminating their dig with the headlights of a van, as they rushed to beat illegal 'nighthawk' metal detectorists to the draw. What they found was the extraordinary grave of a pan-European traveller who possessed gold ornaments and his own metal working kit.

The Amesbury Archer's burial was particularly rich in grave goods, including archery paraphernalia, with fifteen flint arrowheads and two stone wrist guards or 'bracers', drilled with holes for the leather straps, earning him the name of the Amesbury Archer. There were also five, characteristic Bell Beaker pots and he had two copper knifes and a copper dagger, however, it was the glint of gold that set archaeological pulses racing when they found two trug, or basket shaped, golden hair ornaments. Perhaps more significantly, a black metalworker's cushion stone and a boar tusk, typically used for 'planishing' or smoothing out metal. His golden hair fastenings and the copper blades, seem to place him in the relatively short window of the Chalcolithic or Copper Age, but notably they're the oldest metalwork found so far in Britain, marking his grave as exceptional.

Burial archaeology these days is a game of two halves, first a consideration of the physical artefacts found in the grave, then the chemical and genome analysis of any skeletal remains and the Archer's true magic was revealed in his bone chemistry, which showed he had been born and raised eight hundred miles to the east of Stonehenge in the Italian Alps.

It's an incredible testament to the far-reaching fame of Stonehenge as a temple and, some say, a place of healing in those times, as the Archer was significantly disabled by a leg injury that had robbed him of his kneecap and, no doubt, left him with a pronounced limp and crippling pain. He also had a tooth abscess so severe it had rotted away part of his jawbone and I'm guessing his overall pain levels must have been off the scale. The Archer's injuries have contributed to the continuing debate about the purpose of Stonehenge with Prof. Tim Darvill and Geoffrey Wainwright citing it as evidence of a Neolithic place of healing and pilgrimage, a latter-day Lourdes. I'll be addressing that important debate later in the book but no doubt the Archer's arrival at Stonehenge poses the question was he a patient, a pilgrim, a migrant or perhaps all three?

However, the presence of another skeleton, known as The Companion, buried just fifteen feet away and found soon afterwards by Wessex Archaeology, add another dimension to the story because DNA analysis suggests they were distant relatives, thrice removed, although in the context of a clan they may well have been much closer kin, socially and emotionally.

The Companion's grave wasn't nearly so rich although he also had two golden 'trug' hair adornments, but the really interesting revelation is that he seems to have been born on the chalk of Southern Britain, maybe somewhere on Salisbury Plain, then travelled to and from the Alps when he was quite young; apparently returning with the Archer.

This implies is a cultural and societal link between Stonehenge and the Alps and we can also speculate that one reason they are buried close together is that The Companion made the journey to Cisalpine Europe to return to Salisbury Plain and Stonehenge with his handicapped relative. I can well imagine it would have been an act of religious devotion for both, and we only have to consider the long and difficult journeys undertaken today, such as the Haj to Mecca or the Camino Compostela trail across Spain, to recognise how the power of pilgrimage compels mankind. Such a Neolithic wayfare from the Alps, as remarkable as it was, doesn't then seem out of place.

However, the same circumstances could easily provide us with a different narrative, one which sees the Amesbury Archer wanting to see clan members who'd left the Alps many years earlier to migrate north and west, in order to dedicate themselves to Stonehenge, religious migrants with a sacred vocation, perhaps to help with the building project. Who will ever know?

There's a strange and enigmatic feature of the Archer's grave goods, and that's the seemingly careful, colour co-ordination of some of the items buried with him, so that one of his protective wrist guards is fashioned from red stone, and the other black. Similarly, the five Beaker vessels in the grave are also split between red and black hues, with three of the pots displaying the natural red of the clay while two were deliberately over-fired and burnt in the kiln to turn them black. I've not heard any explanation for this burial practice from archaeologists who seem puzzled by it, and so I turned to my partner Stephanie to see if she could cast any light on this practice from her knowledge of Native American, shamanic practices.

A few words here about Stephanie, who's American and a native of Las Vegas, and has a mixed Native American/European heritage with Ogalala Sioux and Paiute blood from the First Nations and, in a startling coincidence, mostly Welsh from both parents' European lineage. She's taken a natural interest in her Native side and, whilst studying for her doctorate Stephanie took some time to learn about First Nation rituals, traditions and Native medicine, guided in this for two years by an Elder of the famous Lakota Sioux tribe. The insights Stephanie gained then have informed me at several points in this book.

What about the Archer's colour-coordinated grave goods then? According to Stephanie, the colours red, black, and yellow feature in most tribal traditions and are taken to denote direction and space in both literal and metaphysical terms, however it's complicated because different tribes put different meanings to different colours. She thinks a deliberate colour harmonisation, found in the Archer's grave, may indeed be a visual reference to his journey from the Alps, both in life and in the afterlife. It's a wonderful and thought-provoking idea, and that tribal explanation works for me and serves to highlight the strands of shamanism the ancients embraced in their belief systems.

This element of long-distance travel, with Stonehenge as the tangible hub of a spiritual galaxy, absolutely fascinates me and we have more evidence of this spirit of odyssey in a family group who were contemporaries of the Archer and buried only four hundred metres north of him and his Companion. They were found in 2003 during trench work for an electricity cable, and because there were flint arrowheads placed in the grave they're known as the Boscombe Bowmen, and in their own way the nine people buried there are as extraordinary as the Pan-European Amesbury Archer and his cousin. There were five adult Boscombe Bowmen in the grave, two teenagers and two children, and they all shared skeletal idiosyncrasies suggesting they were members of the same family. Buried with them were seven distinctive pots marking them out as Beaker Folk and even though they had no metal in the grave with them, they are certainly from the transitional epoch when metalwork was making the existing Stone Age technology in Britain increasingly redundant. Better than that, the science shows the Boscombe Bowmen, like the Winterbourne Chieftain and the people from Aubrey Hole VII, were from Wales and at an educated guess likely to be part of an enduring link between Stonehenge and Preseli.

Great works were going on around Stonehenge in the days of the Archer, his Companion, and the Boscombe Bowmen, with the first of the giant Sarsen stones, fifteen of them in all, arriving from West Woods for the ponderous and time-consuming work of shaping them with hammerstones on site. The new metalworking tenants of Stonehenge had their own ideas of how it should be configured to meet their ceremonial needs, and they were re-arranging the assemblage of Bluestones in harmony with the much bigger sarsen megaliths.

The Archer, and the Bowmen too, would undoubtedly have witnessed some of this bold expansion of the Stonehenge complex, known today as Phase III, which began around 2500 BC and took some 300 years to complete. Remember, there were two sets of Bluestones being re-arranged, the fifty-six in the Aubrey Holes, together with the twenty-four from Bluestone Henge on the banks of the river at West Amesbury: a smaller circle about one hundred feet in diameter. They were later dragged up to Stonehenge, no doubt with great ceremony, to join those already present.

The twenty-four West Amesbury stones were carried along the contours of the most naturally convenient route from the Avon, and this pathway seems to have been commemorated earlier by the epic construction of the two mile long, ditch and bank structure of The Avenue. It's a boomerang-shaped ascent from the river valley to the Plain sixty to one hundred and fifty feet wide in places, which bends around the eastern flank of the monument so that when it enters Stonehenge, the last sixteen hundred feet of The Avenue are aligned with the solstitial lines of the Talon Marks of the Gods.

Then, with the transfer of the much larger sarsen megaliths from the Marlborough Downs complete, the entirety of the Bluestones were rearranged into two concentric circles known as the Q and R Holes, closer to the core of the henge and surrounded by sarsens but very much centre stage. At around the same time a sister Avenue was constructed reaching out from the impressive, wooden Southern Circle at Durrington Walls to the River Avon, which is so close the pathway it's only five hundred and sixty feet long and one hundred feet wide. However, both are auspiciously aligned to the Solstice with the southern circle facing the Winter Solstice sunrise, while the Durrington Avenue reflects the Summer Solstice sunrise.

It's Professor Mike Parker-Pearson's Riverside Project which identified this plausible link between Woodhenge/Durrington Walls and Stonehenge, connected by the two Avenues and the river itself. He proposes this was a specific, ceremonial passageway between Woodhenge, with its timber totems, representing the Place of the Living, and the apparently lifeless megaliths of Stonehenge, representing the Place of the Dead. At auspicious times, such as the Solstices, a procession of communicants, probably carrying the cremation remains of their loved ones, would follow a path from Woodhenge through the Durrington

Avenue, along the riverbank to the West Amesbury henge before climbing The Avenue to Stonehenge. My own analogy is that of a battery created in the ritual landscape with two terminals, one at Woodhenge acting as an anode, whilst the cathode is at Stonehenge; the path along the river and the avenues act as a conduit. This is a metaphysical notion which will also appeal to those who believe there are electro-magnetic variations on the landscape, such as ley lines, which our ancestors may have been more sensitive too and harnessed for their religion and wellbeing.

But first some thoughts on the presence of the Boscombe Bowmen at Stonehenge during this major realignment of the Bluestones within the newly imported sarsen megaliths, and I've considered whether they may have had a specific role in this complex upgrade. I wonder whether the Bowmen might have been a family of big-stone specialists who'd come from Wales to help with the job. Intriguingly, the eldest male's skeleton showed he's suffered a traumatic break to his femur, which had healed but would have left him with a severe limp. I've read expert assessments his broken leg is typical of a fall from a horse, but I can't help wondering whether that large bone fracture was actually caused by an accident whilst moving a Bluestone. And then I ask myself, which of those two causes of his injury would have been more likely in the context of Stone-henge at that time: horse-riding or stone moving? It also occurs to me the priests of Stonehenge may have believed it would be bad karma to have anyone but 'Star Stone' people from Preseli, to shift the sacred Bluestones around and called them from Wales to perform some sort of Early Bronze Age feng shui. Were the Bowmen summoned from faraway as specialist contractors? Maybe they performed shamanic rituals pecu-liar to the Bluestones, before repositioning them? Perhaps they were the only ones who knew all the correct prayers and incantations for the placing of Bluestones. Who knows? It's fascinating too, that the Bowmen were contemporaries of the Amesbury Archer and wonderful to think this group from Wales may have rubbed shoulders with a bloke from the Swiss Alps at Stonehenge, when it was morphing into the imposing structure we recognize today. Four hundred years or so after the Bowmen and the Archer were buried, others were on the scene, people who were part of a much more sophisticated and established

Bronze Age culture, one where bronze and gold were more available. I'll be telling their story over the next chapters but the Amesbury Archer, his Companion, and the Boscombe Bowmen have given us a precious window into the Pan-European nature of their era.

Our view of the prehistoric past may be distorted by the Medieval, when most people were serfs and villeins held in bondage to the nobility and forbidden to leave their village without the express permission of the lord of the manor. It seems those much earlier people of that transitional time between stone and metal technology, were free to follow their hearts, and the eleven people in those three graves close to Amesbury are a snapshot of a time when people travelled great distances to be part of the Stonehenge story. Humbling then that we can scarcely begin to count the steps of their journeys as they walked the paths of long ago in our imaginations.

There's one last individual from that time, whose own path led him to a gruesome fate within the sacred environs of Stonehenge itself, an individual who seems to have been the victim of ritual sacrifice or execution. His enigmatic death came to light during an excavation in the ditch surrounding the henge in 1978 when archaeologist Richard Atkinson, an insect specialist, and his colleague John Evans, were looking for ancient snail shells for dating purposes. They got more than they'd bargained for when the skeleton of a once fit, strong man in his prime popped into view. He was a contemporary, there or thereabouts, of the Amesbury Archer and the Boscombe Bowmen during that exciting phase of the Stonehenge development when the Bluestones were being re-positioned around the giant sarsen megaliths from the Marlborough Downs.

Aged about thirty, he was wearing a stone wrist guard or bracer, marking him out as yet another bowman, and so he was named the Stonehenge Archer as truth to tell, archers are relatively thick under the ground in Neolithic Britain. In any event the Stonehenge Archer's violent death has led to much speculation, and the Crime Scene was still pretty rich, even after nearly five thousand years, revealing he was shot from behind with at least four arrows and maybe as many as six. The first arrow seems to have been shot from further out than the others, piercing his chest and probably felling him, to be followed by others from very close behind, leading to many theories about the circumstances of his death. Was he discovered trespassing in the most sacred inner temple? Was he taken there to be executed as a human sacrifice? Why was his burial in the outer ditch quite deliberate, yet apparently hasty?

Archaeologist Dennis Price, formerly of Wessex Archaeology, thinks the Stonehenge Archer offers proof the temple was once guarded by sentinels and was an arena for gladiatorial fights. He imagines these sentinels only earned this coveted role through ritual combat and cites the many weapons such as daggers and maces found in graves surrounding Stonehenge, together with the traumatic wounds found on one of the Boscombe Bowmen and the Amesbury Archer. It's a romantic if contentious idea, one I don't credit, but ultimately who knows?

However, I've had my own thoughts about the Stonehenge Archer's death with the apparently hasty burial suggesting that perhaps there'd been some trouble in the environs of Stonehenge; some insurrection or factional dispute that had turned nasty. After all, we know the victim was a bowman who might have been captured nearby then despatched by those defending Stonehenge. Was the burial, in such a sacred place, done in haste because fighting was still going on and those who'd shot him had to rush off to another flashpoint?

Indeed, was the burial done with some reverence as a nod to his status within the community? Did they intend to come back and bury him elsewhere, with events overtaking that intention? As with so much in the Stonehenge story, I find myself searching desperately for the 'shrug' emoji on my keyboard.

But my gut reaction when I first read about the Stonehenge Archer's grisly death, was to make an immediate connection with the slaughter of pigs brought from all over Britain for mid-winter, Solstice feasting at Durrington Walls. Don't ask me why I made that link but, incongruous as it may seem, the simplest way of killing a pig is to slit its throat and let it bleed-out. The evidence shows that's not what happened at Durrington Walls, a place intimately wrapped up in the doings of Stonehenge. Instead, the pigs were shot with arrows from behind, sometimes with a number of arrows, leading to a theory this activity may have been a sort of annual competition, a test of archery skills on the beasts that were to be feasted on. which over time had become a ritualised tradition, a test of skill, and an important part of the festival.

I wonder whether the Stonehenge Archer's transgression had been so beyond the pale, so utterly blasphemous, he'd been subjected to a ritual execution mimicking the method used to slaughter those swine, marking his demise as a deeply humiliating death. In other words, I wonder whether he'd literally been killed like a pig?

One thing's for certain, we wouldn't be able to count the Stonehenge Archer's steps through the afterlife because, like the Winterbourne Chieftain, his feet were cut off and he was buried adipose. I'm convinced the reasons for the two notable arthroscopic amputations were entirely different, with a desire by family and clan to keep the Winterbourne Chieftain close-by in the afterlife, while in the case of the Archer, for me at any rate, it swings the argument in favour of a ritual sacrifice. I think the Archer's feet may have been hacked off as a further, post-mortem humiliation, to handicap his wanderings through the afterlife.

When I visited the Salisbury Museum, in the exceptional setting of the Cathedral Close, to view his remains with my friend Les Wilson, the Mail on Sunday photographer, we were pondering the Archer's skeleton when one of the museum guides hove too and told us one theory suggesting why his feet had completely vanished was they may have been fed to the pigs! What a grisly reminiscence of the pork feasting rituals at Durrington Walls on the Winter Solstice.

THE AMBER PRINCESS

A rolling, eight mile walk over the sheep-cropped downland to the west of Stonehenge, with a dramatic descent down the coombe at Bagbury Track, brings you to the village of Upton Lovell in the winding valley of the River Wylye. All the evidence suggests the Wylye Valley was a place where high-status folk sought tranquillity away from the hustle and bustle of the temple complex, and I imagine it to be a Neolithic version of Kew Green in West London, just far enough away from 'town,' resource rich, and sitting on the fashionably sought after riverbank. Three fantastic barrow graves on the edge of the village tell us this story of privilege but importantly, like Aubrey Hole VII, they also describe a cultural framework where women were powerful and held great influence.

The barrows at Upton Lovell were excavated by the pioneering Antiquarian, early archaeologist William Cunnington, and I'll be going deeper into his fascinating story later but suffice it to say, chance brought him to live in Heytesbury in 1775, at the age of twenty-one, where he embarked on a career as a wool merchant. In his forties, his health declined and on his physician's advice to get plenty of fresh air, Cunnington re-invented himself as an Antiquarian and began the extraordinary investigation of hundreds of barrows in Wilshire and the neighbouring counties. Heytesbury is just a mile from Upton Lovell and it's no surprise the first barrows he investigated were the ones on his own doorstep so, in 1803 he investigated a long barrow, which stood on an area flooded in Medieval times to create a water meadow.

About two feet below the barrow surface Cunnington found a cist, a stone box creating a coffin, holding the cremation remains of a woman with some of the most stunning and culturally important Bronze Age grave goods ever found in Britain. Perhaps the most visually captivating of the artefacts is a huge necklace, originally made of a thousand amber beads (only three hundred remain), set on six strings with amber 'spacers' to hold and regulate the shape of the piece. The beads were sourced, and perhaps fashioned, across the North Sea in Denmark, emphasising again the pan-continental nature of Bronze Age Britain, and their owner is referred to in academia as The Lady of the Amber Necklace, though I prefer to call her The Amber Princess.

Her necklace wasn't all they found, as other pieces emerged flashing from the cist, including a rectangular plaque of incised, paper-thin gold, which would have been backed onto wood and stitched onto a piece of clothing as an impressive badge of office. There were also eleven thumb-nail-sized, barrel-shaped golden pieces, which may have been strung into a bracelet, necklace or stitched prominently onto clothing. These tiny 'barrels' are not hinged but the golden ends can be folded over to enclose each of them, giving rise to the idea they are shamanic in nature, and each may have held some small quantity of a healing herb or maybe a psychotropic substance.

More gold with two 'caps' that may have adorned the end of a wooden staff or sceptre of office, and an enigmatic piece of black shale worked into a cone-shape then decorated with a beautifully incised golden cover, known as the Upton Lovell Button. There were also two bronze pieces, including the sort of pointed awl used in tattooing and a small, decorative bronze knife, typical of a high status, female burial. The most poignant funerary item was an incense vessel, known as a 'grape cup' with perforations in the side to allow the scent of herbs and hallucinogens to waft around the funeral ceremony, and it's thought such small clay pots may have been fired in the cremation pyre itself as a sentimental farewell.

All this adds up to a woman of immense prestige, a woman who might well indeed have been a high priestess at Stonehenge, perhaps a healer or a seeress, certainly someone exalted in the community, a famed

Bronze Age princess and a power in the land. Little wonder her grave is known as the Golden Barrow and when it was excavated it caused an immense stir in the drawing rooms of Georgian England and made Cunnington's name in fashionable society.

Sad to say, little remains of the barrow itself, except an imperceptible rise in the ground, because as soon as the burial hoard was removed the local landowner saw that as licence to plough the barrow into oblivion. Even sadder, the funerary remains of the Amber Princess were simply discarded to the four winds, as were the cremation ashes of someone placed nearby, perhaps one of her relatives. The grave goods survive on display in the Wiltshire Museum, and later in this book I intend to show the cone-shaped golden, Upton Lovell Button has huge cultural significance of global importance.

Cunnington excavated two more graves in the Upton Lovell assemblage, officially designated G2 and dated around 1900 to 1700 BC at a time when the great trilithons were being shaped on site and erected. One was G2e another female burial, this time in a large Bell Barrow on higher ground where a beautiful, but far less grand necklace, made of amber and faience beads, was discovered. Judging by her grave goods, this woman had not been as posh as her neighbour in the Golden Barrow, but she does reinforce the idea that women in Bronze Age society were powerful individuals in their own right.

Perhaps, they held a status similar to that of the Celtic women who'd follow them in a thousand years or so, as their Iron Age sisters held sway in a strongly matriarchal society where women could choose whom they married, divorce if they wished, buy and sell land, become tribal chiefs and war leaders, and serve as Druid priestesses too. The Amber Princess and her neighbour seem to be telling us that may have been substantially true in the Bronze Age as well.

A third grave on the Wylye water meadows known as Upton Lovell G2a, is one that needs to be given much wider attention for the amazing insights it gives us into Stonehenge society. It's commonly known as the Upton Lovell Shaman Burial, but I prefer to call it the Wylye Shamans' Grave because there were two people in that burial, a man and a woman, bound together for eternity and I believe they were both shamanic priests. What Cunnington found almost beggars' belief, representing a very rare internment indeed and although it contained only a microscopic glimmer of gold, Upton Lovell G2a held the bones of one of the first goldsmiths known in Britain and the burial tells us an enormous amount about the Bronze Age. The Wylye Shamans were laid to rest with their most prized worldly goods, then a barrow was raised over them, signifying their high status in society and I can do no better than repeat the description of the grave offered by the Wiltshire Museum in Devizes where the artefacts are housed:

Buried in a barrow at Upton Lovell, the Shaman was a metalworker and religious leader, in touch with the spirit world. He was buried in his ceremonial cloak, decorated with pierced animal bones. These would have jangled as he walked and danced. He carried a magnificent dark coloured battle axe, made from greenstone brought from Cornwall... The Shaman was also buried with stones used for smoothing and burnishing gold, suggesting he was one of the very few who understood the magic of metalworking.

Placed next to him in the same grave was the body of a woman. She was carefully placed sitting upright, her head close to the surface of the barrow. She was buried with a necklace of polished shale beads and a fine shale arm ring. They were buried together on top of the ridge looking out over the river valley that led towards Stonehenge. Perhaps this was one of the routes that traders took, bringing rare objects and raw materials to the ceremonial centre at Stonehenge...

I don't doubt the shamanic couple had chosen the Wylye Valley to set up business in the most convenient spot for their important, high-status customers and co-religionists in the orbit of Stonehenge. I hope this enigmatic couple had a good life on the banks of the gin clear, chalk stream because the question of the woman's demise is perplexing and macabre. The consensus is she climbed down into the grave and sat in a symbolic position of overwatch above her man then died, probably with her wrists slit so that she would bleed out. She was, if you like, the ultimate 'possession' to take into the afterlife, a thought I

VIEWED WITH HORROR UNTIL I SPOKE TO MY FRIEND DAVID DAWSON at the Wiltshire Museum who prefers to characterise her death as an ultimately heroic and unselfish act of love, and offered this, "I've always thought she might have been the subject of a Bronze Age ceremony of ritual suicide. Her belief system may well have seen her go happily to her death and she may even have been helped on her way by psychotropic drugs. We'll never know."

That's especially true as Cunnington and his Antiquarian crew working in 1801 only kept the good stuff, the grave goods, while they scattered the couple's bones about to be ploughed into the ground, denying modern science the opportunity to tell us so much more. Having said that, six of the artefacts Cunnington kept certainly illuminate the Shaman's skills as a goldsmith, as they comprise what archaeologists call a chaîne opératoire, or sequence of processes, in Bronze Age gold work.

One of the stones had been used as a small anvil for the planishing or flattening of gold and this milky coloured cushion stone, as they're called, must have been of great spiritual significance as it was placed on his chest in the grave. The Shaman also had four hammers, repurposed from the pieces of a shattered stone axe, and the sixth stone implement was first thought to be a burnishing or polishing stone until scientists realised it was a 'touchstone.' This tool shines an extraordinary light on the art of ancient goldsmithing, a skill which must have given our Shaman an aura of wizardry within his community and goes to confirm the duality of craftsman and priest.

The touchstone had minute traces of gold across its face, and these are believed to have come from small ingots of the element the Shaman's was thinking about trading. The nearest sources of gold were in Wales or Cornwall and further afield across the sea in Ireland, and by marking the touchstone with any gold he wanted to 'buy' our Shaman could assay the purity and workability of the metal by eye and experience. Just think of it, to you and me gold is gold, but to him its qualities could be divined from the streaks made on a piece of dark, red sandstone held up to the light. Different purities, different coloured streaks. In fact, modern scientific analysis tells us those gold streaks still visible four thousand years on, contained around 15% silver and 1% copper, a quite typical alloy of gold for the Early Bronze Age, and the Shaman's eye would have told him that, unlike pure gold, it wouldn't be too soft to work successfully because of the hardening presence of silver.

Touchstones are extremely rare items, and at present the one buried with our Shaman is the oldest known example in Europe. Wonderful! So wonderful, no less an authority than Phil Harding, Time Team's famous, Wiltshire born archaeologist believes the Upton Lovell Shaman was one of the first goldsmiths on these islands and may have been responsible for crafting many of the golden artefacts found around Stonehenge.

I have a personal postscript to this story as a year before lockdown a friend was having an extension built at her home, which required new footings to be excavated. She lives less than half a mile from the Wylye Shamans' Grave and it so happens Austin Shepherd, a friend of my son Morgan, was tasked with the spadework and had the good sense to stop digging when he spotted the hint of a sparkle on a stone at his feet. It turned out to be a perfectly shaped Bronze Age cushion stone, with a rime of gold on the upper surface where artefacts had once been worked. I was allowed to examine the stone, which appears to be Old Red Sandstone (ORS to geologists) and fits perfectly into the hand. What a thrill to hold such an implement, which no doubt has a four-thousand-year link to the goldsmithing tradition of the Upton Lovell Shaman. I'd love to tell you more about the provenance of this cushion stone, particularly the significant position of the house where it was found but sadly I'd be inviting a plague of illegal 'nighthawk' metal detectorists to descent upon my friend's home.

Such artefacts are beautiful and modern, micro-examination is beginning to work out whether different artefacts are the handiwork of the same artisan, rather like the brush strokes on an Old Master's oil painting, although they'll never be able to tell us just who the goldsmith was, of course. The shamanic nature of the Upton Lovell couple was revealed by the boar tusk decorations but also by an extraordinary tattooing kit found at the feet of the woman. It comprised four ink cups made from fossilised sponge nodules and a bronze piercing awl, and I think we can safely bet both shared shamanic roles, while he was also a skilled goldsmith.

This was a Bronze Age power couple, he owned the allegorically mystical skills of goldsmithing, while she was possessed of the occult of the tattooing needle and together they strode the by-ways of Salisbury Plain, a couple set apart and otherworldly. As it is, the Wylye Shamans probably lived and died at Upton Lovell, on the graceful banks of the river, perhaps three hours walk away from Stonehenge on a fine day, and I have little doubt they were familiar acolytes at the great temple.

12

THE STONEHENGE GIANT

There's another round barrow burial which, above all others, symbolises the heady days when Stonehenge reached its zenith in terms of architectural achievement and cultural opulence around 1900 BC. As we'll learn later, it's undoubtedly the most important Bronze Age grave in Britain, and the giant of a man who was laid to rest there is emblematic of the astronomical power of the temple.

Bush Barrow stands just a kilometre away and eye-to-eye with Stonehenge, in a situation which couldn't be more auspicious because, at the moment of the Winter Solstice sunset, the solar disc expires directly behind the barrow forming a golden halo around the once chalk-white grave. The paramount chieftain who was interred there, doubtless with arcane rituals and high drama, was six feet tall when most men were five feet eight and the regalia laid around his body is nothing short of stupendous. There's little doubt he was the man who ruled over Stonehenge when the temple was at its height as a masterpiece of Trilithons and Preseli Star Stones.

The Bush Barrow grave goods certainly lend the megaliths of Stonehenge a regal, human context and give us the most explicit pointers to the way the temple was used, and a vague idea how its ceremonies may have played out. As it was, the fifteen feet high grave held its secrets for four thousand years, until the age of the Antiquarians when William Cunnington, the most prolific of these early proto- archaeologists, directed the Bush Barrow excavation on either the 10th or 11th of July

1808. In the burial he discovered a hoard of gold and bronze artefacts of unsurpassed quality, together with an elaborately polished stone orb, representing royal regalia. I'm going to describe the Bush Barrow treasures in some detail here, with the intention of returning to a couple of them later, when I'll reveal more of their astonishing secrets.

On first sight, the most striking of the grave goods is a golden lozenge, decorated with perfectly executed lines, inscribed onto the gold. It was laid on the giant's chest when he was placed in the grave. A similar but much smaller golden lozenge graced the top of a rather wonderful, polished stone orb found close by his skeleton. The orb is fashioned from a fossilised colony of turbellaria or sea worms, believed to have been sourced from Brixham on the Devon coast. It's egg-shaped, dun in colour and superbly worked and polished into its distinctive and symbolic form. It was drilled through, probably by a Bow Drill similar to the fire-starting awl used since the dawn of time, but instead of tinder at the point of the spindle, abrasive grit and lubricating water would have be used to grind the hole. This was labour-intensive, time-consuming work, which took an estimated five-hundred man-hours to complete.

Who knows how long it took to polish the lump of fossil into a near perfect egg form before the drilling began, but as I often rather glibly remark they had no TV in those days. The result was a pretty much perfectly round slot to accommodate a stick, which transformed the Egg from an orb into a sceptre and in my view gave it an enhanced majesty. Whilst the stick had long since disintegrated Cunnington did find the collars that decorated its shaft, crafted in zigzags of bone to look like flashes of lightning. After examining the sceptre, the Antiquarian Sir Richard Colt-Hoare who funded Cunnington, was moved to describe this enigmatic object as 'an Insignia of Dignity' and it is indeed the visible symbol of the authority of a very powerful man, the King of Stonehenge and probably an astronomer priest too. The giant in the grave also had a gold-plated buckle, either for a belt or to hook on a knife scabbard, and two of the finest and largest bronze knives ever excavated from those times; thought to have been forged in present day Brittany. A beautiful stone axe was also among the grave goods, perhaps giving a nod to the Neolithic past, together with a very finely moulded-bronze axe acknowledging the relatively new, metal technology of those times.

However, a third bronze dagger eclipses practically every Bronze Age blade excavated in Northern Europe because of its twelve inch long, wooden hilt decorated with an estimated 138,000 tiny gold pins, each about a millimetre long and fine enough to pass through the eye of a needle. Using a tiny bronze awl, the artisans set and glued the pins into the hilt at a density of a thousand pins per square centimetre and here's the thing, the tops of these hair-like pins were chamfered at different angles, so that when the light shone on the hilt it displayed a herringbone pattern. Utterly, mind boggling!

We know the what the hilt looked like, and its extraordinary visual impact, because illustrator Philip Crocker was employed on the excavations, and he'd managed to execute a wonderfully evocative watercolour of the hilt in the hours before its wooden stem mostly disintegrated on exposure to the atmosphere. Many of the gold pins had already been scattered by the slip of a trowel, and only a few remain witness to the wonder of that hilt. What a tragedy, but of course the Antiquarians were the founding fathers of modern archaeology and would doubtless have given their eye teeth for access to the scientific preservation and 'lifting' techniques developed by those who followed over the next couple of hundred years.

Expert assessments of the optical powers of the goldsmiths who created this stunning work, suggest they would have been children, or maybe adults who'd been used to this close work from childhood. At a time when an average life span was short, that's not so surprising nor is it surprising to think that some of the greatest modern jewellers, the likes of Faberge or Cartier, would have been pretty much gobsmacked by this level of skill and artistry and hard-pressed to replicate it. David Dawson, the guardian of the Bush Barrow artefacts at the Wiltshire Museum has no doubts, "The dagger hilt is quite rightly described as 'the work of the gods, it's utterly remarkable."

As I've already mentioned, I was mesmerized when I first saw these wonderful grave goods in their display cabinet at the museum in Devizes, so dazzled I missed the card placed discreetly in one corner advising visitors the 'gold' objects on display were facsimiles, counterfeits if you like.

On my next visit, I did read the notice, but they were bloody good imitations and undeterred by their provenance, I kept visiting to gaze at them over the months that followed, just to wonder about the man who'd owned them and daydream about those long-ago times.

It was around 2009 and through my frequent visits to the museum I'd got to know David Dawson, so I asked him why duplicates were on display, and where were the originals? He explained that for over thirty years the real Bush Barrow gold had been reburied, more mundanely this time, in a bank vault because the Georgian-era gallery where they were displayed, wasn't secure enough to satisfy the justified demands of the museum's insurers; at least not without a lot of money being spent. The Society were hoping to raise the cash to make the gallery burglar and fire proof, but it was proving to be a long haul. Hang on a minute, I thought. I'd been chewing over the nature of the Bush Barrow Hoard for months and my thoughts seemed to coalesce in that moment, "David, could you call the Bush Barrow Collection the first Crown Jewels of Britain?"

I remember him being a bit taken aback and he gave me an old-fashioned look before he said, "Well, you might Alun but then you're a journalist. I wouldn't but then I'm a scientist."

Invariably polite and understated, David had a point. I am indeed a journalist first, and my view of the world is informed by years of experience in crystallising ideas and concepts, to express them to a wider audience, so I asked whether that statement could be true in principle. David pointed out the Antiquarians had indeed used the descriptive 'Insignia of Dignity,' and indicated it wouldn't be wildly inaccurate to characterise them as such, especially as nothing so regal, pre-dated them in the UK. I took this as a yes, and wasted no time in contacting Paul Harris, a feature writer on the Daily Mail. An old friend, Paul and I had been together in Israel covering Saddam Hussein's Scud rocket attacks on Tel Aviv at the onset of the Gulf War, and I put the case for a piece on the Bush Barrow collection, asking him if he'd like to write an article on the First Crown Jewels of Britain. A week later he arrived in Devizes, as keen as mustard.

In the intervening few days David suggested I might like to see the real thing for myself. Was he kidding? A couple of days later I was in the Museum conference room, with my old Fleet Street photographer mate Les Wilson, who conveniently lives a couple of miles away from Stonehenge. Les would take the photos ready to accompany Paul's feature, and we found ourselves looking at a matt black, rectangular box, sat on a green baize table under a large window, with David and the museum Curator, Lisa Brown, next to it.

Lisa removed the lid from the vault box, then produced the Golden Lozenge in her white-gloved hands; for all the world a magician performing her showstopper; a rabbit from a hat. It was a moment of complete magic for me, and Les Wilson too, the same for Paul Harris, when the Collection was brought out of the vault again for him to view. As he left Devizes, we shook hands and Paul told me, "You and I have seen a lot of things Al, but I've never felt the hairs on the back of my neck go up quite like that before."

Paul's two-page spread, under the unambiguous headline 'The First Crown Jewels of Britain', was perfect, placing the Bush Barrow Hoard in its true perspective and eventually helped swing the grants that would make a new, secure gallery possible. Money was just the start of it, of course, and it took four more years of patient commitment and hard work on the part of the inestimable David Dawson, until I was delighted to receive an email from him, thanking me for my small part in it all, and inviting me to the grand opening of the new gallery, by the Princess Royal. The Bush Barrow Collection, the Amber Princess and the Wylye Shamans grave goods have all been displayed in that wonderful gallery since, after decades out of sight interred in a bank vault.

THE BUSH BARROW LOZENGE

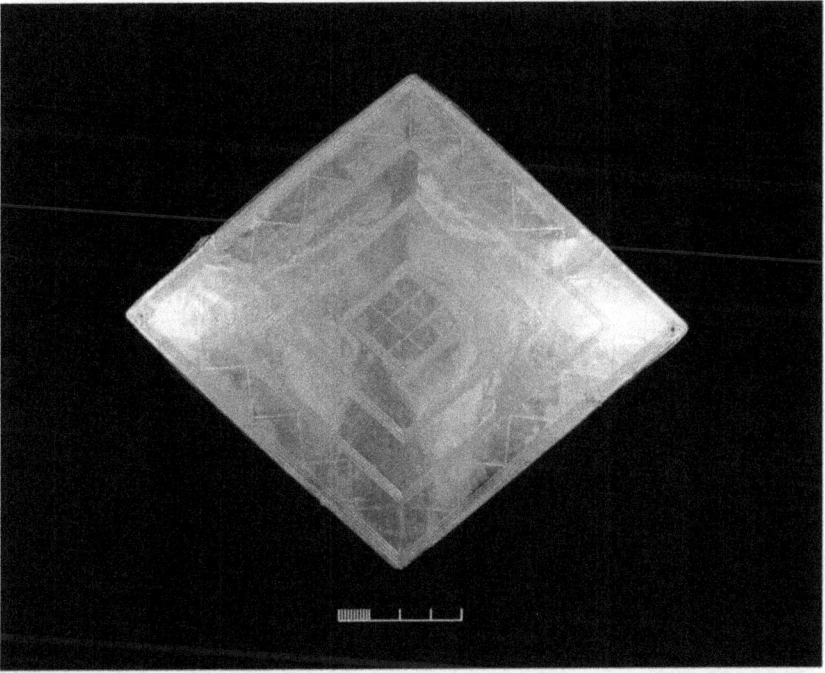

The delineations finely etched into the gold contain the precise angle of declination between the Summer and Winter Solstice and the nine arrows inscribed along each of the four sides point to an astonishing provenance revealed in Chapter Nineteen.

(Photograph courtesy of the Wiltshire Museum)

I fear these wonderful creations of our Bronze Age ancestors have been woefully neglected, certainly not by David Dawson, and the stalwarts of the Wiltshire Museum, but metaphorically forsaken by the archaeological establishment allowing Bush Barrow to be 'unremembered' by a generation of writers and documentary makers, engaging with the story of Stonehenge, in favour of the Amesbury Archer. I believe the answer's simple. Bush Barrow was excavated in 1808, and all the artefacts removed while the Giant's skeleton was left in the barrow when it was backfilled. No strontium analysis, no DNA, no media frenzy and then to seal Bush Barrow's anonymity the grave collection was locked away in a bank vault for decades. On the other hand, the Amesbury Archer was uncovered just twenty years ago, and the skeleton subjected to all the revelatory scientific analysis available.

So here we have two skeletons, one of them old hat, and let's be fair, buried out of sight for more than thirty years, the other brand spanking new and the focus of huge 21st Century media attention. I fear historians and archaeologists have fallen into a waiting trap and bedazzled by the more recent discovery, they've neglected the older one, casting themselves as victims of fashion. Not a good look, and its surely time Bush Barrow is reinstated to its rightful place in the conversation.

As my story unfolds, I'll reveal the Stonehenge Giant's true celebrity, and the international significance of his grave goods, in the meantime I believe it's time Bush Barrow was re-excavated. The area around the Normanton Down cluster of barrows, where Bush Barrow stands, is sensitive and permissions to excavate in that landscape are almost as rare as hens' teeth, but I'm sure there are ambitious archaeologists out there who'd be eager for the opportunity. And why not? The skeleton of the Stonehenge Giant lies waiting to be excavated, and it would be the most significant archaeological 'Cold Case' in the UK since King Richard III was identified from a set of bones found in a town centre car park.

13

FUNERAL PARLOUR
OR HEALTH CENTRE?

For well over a decade a seemingly entrenched, but well-mannered debate about the nature and function of Stonehenge has echoed around the world of archaeology. It's been on the back burner lately, while gobsmacked scientists assimilate and assess the mass of Lidar related discoveries made around the monument, particularly at Durrington Walls nearby.

But the fundamental question won't go away. What was Stonehenge for? In the final chapters I'll make the case its primary purpose was that of an astronomical observatory, corroborated by its architectural lay-out and, without placing a 21St Century template on the henge, its religious and astronomical functions may well have been irrevocably entwined. Setting the obviously astronomical nature of the temple to one side for a moment, let's consider the other theories proposed by some of the big beasts in the world of Stonehenge thinking.

They come down to Stonehenge being a 'Place of the Dead', or in a diametrically opposed idea, a 'Centre of Healing', along with permutations of other ways the temple might have been employed thrown into the mix. Essentially, the theories rolled together come down to births, marriages and death, lots of sky at night and the occasional human sacrifice. I think the idea that it was a multi-purpose place of worship is the one that makes most sense to me, and the moment you try to place a single-use template over the Stonehenge it seems to lack veracity.

The concept of Stonehenge as a Centre of Healing, has been most powerfully advocated by two of the leading experts on the monument, Geoffrey Wainwright, and Tim Darvill; academics I've mentioned previously on these pages. Sadly, Geoffrey Wainwright died in 2017 but their two names, Wainwright and Darvill, are forever linked in the world of archaeology so I'll refer to them that way, as if he were still with us, hoping that might please the spirits of the ancestors. There can be no absolute proof of their 'Place of Healing' assertion, and needs must, their ideas are speculative, but I'll examine their theories soon, together with some fresh ideas of my own to add to the debate.

For now, let's consider Mike Parker-Pearson's contrary ideas on the purpose and usage of Stonehenge as 'a Place of the Dead.' It surely deserves careful attention by virtue of the massive contribution the professor has made to our knowledge of Stonehenge as director of the Riverside Project, his work at Waun Mawn and advocacy of the A40 Route for the Bluestone haulage. Parker-Pearson has been an influential figure in the thinking on Stonehenge for the past thirty years or more and derived his Place of the Dead theory from a long-time collaboration with an academic called Ramilisonina, a Madagascan archaeologist, who characterised the cold megaliths of Stonehenge in that way. Similarly, Ramilisonina identifies the huge timbers of Woodhenge nearby as a 'Place of the Living.' Stone for the dead, wood for the living. It's a simple concept and an elegant solution to the debate coming from Ramilisonina's own, lived experience on the Indian Ocean Island, where stones are still conveyed and erected to monumentalise relatives who've passed away.

That's a wonderful practice but does it fit well in the context of Stonehenge? Without wishing to be at all trite, the archaeology shows the sacred circle was indeed a place of multiple burials, and the wider Stonehenge ritual landscape is blistered with scores of barrows where cremations and inhumations have been identified. Certainly, then a place of the dead, no question, but critical thinking suggests Stonehenge was multi-functional with great ceremonies performed seasonally, to mark the passage of the sun and offer oblations to the gods, as well as to cremate, bury or excoriate the remains of the great and the good. And maybe there were marriages, human sacrifice and healing rituals too. Why not?

Like many others, I'm just not convinced by the stark 'Place of the Dead' and 'Place of the Living' demarcation of the Stonehenge and Woodhenge roles. Sure, it has the benefit of simplicity, and I'm quite certain that for designated periods of time in the religious chronology of Stonehenge the processional path from Durrington Walls, along the river valley to Bluestone Henge, then up The Avenue to Stonehenge was indeed a funereal route and the two places took on the mantle of Living and Dead.

I just can't believe that was a permanent differentiation, more likely an order of service in a long and varied, annual liturgical calendar including rites of all sorts. That's because I see an innate spiritual life of Stonehenge embodied in the Bluestones by dint of their unique, audio-visual qualities, through their light and sound. I suspect Neolithic and Early Bronze Age people would have thought so too, perhaps viewing the Bluestones as individuals, as personalities if you like, rather than cold, inanimate statues of death.

That's not such a far-fetched idea, walk around Avebury Stone Circle most days and you'll overhear modern 21st Century tourists endowing the great megaliths with the simulacra of human characteristics in the stone; the broader ones represent females with their hips, the straight, phallic looking stones are male, others conjure visions of witches etc. As for the Bluestones at Stonehenge, you can play chimes on them, literally for the Gods' sakes, and that alone marks them out as expressive of life.

Ultimately, the standing stones erected in Madagascar for the ances-tors are not, to the best of my knowledge, chosen for their lithophonic qualities, and therein lies a fundamental difference as Bluestones can demonstrate the thrilling quality of pitch perfect sound. Why wouldn't our Neolithic ancestors believe that set the stones apart, signifying they were possessed of a liminal and ethereal life force entirely of their own. For me, that's where the analogy of Stonehenge primarily as 'a Place of the Dead' founders, and by saying that I offer no disrespect to the tradi-tions and culture of Madagascar. I'm just saying it doesn't fit a rounded view of Neolithic and Early Bronze Age Stonehenge, and I personally find it impossible to believe 'singing stones' were brought all the way from Preseli to serve as an elaborate set of headstones.

Stonehenge may well have been a place of ritual sacrifice too and the evidence for that comes from the violent death of the Stonehenge Archer we've already heard about. Yet another body had previously been found within the cloisters of Stonehenge in 1923, long before the remains of the Stonehenge Archer turned up. This time it was a man who'd had the ill fortune to have been beheaded, but in the 1920's, only so much analysis could be done on the skeleton before it was packed in a box and stored away. It was presumed lost during the Blitz in World War II and assumed to have been destroyed by German bombs. It hadn't and Mike Pitts tracked the box of bones down to the dusty archives of the Royal College of Surgeons in a remarkable piece of historical detective work. It's a great story, which I have no intention of reprising here, instead I urge you read Mike's own account in his excellent best-seller Hengeworld. Long story, short, 21st Century analysis showed the remains to be Anglo-Saxon, strongly suggesting Stonehenge was a place of pagan worship and dramatic ceremony well into the Dark Ages. Stonehenge, a Place of the Dead certainly and a Place of Death too, as evidenced by at least two executions performed at the scene, obviously a Place of Astronomy and a place of Celestial Worship, with the ringing star stones from Preseli at its very heart. But what about the proposal it was a Place of Healing? Wainwright and Darvill characterised Stonehenge as a Neolithic Lourdes, comparing it to the famous Roman Catholic place of pilgrimage in France, where therapeutic waters, and a vision of the Blessed Virgin, are said to bring about miraculous cures for many conditions.

Their Lourdes comparison has come in for a lot of criticism, although Wainwright and Darvill are a serious duo of scientists and didn't simply pluck their 'Healing' theory out of thin air, but offer thought provoking clues harvested from finds in graves excavated in the Greater Stonehenge area, coupled with some fascinating folk memory and the empirical evidence of a dig they carried out themselves at Stonehenge in 2008.

One of their key points has been to highlight the evident destruction of some Bluestones manifest in the crumble layer around the henge, which they say supplied pieces of the rock to make amulets for the sick, and to place pieces of the sacred stone in graves as reverences. Not so hard to grasp, when we know Bluestone 'souvenirs' are still greatly valued and held as sacred to this day by a widely diverse, New Age demographic, and there's also a pretty much universal shamanic, tradition for the creation and wearing of healing amulets. Wainwright and Darvill also reviewed burials from the area around Stonehenge and found signs of serious injuries in many of them and two skulls in particular with evidence of rudimentary, trepanation or brain surgery, some of the earliest-known operating procedures in Britain. Importantly, dental analysis shows that about half these ailing people were from outside the Stonehenge area, implying they could have been pilgrims seeking a cure.

One particularly famous burial in the orbit of Stonehenge, which circumstantially fits this narrative of a sick and pain-wracked pilgrim seeking relief is that of the Amesbury Archer, who was definitely in need of medical help. Analysis shows his pain must have been off the scale and the theory he'd made the pilgrimage from his birthplace in the Alps, to seek a miracle is as good as any.

As I've already pointed out excavations at Stonehenge are rare birds indeed, but Darvill and Wainwright got the necessary permissions and slotted a trench near the Stones in 2008. Their major conclusion was the Bluestones had been put in place between 2400 and 2200 BC, three centuries later than the previous estimate of 2600 BC. Somewhere along the process of their analysis, Wainwright and Darvill, cross-pollinated their archaeological clues with circumstantial evidence gathered from ancient Welsh practices and famous legends.

First, they considered the age-old belief in Wales, which perpetuates to this day, that Bluestones hold the power of healing. There's a particular belief that freshwater springs, around the well-known source of Bluestones at Carn Menyn have that power. Bearing in mind Wainwright was a native of Pembrokeshire, he was already familiar with this cultural story and, as a native of Wales, so am I. But when they looked on the ground the two colleagues also found evidence springs had been formalised by Preseli people over millennia. Bluestone rocks and boulders had been used to form small pools at the point of eruption to form what they call, 'enhanced springs.'

Make no mistake, this is a very wet bit of landscape, with not much need to dam-up springs on the hillside to get a drink of water. However, you may do that if your aim is to anoint yourself with healing waters, and

Wainwright and Darvill found one of these indigenous pools near Carn Menyn has a rock at its head with a Neolithic circle and cup decoration inscribed on it; a telling find indeed.

The two archaeologists realised the physical evidence of these 'enhanced springs' resonates strongly with the writings of the 12th Century cleric Geoffrey of Monmouth, who alludes to the therapeutic qualities of Bluestones, saying they were first used by the Irish on Mount Killaraus, for rituals and healing. In fact, the British poet Layamon described in some detail the therapeutic procedures carried out with Bluestone water in this couplet:

The Stones are great, And magic power they have, Men that are sick, Fare to that stone, And they wash that stone, And with that water bathe away their sickness.

Essentially, Wainwright and Darvill are pointing to an ancient and often reiterated belief that waters bubbling from, or passed over, Bluestones become fused with healing properties. Not hot enough for a spa, but frigid enough for cold water therapy you might think, and I've no idea whether there's any chemistry to back-up a connection between the mineral content of Bluestones and any associated health benefits, while there's ample evidence that people in Wales have believed it to be the case for a very long time indeed.

Wainwright and Darvill, have been criticised for introducing the musings of Geoffrey of Monmouth into a scientific analysis of the fundamental purpose of Stonehenge, with Mike Pitts notably dismissing it as 'fairy-tale.' As a great believer in the powerful messages held, albeit enigmatically in folk memory, I don't agree. I like to call those communal memories, smoke from the flames of history, and I think Mike's criticism is a bit harsh.

Mike Parker-Pearson is also happy to cite the writings of Geoffrey of Monmouth, and his famous description of Merlin magically transferring the Bluestones to Stonehenge, after they'd been taken from the Irish in battle. I think Prof. Parker-Pearson was entitled to evoke Geoffrey, and so are Wainwright and Darvill. It's also important to realise Geoffrey of Monmouth was only a staging post in these folk memories, having harvested them from very much older Welsh tribal legends from the Iron

Age, to create his resounding, literary success, featuring the bestselling Arthur and Merlin dynamic duo.

Tim Darvill was also involved with the investigation of the campanological qualities of the Bluestones as mentor to the Landscape & Perception Project on Preseli. Those qualities are truly awe inspiring, but not in a month of Sundays would I have connected the ringing stones of Preseli, directly to the Wainwright and Darvill theory of Stonehenge as a Place of Healing. At least, not until I was discussing this chapter with my partner Stephanie who you'll recall, spent time studying First Nation rituals and Native medicine. The conversation we had went along the lines of me thinking there was something authentic in the healing theory. It made sense and 'spoke' to me, but I felt something was missing and there must be another ingredient.

Without hesitation Stephanie suggested I should consider Sound Healing, which ancient and more modern cultures have practiced for millennia. "Why not the people of Stonehenge? After all Bluestones are lithophones, perfect for Sound Healing," she said.

All I had to do was join the dots, and sure enough a cursory search online told me she was absolutely on the money. More than that, some of the ways sound has been used in the healing process are ancient and mind-boggling. Sound Healing has been an ever-present aid to wellness for body and spirit in multiple cultures, throughout our time. From the outset, it's important to realise that a great deal of Sound Therapy or Frequency Medicine, is based on what is perceived to be a universal harmonic, the sound of the cosmos, if you like, expressed in the repeated Buddhist note of OM, said to be a frequency of 417Hz.

Whilst we all accept good feelings come from listening to music, there is a difference between music and Sound Healing and that seems to come down to the notes achieved and a degree of hypnotic repetition. Observing the way shamans still practice Sound Healing in many albeit small, often remote and usually tribal cultures, I think our Neolithic and Bronze Age forbears must have made those differentiations too. They may have accepted music was good for the soul on one level but knew that healing required a different set of sounds. I've taken part in a shamanic ritual myself whilst researching another book, in a ceremony meant to explore other aspects of self, rather than physical healing, and the experience centred completely on the repeated, rhythmic notes of a drum. I wouldn't pretend for a second to be an expert on harmonics and the effects of music on body and mind, just as I was completely baffled by the stupefyingly complex equations experts used to declare Stonehenge had been purposefully built to gather in and reverberate sounds acoustically. However, the conclusions of experts are a different kettle of fish, as I can understand them, interpret them, and triangulate their meaning with other pieces of information. In this sense, I've seen many studies that claim various forms of Sound Therapy can reduce stress, decrease anxiety and depression, bring high blood pressure down, inhibit heart disease and stroke, lower cholesterol and, importantly, reduce and control pain.

It's tempting to write-off the therapeutic effects of oscillations and frequencies as 'hippy hogwash' but make no mistake Sound or Frequency Medicine is already with us and has been for decades. It's in everyday, 'conventional' use in hospitals around the world benefitting countless patients and saving millions of lives every year. You only have to think of magnetic resonance imaging, better known to most of us as MRI, routinely used around the world for the diagnosis of a whole catalogue of conditions and serious internal injuries. It's an adaptation of radio frequencies, through the harnessing of sound oscillations. Frequency Medicine by any other name.Similar, medical applications of radio frequences include diathermy and hyperthermy used in cancer treatments and electro-scalpels, in everyday use making incisions and cauterizing tissue during operations. Diathermy harnesses megahertz levels of radio frequency to treat pathological lesions, such as cancers within deeper body tissues, and in neurosurgery and eye surgery too. NASA has been experimenting in this field and reports some success in healing bone tissue with another oscillation-based treatment called Pulsed Electromagnetic Field therapy, and so on.

The reality is Frequency Medicine, and the related field of Sound Healing, are here to stay and certain to develop further as major pharmacy companies have started making significant investments in research. No less a figure than Albert Einstein was unequivocal about its potential a hundred years ago when he said, "Future medicine will be the medicine of frequencies." Perhaps, we just need to gather ourselves up and admit that not for the first time our ancestors may have known many things we are only just coming to relearn.

There's another, important point to be made here. You may be personally sceptical about these claims; you may not believe the delivery of specific sound frequencies could bring about the health benefits claimed. Perhaps you believe modern, pharmaceutical interventions are the appropriate way to treat people with heart disease, depression, stress etc., but that's not the point. The fact is that millions upon millions of people, over thousands of years, across most of the inhabited planet have at some time or other believed Sound Healing works and sought its benefits. That includes Stone Age cultures, clinging to existence, in remote parts of the world who still practice Sound Healing to this day. Pardon the pun, but does that ring any bells? Of course it does, because our Neolithic ancestors were Stone Age people too, and they had their ringing Bluestones.

Traditionally, Sound Healing has been closely linked with shamanic practices, and drumming has obviously been a huge part of that process from the dawn of our time. From drums we seem to have moved on to flutes, then simple string lyres and lutes, and onwards again to harmonic bowls, like the Tibetan singing bowls so important in Himalayan healing practices. We shouldn't forget singing, more properly mouth music in this context, with repeated harmonics, which has also been a staple of Sound Healing over millennia.

Sound Healing is integral within much Native American culture with a belief, spanning many tribal groups, that every person is born with a 'voice.' When you become ill, whether in body or mind, then singing various cadences to the rhythm of a drum is seen as a way to realign your 'voice.' The Cherokee have a strong belief that the voice is the best sound medicine. Variations on this general belief are not confined to the North American continent with African tribes such as the !Kung of the Kalahari, (where '!' denotes a click sound) carrying out song-healings that can last all night. Harvard University researcher Richard Hartz witnessed a song healing, carried out for a young man bleeding profusely from wounds inflicted by a lion. He attested a group of about twenty hunters gathered round the victim to chant and dance to drumbeats until, by morning, the bleeding had stopped, and the wounds had closed over. Remarkable, indeed, and a reminder that we shouldn't always view reality through the prism of our western, technological mindset. The Shona of Southern Africa use song healing, the Dagara of West Africa, and pretty much every tribal grouping in the Sub-Saharan regions of that vast continent too. Back to North America for a moment where the Navajo have medicine men known as 'Singers' who first diagnose the problem, then prescribe the appropriate chant from a dispensary of more than sixty songs. These Singers are held in high regard and must undergo a long apprenticeship to learn their trade by rote. This Native, ritual healing resonates with the methods of the 'harmonic healing houses of Turkey,' known as the Darusiffas, established in the 13th Century, then formalised by the Ottoman Empire. They had a similar idea to the Navajo and prescribed specific music for an individual patient's ailments. I find this fascinating, as it appears to be a half-way house between tribal, shamanic practice and institutionalised, formal medicine. If you want to know more, doctrinal student Asude Ucal wrote a great article on the Darusiffas in The Psychologist magazine.

Around the world, we find a similar picture among the Aboriginal tribes of Australia, and across the great ocean span of Polynesian cultures, all practicing Sound Healing. It's the same in Europe, where the Sami reindeer herders of Arctic Scandinavia, still use their extraordinary pentatonic singing, known as the joik, in shamanic healing rituals, despite repeated attempt to suppress the 'pagan' practice by Christianity. Lots of Sound Healing through time and space then, but does this mean it was practiced at Stonehenge? We simply don't know but if, like me, you accept the empirical evidence of two exhaustive, scientific studies into the lithophonic nature of the Bluestones and the acoustic architecture of Stonehenge, then surely, it must be a possibility. In any event, the balance of probabilities and physical evidence of the Stones being struck from the 'Perception' study mentored by Tim Darvill, suggests the Bluestones were indeed chimed during great ceremonies at the monument, to mark such momentous occasions as the Solstices. Possibly, they were rung for many other religious and socio-religious observances too, ones that we can't begin to imagine, making it easier to believe Bluestones, may also have been chimed for healing ceremonies. Why not?

But there's another ingredient I'd like to add to the proposition Stonehenge was a Healing Circle, and once again it was suggested by Stephanie, and again it's drawn from her knowledge of the practices embodied in Native American culture. We were talking about aspects of aboriginal healing practices, when Stephanie mentioned our friend the Upton Lovell Shaman. Like me, she's fascinated by the Shaman and the woman who was buried with him in the Wylye Valley, no doubt his partner in life, religion and death, and reminded me the couple were buried with a tattooing kit, before enlightening me about the important healing function of tattooing in shamanic cultures. Right again Stephanie, because inking has been used since time immemorial to aid healing as well as to describe clan loyalties, acts of courage in the hunt or in battle, and to signify wisdom.

No less a prehistoric celebrity than Otzi the Ice Man had a set of crosshatches and circles inked onto his lower back and legs, and significantly most of his tatts coincide with the acknowledged acupuncture points associated with rheumatism. And yes, Otzi's bones show signs of rheumatic infection. It's also believed that herbal infusions were added to tattoo inks in some parts of the world and introduced into the system during the procedure; an early form of injection if you like. The Upton Lovell, Shaman's grave goods are on display at the Wiltshire Museum and here's their summary of his tattooing kit...'*Another interesting item found and considered to be associated with the shaman was a tattooing set. Four flint nodule cups made from decayed fossil sponges and a bronze awl were found together at the feet of one of the bodies.*'

The positioning of the tattooing implements within the burial is ambiguous and suggests it might equally have belonged to the Shaman's woman, or maybe they were shared possessions. Perhaps she did the tattooing and was integral to his healing rituals too, if not his goldsmithing, as I can't imagine she would have been disassociated from his shamanic activities; that wouldn't make much sense at all. And then Stephanie intervened again, this time sending me a quote from psychologist and anthropologist Dr. Alberto Villoldo, a scholar of shamanic practices in the southern and central Americas, who wrote, *"Stonehenge in England and Maccu Piccu in Peru are perhaps the most well-known examples of places grounded in the land and the cycles of nature. Dominant features of both sites are massive stones oriented to the movement of the sun. Each (of the two) can be thought of as a great medicine wheel placed on the earth."*

A Medicine Wheel, what's the doctor talking about? Surely, not one of those drum-skins, decorated with Native symbols and feathers, found on the walls of New Age adherents and seekers of spiritual truth? What have they got to do with Stonehenge? Stephanie quickly followed-up with more information and some photographs, and it turns out you can't hang an original on your wall because, wait for it, the real Medicine Wheels are gigantic stone circles set in wilderness landscapes.

The best known of them is the Big Horn Wheel in Wyoming, which is a truly impressive structure of white limestone rocks laid out on a mountain top 10,000 feet above the Big Horn Basin. It's around 10,000 years old, eighty feet in diameter, and has 28 spokes radiating from a central cairn, the same as the number of beams use to roof ceremonial lodges and some interpret as a calendrical link to women's menstrual cycles. The stone cairn forming the hub of the wheel, aligns with Solstice sunrise through a line with another, outlying cairn on the ridge.

Crow tribal tradition (their authentic name is Apsaalooke) says it was already there when they took those mountains from other native clans by conquest, and many tribes have revered the Big Horn Wheel over time so, during periods of peace, all were allowed to make pilgrimages there with impunity. I can see why they'd want to, and it's now on my bucket list too although quite properly, you can only approach the sacred site in the company of a Tribal guide these days.

There are some 200 surviving medicine wheels in the USA and Canada, many of them in Alberta and Saskatchewan, and they are defined by that central cairn, concentric stone circles and at least two spokes radiating from the centre. Some experts believe they are also aligned with certain constellations and were observatories as well as places of sacred rites and healing. A gambler would wager that if two hundred medicine wheels are still present on the ground, then hundreds, maybe thousands more have already been destroyed by development and agriculture when the wave of European farmers ploughed relentlessly across the Great Plains and Rocky Mountains. Indeed, there are well founded concerns on that count for the Medicine Wheels that still survive.

We have a fair idea of how indigenous tribes used Medicine Wheels from tribal accounts given in the 19th and early 20th Centuries, remembering the aggressive colonisation west of the Mississippi only began a little over a hundred and fifty years ago in the 1860's. Complex rituals were carried out inside the Wheels, according to the tribes, where different segments delineated by the spokes were used for different ceremonies and different healings, including mourning, temporal and spiritual journeys, rites of passage and physical and mind healing too, all within the sanctuary of the Wheel.

The cardinal points are recognised around the wheel in the Four Directions together with the spirits of Mother Earth, Father Sky, and the Tree of Spirits. The various segments of the Wheel are also associated with spirit animals and sacred plants like sage and tobacco, so the complexity becomes a cats-cradle of different interpretations and esoteric ceremonies of the various tribes and clans. We can be sure though the participants knew exactly what they were doing and what they were trying to achieve.

But can Stonehenge be characterised as the Medicine Wheel proposed by Dr. Alberto Villoldo? Well, I guess Stonehenge has extraordinary levels of complexity too and I see no reason for dismissing the proposition out of hand, in fact the reverse. After all, Stonehenge is its own wheel with directional values built into its architecture and I'm guessing some of the arcane ceremonies performed at Big Horn and Stonehenge would have been at least vaguely familiar to priests and worshippers at either shrine.

More than that, I suspect that if the Upton Lovell shaman had been born in the great valley of the Big Horn River, he'd have become a shaman there too, neither would a Medicine Man's clothing have been entirely foreign to either culture, deerskin suits, woven textiles, moccasin style footwear; not so different at all.

As it is, our Wiltshire shaman and his woman lived and died at Upton Lovell on the lyrical banks of the Wylye River, a pleasant walk away from Stonehenge, perhaps three hours on a fine day. And in my mind's eye, I can see them arriving at the great temple, the boar tusk decorations on his ceremonial cloak clacking rhythmically as he drummed and danced at great ceremonies. Perhaps, the two of them were temple musicians who played the Bluestone chimes as they exhorted the gods for a healing inside Britain's own gigantic, megalithic Medicine Wheel.

14
TEST TUBES & TROWEL

Scientific advances in genomics and chemistry have transformed the study of our prehistory over the past two decades, mapping our cultural geography and revealing population trends from our DNA and the isotopes laid down in our bones by diet; markers trapped like dragon-flies in amber.

My first encounter with the mind-blowing, archaeological applications of genetic science came in my role as correspondent when I found myself in one of Britain's most famous cave complexes, surrounded by many of the UK's top archaeologists, including the late and wonderful Prof. Mick Aston of Time Team television fame together with a gaggle of media types like me.

It was the morning of Friday, March 7th, 1997, and at the time I was a staff correspondent for the Daily Express, standing in the cool, damp entrance to Gough's Cave, just a few feet away from the spot where the skeleton of Cheddar Man had been found in 1903 at the source of the River Yeo, which rises in the cave to run down the Gorge seeking a way out to sea.

Hand on heart, I'll never forget the subterranean drama that unfolded there at what was perhaps the strangest and at the same time most personally thrilling press conference I've ever attended. It was called by TV production company HTV who'd been filming a documentary about Cheddar Man, who was in his 20's when he died, and at 9000 years antiquity represents the oldest, complete skeleton in British prehistory. It's also the country's oldest cold case murder as young Cheddar Man was brutally despatched by blunt trauma to his skull before his legs were butchered to prep a cannibalistic meal and the rest thrown into the subterranean source of the Yeo.

Dr. Bryan Sykes, of Oxford University's Institute of Molecular Medicine, opened proceedings and explained his team had isolated DNA samples from one of Cheddar Man's teeth. So what? You may well ask, but 25 years ago that was a completely novel concept at a time when the average person in the street was just becoming used to hearing about DNA solving crimes, but most people assumed samples could only be taken from relatively fresh biological material, certainly not from the molar of a man who'd been dead for nine millennia.

There was more, as Dr. Sykes revealed the team had hit on the idea of going to the local comprehensive school, The King of Wessex, on the outside chance of finding a descendant of Cheddar Man in the local area. They'd taken cheek swabs from fifteen pupils and five adults; all bar one from old Cheddar families. At this point Dr. Sykes introduced the history master, Adrian Targett, who was officially representing the school that day, and then declared his team had indeed found a direct match on the mitochondrial (female) line. Dr. Sykes paused for dramatic effect before pulling his rabbit out of the hat, and there was a collective gasp as he announced, "Cheddar Man's sample directly matches the mitochondrial DNA of Mr. Adrian Targett who, as you've heard, is the school's history master."

I felt the hairs on the back of my neck go up, there I was in the mouth of a cave where clans had sheltered in the aftermath of the Ice Age, and incredibly I was sharing that space with a man whose ancestor had been one of those hunter-gatherers. In that moment my growing passion for pre-history sparked by Stonehenge, was given a turbo boost. I interviewed Adrian, a lovely bloke, who told me Cheddar Man's family hadn't gone too far in the 9000 years, as he'd been brought up in Bristol, just twenty miles away. In hindsight, I realise his lineage also represented the small percentage of Mesolithic hunter gatherers, less than ten per cent, who fled to the margins of moorland and sedge marsh to avoid obliteration during the Neolithization of these Islands, a genocide perhaps heralded by the Coneybury Feast.

I remember trying to formulate the words I needed to write my piece and finding it uncharacteristically difficult because I wanted so badly to do justice to that wonderful revelation in Gough's Cave. In the end I came up with an expression that went something like 'Adrian Targett's lineage pre-dates great religions and dwarves royal dynasties' and when it was published as the front-page splash of my newspaper, that phrase was picked up by the wire services in the days before social media, and went around the world.

It's only in a very recent moment of hindsight, that I've come to realise that I was present that morning at the birth of the DNA ancestry industry that's since given countless millions of people tangible insights into their forebears and cultural roots. Cheddar Man then, was a genome first in the world of archaeology and genealogy and a far cry from the world inhabited by those founding fathers of the science the Antiquarians, who first dug into our past in the 18th and 19th Centuries.

I passionately believe theirs is an essential part of the human story of Stonehenge, not only because of the exceptional grave goods they excavated from burial barrows in the wider hinterland of the henge, but because of their role in the creation of the science of archaeology. One very disparate group of men in particular are central to my story of Stonehenge, and I call them Team Cunnington, named for their leader William Cunnington, the well-off wool merchant who lived in the village of Heytesbury, twelve miles west of the henge.

Cunnington emerged as a proto-archaeologist in the years around 1800, a time of seismic cultural and political unrest in Britain and pure mayhem on continental Europe. America had already freed itself from the grasp of their English rulers, Mad King George III was still on the throne, despite two assassination attempts, and slavery continued to mint money for the immoral upper classes. The poor starved after successive, failed harvests caused by distant volcanoes and the Bluestone chime, which had called the congregation to evensong in Maenclochog had recently been demolished along with the entire church, and any evidence whatsoever of pagan practice under the steeple Cross.

Abroad, the French Revolution had already guillotined itself into exhaustion opening the way for a takeover by the military adventurer Napoleon Bonaparte and this had some unforeseen consequences for

British prehistory and the nascence of archaeology, and geology too. As a consequence of the Napoleonic Wars the fashionable Grand Tours around the continent enjoyed by the Upper Classes ended abruptly. Instead of gasping at the spectacular scenery of the Alps, then marinading themselves in the ancient histories of Rome and Greece, the war forced the well-heeled to look closer to home, to the less exotic but equally exciting delights of the British Isles, with journeys around Scotland and Wales replacing the Grand Tour.

What followed was an explosion of British landscape painting and epic poetry, and a new appetite for our own, homegrown ancient history. It kindled a fascination with the mysterious Druids and the wealthy amused themselves among the 'Celtic Sepulchres' of Stonehenge and Avebury. Wiltshire has more than its fair share of standing stones and barrows, and they piqued Cunnington's curiosity as he followed doctor's orders and wandered around the profusion of mounds and barrows on Salisbury Plain.

At some point he decided the best way to discover what these features were all about, was to physically investigate them by excavation, a process he began in 1798. Not that Cunnington, good bloke though he was, did any excavating himself, his social status as a merchant was too elevated for him to get his hands dirty digging. Others did the backbreaking graft for him, hired labourers he called his 'barrowmen' or 'spadesmen' and in 1799 he was introduced to Stephen and John Parker, a father and son duo of agricultural labourers, who also lived in Heytesbury. I'll pause for a moment to lead a round of applause for Dr. Paul Everill of Winchester University, who unearthed the story of the Parkers from the archives of the Wiltshire Museum and wrote a fascinating paper on father and son, which I've drawn on to inform my own less academic account.

In any event, Stephen and John Parker were pleased to get work that paid significantly better rates than the agricultural labouring they were born to endure, and Cunnington was pleased to declare they had a natural facility for the work, while young John in particular, quickly caught on. In a relatively short space of time, Stephen and John became the working engine of a team that would excavate an astonishing four hundred burial barrows across Wiltshire's ritual landscape in just a decade. It was the Parkers' back-breaking toil and their intuitive feel for the soil that transformed Cunnington's ideas into reality and brought their boss great prestige.

One excavation they were engaged on at Upton Lovell in 1802, was to cement Cunnington's reputation as an Antiquarian treasure hunter. It became known as The Golden Barrow, where the Amber Princess was laid to rest with her remarkable artefacts, including her magnificent necklace and the enigmatic Upton Lovell Button. Some discreet, drawing-room jostling followed as members of the gentry vied to fund William's digs and share the limelight and the treasures. Sir Richard Colt-Hoare, the owner of Wiltshire's grandest house at Stourhead, eventually sealed an exclusive deal with Cunnington, and bought his existing collection.

Before we move on, it's important I reprise the life of the money-man Sir Richard Colt-Hoare, the archaeological 'angel' who was the product of two influences, first the enormous fortune that dropped on him from his family's bank, and secondly the Napoleonic War travel ban, preventing him promenading around Europe on the Grand Tour. Unwilling to take the helm at the family bank and unable to travel abroad, Colt-Hoare began travelling in Wales where he fell under the spell of all things Antiquarian, Celtic and Druid. He was the man who bankrolled early archaeology, but I find him a difficult and paradoxical fish who demonstrated the signature lack of empathy with 'common people' that was the hallmark of Georgian society and its ruling classes. At the same time, he was a self-taught classicist and a decent writer, and his two prodigious volumes of 'Ancient Wiltshire' are his invaluable legacy and still informing modern archaeologists. Sir Richard also developed a genuine friendship with his business partner Cunnington, giving him fulsome praise in his writings, while the Parkers got only fleeting mention, commensurate with their lowly station.

It wasn't long before the talented artist and cartographer Phillip Crocker joined the team, plotting the barrows they excavated and illustrating the finds as the team roles were divided out by class and to some extent talent, with Colt-Hoare signing the cheques while Cunnington identified suitable barrows to excavate. Literally at the bottom of the barrow, were the calloused hands of the Parkers, the men who did the hard work braving the dangerous trenches they dug, enduring the summer heat and dust and winter's freezing rain out on Salisbury Plain's cruelly exposed terrain. Here was Team Cunnington, the disparate group that went on to excavate some of the greatest Bronze Age treasures of the British Isles until, at their pinnacle, they brought the priceless pre-history of Bush Barrow and Upton Lovell into the light of day after nearly four millennia in the ground. Their discoveries are absolutely central to my story of Stonehenge.

The did a lot of collateral damage with their haphazard digging, and hindsight tells us Cunnington's most unfortunate omission was to discard the skeletal remains they found during their excavations. But every science has to start somewhere, and no doubt Cunnington, his two 'spadesmen' and the artist, were true pioneers in the field. They also gelled as at group, despite their social distinctions, and Cunnington looked out for them as was demonstrated by his dramatic intervention into a looming family tragedy for the Parkers, in situation that couldn't have been more grave.

Four elements were involved in this Georgian melodrama, one was hunger, another a pig, the third Stephen's eldest son, and last the penal system of the era known as the Bloody Code, guaranteeing appalling punishment for trifling offences. In any event Stephen's son, also called Stephen, risked all by stealing a pig to feed his family, but he was no master criminal and was literally caught with the bacon, arrested, and held for the offence of theft of a pig at Warminster gaol. He was eventually arraigned before Winchester Assizes in 1802 where, in line with the Bloody Code, a judge sentenced him to hang for his heinous, hunger motivated crime.

Naturally, Stephen Senior was at his wits end, and turned to his employer, begging Cunnington for help. To his credit the Antiquarian readily agreed to do what he could, and true to his word, wrote to an influential local dignitary, who in turn spoke to the Judge in the trial. Because of that informal, extra-judicial intervention Stephen Junior's sentence was commuted to one of Transportation to Australia, and two years later he arrived in Sydney to start his sentence. The story shows a remarkable bond, reaching across social boundaries, between the merchant and his 'spadesmen,' despite the starchily rigid conventions of the time, and surely Stephen Parker would have repaid Cunnington with unquestioning loyalty, in gratitude for the precious gift of his son's life spared.

It's a poignant parable of the Georgian era, but for me the story of John Parker is truly significant in our Island story, because young John was the hero of the Cunnington digs. Just twenty-one years old when he began excavations, his youth and natural intelligence meant he was quick to pick things up and was faster on the uptake than his father according to the correspondence. John was quite simply a natural, and his breadth of knowledge and confidence was highlighted in the autumn of 1804 when the team were excavating a barrow at Sherrington, downstream of Heytesbury in the Wylye Valley.

The Antiquarian Lord Wyndham, once pitched-up on a site visit, and suggested the particular barrow was of Saxon provenance. John Parker knew better and, whilst he was to defer to his social better, John confidently disagreed saying there might be some Saxon material at the top of the barrow, but what lay below was a 'British Tumulus.' In other words, John understood that what lies above must generally post-date what's found below, demonstrating his innate understanding of the layers and stratification of history within a burial mound. When Colt-Hoare came to write-up this conversation, from an existing account sent him by Cunnington, he completely edited out any mention of John and his contrary view to that of the 'expert.'

John was to show his intellectual mettle and self-assurance again, when he was the first to suggest the Wansdyke, an earthwork that snakes across Wiltshire, was not Roman as the accepted wisdom of the time had it. Instead, he insisted it post-dated Rome and was probably Anglo Saxon. Why? Because John had dug with his own hands, down to the cobbles of a Roman road crossing beneath the Wansdyke, and to him, it was obvious the earthwork must have been built over the road. Again, Colt-Hoare viewed John's entirely rational conclusion with scepticism and didn't include it in his Wiltshire histories, perhaps resenting a mere labourer was proving to be so damned clever.

Eventually, the team came to make an assault, for that's best description of the effort, on the huge mound at Marden in the Vale of Pewsey. It's gone now, carted off and ploughed away for agriculture, but several digs on the mound at Marden nearly broke John's spirit, prompting Colt-Hoare to accuse him of 'sulking fits' and insisting that on his next visit John *'must be in sweet temper and await my pleasure for I shall have no sulks.'* In 1809, a year after the Bush Barrow discoveries, John annoyed the boss again with Colt Hoare complaining to Cunnington in a letter, *'John Parker seems to increase in stupidity as he grows in years.'* but to Cunnington's credit he pushed back at Hoare for 'wrongfully' picking on John.

Make no mistake, this proto archaeology was a dangerous activity, and not just socially, as little heed was paid to shoring up the sides of narrow trenches that could be ten, fifteen feet deep and inherently unstable. There were collapses, thankfully no fatalities, but still excavations were extremely taxing and stressful places to work. Other, unexpected dangers were posed too, and Sir Richard had a narrow escape himself when he paid a visit to a difficult excavation at Oakley Barrows in Dorset. The Parkers left their iron tools on the edge of the dig as the group sheltered in the trench when thunder clapped, and a storm swept in with sheets of rain and lightning. The metal attracted a direct hit from a lightning bolt, which sent a shower of rocky debris onto those sheltering below, forcing them out into the storm again.

You'd be forgiven for thinking such a shared, near-death experience might have broken down the rigid social walls between Colt-Hoare and the Parkers, at least partially. Apparently not, as Colt-Hoare's irritation with John continued. Whatever slights Colt-Hoare had decided to imagine, he couldn't take the triumph of the excavation at Bush Barrow away from John Parker, who was only twenty-six years of age when the team arrived there in July 1808. It was particularly hot out on the Plain after a summer heatwave, when work on the barrow began, which also meant it was perfect digging weather as the dry conditions minimised the potential for a trench collapse.

In my mind's eye I can see John, the natural archaeologist, at the bottom of the fifteen-foot shaft they'd created scratching around the skeleton and the grave goods by lamplight. And he was doing so a deal more accurately and successfully than on previous digs, because John had spent the previous weeks pondering what might be the best tool for the close work that had to be done when artefacts and skeletons were revealed in a dig. Spades were far too clumsy and brutal for the job; John was raised working with the soil and had a natural understanding of the 'dirt' under his feet and in his hands. I can almost hear John telling himself, 'just the thing, this'll do,' as he picked-up a humble, bricklayers' tool and, in a moment of pure genius, dropped it into his work bag. It was a trowel!

What a moment, when John Parker's intuition proved right and he used a trowel on a dig, for the first time ever, at Bush Barrow. We know this for certain, because Cunnington thought it notable enough to report to Colt-Hoare, in a letter, that John 'used a mason's trowel' that day. There's something intensely satisfyingly about that innovation, when a largely illiterate person, with few rights and no vote, gifted one of our great sciences with its most useful implement and its instantly recognisable motif. And what an excavation to use a 'mason's trowel' in for the first time, and John must have felt a sense of wonder and elation when the Bush Barrow gold glinted in the light of his lantern.

Inevitably, the story doesn't end well. Cunnington eventually succumbed to twenty years of ill health and died in 1810 at the age of fifty-three, just two years after the Bush Barrow excavation, leaving behind a thrilling legacy as one of the founders of modern archaeology. How delighted William would have been to know five generations of his lineage would carry on that legacy of archaeological endeavour, founding the Wiltshire Museum and obtaining Colt-Hoare's collection for display.

With William Cunnington's passing, the Parkers' archaeological careers ended abruptly, and they were summarily laid off by Sir Richard Colt Hoare. Stephen Parker Senior died seven years after Cunnington in a degree of poverty, as Colt-Hoare felt no obligation to look after the two workmen who'd found him such treasures and brought him such kudos. There were no redundancy packages in those days, no pensions, no payoffs, and despite his unrivalled achievements, John Parker was of low birth and there was no place in history for him, certainly not by the pen of Colt-Hoare. No doubt Sir Richard could have done something to help but we know there was history between those two and the aristocrat turned his back on the sullen 'spadesman' who'd had the temerity to challenge him with opinions.

John fell victim to the economic depression caused by the Napoleonic Wars with little field work or winter threshing to be had, and he spent the rest of his life in poverty. At one point he was living in a makeshift, homeless shack he'd erected in Heytesbury churchyard, which was allowed to stand by a charitable Vicar, and according to the 1851 Census he was registered as resident in the local Workhouse under the rule of the infamous Poor Laws. Still, at the age of sixty-nine this obviously formidable character managed to find love again, and was married for a second time, moving into a small cottage at Knook, a stone's throw from the famous Upton Lovell barrows he'd excavated, before dying in debt in 1867.

John Parker's astonishing contribution to the early days of archaeology still goes largely unsung, despite the sterling work of Paul Everill, but I'm giving John Parker a shout-out as the man who gifted archaeology its essential implement and its unmistakeable icon, the trowel. The evidence is that John had become the most accomplished and experienced exponent of the new science of digging into the past anywhere in the world. Cunnington called him a barrowman or spadesman, but I'm going to call John Parker the first, true field archaeologist, and I passionately believe John should be celebrated in his home county of Wiltshire and nationally too.

John Parker personally excavated many of the treasures exhibited in the museum in Devizes, including some of the most fabulous and significant artefacts of the British Bronze Age, and I can think of no better tribute than a John Parker Gallery in the new Wiltshire Museum building being planned at the moment.

Other inventive people took over Cunnington and John Parker's mantle and developed field archaeology over the next couple of centuries, not least a whole dynasty of Cunningtons. One of them is William's grandson Edward who excavated Clandon Barrow in 1812 and found the stunning Clandon Barrow Lozenge, very similar to the Bush Barrow Lozenge; artefacts I'll be saying a great deal more about later in the book.

And that brings us to the 21st Century heroes of Stonehenge

archaeology, most of whom we've already encountered on these pages, starting with the archaeological duo of Darvill and Wainwright who've done so much to reveal a new, alternative face of the monument with their healing theories. Tim Darvill has also been instrumental in revealing the truly amazing visual qualities of the Bluestones when polished and their lithophone properties as sacred bells, providing convincing reasons for their long-distance transportation to Salisbury Plain. My friend Mike Pitts ranks with the best of them too, and he's translated his digging at Stonehenge into two best sellers on the iconic monument and his brilliant Digging Deeper blog. A word also about Francis Pryor, whose Bronze Age archaeology at Flag Fen, near Peterborough, has been a revelation and his brilliant book, Britain B. C. published in 2004, left a deep impression on me and has been a personal inspiration.

There were so many excellent archaeologists involved with the Stonehenge Riverside Project I don't have space to mention them all, but Josh Pollard stands out. Perhaps, Mike Parker-Pearson has emerged as the country's greatest contemporary archaeologist for leading that seminal investigation in 2008 and for his subsequent, ground-breaking work in Preseli, with the discovery of the Waun Mawn proto-Stonehenge circle, and three more Bluestone quarries. These are reasonably familiar, front-of-house faces of archaeology, but we owe a debt of gratitude to the backroom people, who do the largely unsung conservation work and the painstaking laboratory analysis, which provides the field archaeologists with answers to a host of questions.

Before I move on to the concluding chapters let's pause for a moment to reflect again on the life of John Parker, who excavated two particularly significant golden artefacts, the Bush Barrow Lozenge and the Upton Lovell Button. What memories he must have had during those long nights, sat at the hearth before his pauper's death. I don't get the sense John was in any way an unhappy or bitter man, but still he must have glimpsed the glorious long-ago, dug from the earth with his own hands, as he peered into the embers of kitchen fire.

Visions of the Golden Lozenge and the Golden Button must surely have crowded in on John Parker's dreams of ancient treasures, but sadly he would never come to know just how uniquely precious those two artefacts are to the Stonehenge story and to British, European and world prehistory.

Over the next two chapters, I'll relate the thrilling truth about those golden artefacts, which reveal Stonehenge to be a precisely constructed astronomical observatory, but not for a moment will I forget John Parker's role in bringing the story to light and, as we're about to discover it would have been, as the saying goes, beyond his wildest dreams.

15

MOON GAZERS

F ive thousand years ago our Neolithic ancestors planned and laid out the first circle of megaliths at Stonehenge as an al fresco planetarium, a place where they could observe the movements of sky and use their standing stones as waymarks and checkpoints for the passage of heavenly bodies.

There can be no doubt the primary function of the monument was that of an observatory. I say its primary function because it's impossible to separate the astronomical observations of the Neolithic and Early Bronze Age people from their religious convictions. In other words, the heavens above, the sun, the moon, and the stars, must surely have been inextricably linked to the gods that were both observed and worshipped at Stonehenge.

The explosion of standing stone and henge building in both Neolithic and Early Bronze Age Britain was directly linked to this old astronomy which had probably been motivated in the mists of time by the dreadful, primal fear of the sun abandoning us. It was a terror engendered in those people through powerful Tribal Memories of global climate events such as major volcanic eruptions, dimming the sun's power, causing disaster in the biosphere, and famine in the population. The Neolithic and Early Bronze Age preoccupation with the sun has dominated the debate about the astronomical use of Stonehenge for at least four decades with no less a body than the Royal Astronomical Society concluding the great Trilithons of Stonehenge were deliberately aligned to predict and observe the Solstice sun. Because of the implications for mankind's history and the astronomical legacy of our stone monuments, the Royal Society was moved to officially endorse a relatively new branch of their science called Archeoastronomy, supervised by a very active committee.

They follow in the footsteps of no less an astronomical pioneer than Edmond Halley, of Halley's Comet fame, who, in 1720, came up with an equation, using magnetic deviation and the position of the sun, to date Stonehenge at around 460BC, which gave weight to the 'Druid Temple' school of thought, prevailing in Halley's days although, it has to be said, for once the great man was out by three thousand years.

Even those of us with only a passing interest in Stonehenge are aware of its alignment with the sun, if only from the publicity surrounding the Solstice celebrations at the monument. But I'd like to focus first on the far less familiar, lunar applications of the henge as our ancestors tracked the moon's phases and even positioned elements of the henge to act as a stone ephemeris, a megalithic calendar allowing them to pace time, observe the turning wheel of the year and plan their oblations to the gods. As with many things Neolithic there's controversy over these ideas, but I maintain we can be certain the ancients were perfectly familiar with the moon's regular cycle as it waxes and wanes every twenty-nine and a half days over the lunar month.

It's also very evident they'd worked out for themselves the longer, lunar phases known as Major and Minor Standstills, which occur every 18.6 years. Eloquent proof of this lies seven hundred miles north of Stonehenge in the Outer Hebrides where in 2900BC, shortly after the first Bluestone circle was erected at Stonehenge, a unique and complex stone monument was being raised on the Isle of Lewis off Scotland's wildly romantic west coast. The Stones of Calanais (pronounced 'calanesh') comprise a cross-shaped Henge with a central cluster of thirteen giant stones around a small tomb, and one of the arms of the cross forms an avenue of nineteen stones running off to the Northeast. Calanais is indescribably beautiful, but the monument also represents the minute attention our forebears paid to the passage of the moon and here's the really wonderful thing, the stone circle at the centre of the temple is positioned so that every time the moon is in the extreme south at a Major Standstill, its silver disc appears to roll slowly along the hills of the neighbouring island of Great Benera then sets by appearing to drop into the Stone Circle, like a snooker ball falling into a pocket. Truly astonishing, and the more so when you realise this event only happens once every 18. 6 years, roughly five times a century. How then did the inhabitants of Lewis, hit upon this awe-inspiring Neolithic conjuring trick, fully five hundred years before the Pyramids were built?

I imagine the leaders of a clan of farmers and sea harvesters, standing on the spit of land that winds its way to the northeast, watching the passage of the moon one Major Standstill night and observing it suddenly plunge out of sight, apparently into a spot on that promontory. Such a sight must have fired their curiosity, and I can see them deciding to mark the spot with a timber upright, or maybe a pile of rocks, before watching the night sky for many years hoping to see that optical illusion again. Then on the next Standstill 18.6 years later a storm rushes in and rain clouds blot out their sight of the moon. Nothing for it but to keep watching, until they confirm their original marker is indeed in the right spot and so the process went on, perhaps for centuries, depending on the weather, and the wellbeing of the clan. We'll never know how long it took, but what we do know is the clan must have been inspired by the original vision, and multiples of eighteen point six years may have passed while their descendants, weather permitting, checked the passage of the rolling moon as they measured and plotted their Stone Circle with poles and string.

Weather permitting is the key phrase, but around 2900 BC their patience was rewarded, and their dreams came to pass when they built their temple and doubtless watched in awe as the ball of the moon rolled along their lunar snooker table to drop into the pocket of the Stone Circle. A speculative account on my part for sure, but Calanais is so exceptional that nearly three thousand years after its inauguration the Ancient Greeks had heard of it by legend and in the First Century BC the historian Diodorus, wrote of *"a northern island with a spherical temple dedicated to the moon, who returned every nineteen years and skimmed the earth at a very low height."*

Calanais is telling us, loud and clear, the passage of the moon was nearly as important a preoccupation for the early farmers of the Neolithic as their well-known fixation with the voyage of the sun across the sky. Further testament to the importance of moon cycles during the Neolithic and Bronze Age are some fascinating monuments, about two hundred of them in total, known as Recumbent Stone Circles, found in the Aberdeen area of Scotland, Cork, and Kerry in Ireland. They most often feature a large stone lying on its side guarded by two upright monoliths at either end, aligned to the passage of the moon in its southern arc, proof yet again of the ancients' astronomical skills and the importance of the lunar cycle.

No one truly knows why lunar observations were made at these recumbent monuments but my partner Stephanie, who's a food neuroscientist, believes they had important implications for farming. Her theory is that most of the two and a half thousand surviving stone circles on the Islands of Britain are aligned to read the passage of the moon for a very good reason. Why? Because even the most technologically savvy, 21st Century, chemical-input farmer, knows it's always best to plant seeds at the new moon. So, she suspects the allotment tenders of the Neolithic, and certainly the more sophisticated farmers of the Bronze Age, were early proponents of biodynamic agriculture, predicated on a detailed knowledge of the passage of the moon to guide planting and other farming practices; a theory that sounds plausible to me.

Calanais is also an eloquent parable illustrating the extraordinarily long-term and generational mindset of Neolithic and Bronze Age peoples, as was the case with our friend the Winterbourne Chieftain who wandered the downland around Stonehenge fully five hundred years before the first Bluestone circle was erected there. Was he part of a generational project to erect a stone circle at the place marked by the Talons of the Gods, those glacial striations at the site of Stonehenge? Was he involved in a pact with his ancestors back in Wales, and by implication his descendants, to make the observations needed to create an astronomical temple as they did at Calanais? Is that why he travelled so frequently between Pembrokeshire and Wiltshire, to advance the contract made between the generations?

I believe that may well be the case, and that's backed up by strong evidence the Stonehenge site was already a cosmological observatory, first set-up to perform its function as a solar and lunar tracking station as early as the time of the Blick Mead Mesolithic foraging clan. Remember the three post holes found when the old Stonehenge visitors' car park was extended? They were forty feet apart on a line running directly east to west, close to the Talon Marks of the Gods, and were tree-trunk 'totems' standing an estimated thirty feet high on the landscape. It's believed there may have been other posts, obliterated or yet to be found, while calculations carried out on those three Car Park Post Holes in the 1960's revealed they aligned precisely on the positions of the setting sun, and the setting moon, with 'extreme accuracy' making them the first astronomical observation points at Stonehenge, and demonstrating a very strong lunar function.

A mind boggling four-and-a-half thousand years after the Post Holes were first erected, the Bluestones were brought from Preseli and raised in a simple circle of fifty-six standing stones, represented by their empty Aubrey Holes 'sockets', which many experts now believe may have been used as a prehistoric lunar calendar.

Putting it as simply as I can, you take Aubrey Hole settings twenty-eight and twenty-seven as the base line marking the beginning and end of the year, each space between the Aubrey Holes represents one day. Using a marker pole to circle the stones in an anticlockwise direction gives you a count of three hundred and sixty-five days or one solar year. In addition, the circle was erected in such a way that the direction of the sunrise on the Summer and Winter Solstices divides the whole into two concise semi-circles.

In later, Bronze Age iterations of the henge the four Station Stones played an important lunar as well as Solstitial function. Only one is still in place today, but the four of them formed a rectangle around the central monument with the North and South stones placed on low humps raised within the outer ditch. The shorter sides of this box, align with the Solstitial Axis, while the longer sides match the southernmost and northernmost possible moonsets during Major Standstills every 18. 6 years.

Thoughts return again to our friend the Winterbourne Chieftain, and I wonder if he may have been one of many down the decades and centuries who worked on a Calanais-style, long term observation and measurement project to achieve this solar and lunar function for the still dreamt-of circle at Stonehenge. Did he pass on his observations to his descendants because, just like Calanais, the sky needed to be watched decade after decade, using marker poles, ropes, and small piles of stones to lay out, adjust and then mark these powerful lunar aspects on the ground before committing the huge resources needed to transport the vitally important Star Stones from Preseli.

There's another moon calendar theory, one proposed in 2022 by Professor Tim Darvill, who reasoned this lunar application was developed with more sophistication, much later in the life of Stonehenge when the unique, lintelled trilithons were raised in the Early Bronze Age. A ring of thirty sarsens were erected within the boundary of the henge, representing the days of the lunar month and three-hundred-and-sixty-days of the year, with the additional five days needed to complete a solar year, represented by five stone structures within the Trilithons and four outside the circle, to facilitate the tracking of the quadrennial Leap Year. The Altar Stone, neither Welsh Bluestone nor English Sarsen but a Scottish one-off, lies recumbent inside the circle directly opposite Stone 56, a slim sarsen megalith perhaps representing the remnant of what was once the tallest Trilithon at Stonehenge. The Altar Stone lies along a primary axis of the temple, marking the sunset of both the Summer and Winter Solstices, which runs directly down the centre of its sixteen-foot length. There's long been a debate about whether the Altar Stone was deliberately laid flat or had once been upright and then fell or was toppled over by a falling sarsen.

However, I think this new Scottish provenance may link it directly to the tradition of the Recumbent Stone circles of the area where it was sourced, north of the Great Glen. The recumbents of Northern Scotland sit with two uprights and a flat central megalith, like stone sofas that track the voyages of the heavenly bodies, and my own theory is the Altar Stone was already in an auspicious, recumbent setting before it was acquired for the Stonehenge project, perhaps as a special gift from a northern dynasty to the rulers of Salisbury Plain.

There has been speculation that this diversity of provenance, Welsh, Scots and English stones paints Stonehenge as a unifying project to bring all the areas of Neolithic Britain under one umbrella. I don't really buy that as it's pretty obvious the primary purpose of Stonehenge was that of a solar and lunar observatory and the Bluestones from Preseli were particularly special in any event. Not only that, but the notion that Neolithic Britain was already united, possibly by religious observance, holds just as much water as this new unification theory. What the provenance of the Altar Stone does describe is a very sophisticated, island-wide Bronze Age society where diplomacy and trade fostered relationships; a society where trade goods, news, ideas and even stones travelled.

As I write in the autumn of 2024, there's been a sudden flurry of interest in the Moon/Stonehenge relationship precipitated by the advent of a Major Lunar Standstill beginning in the Spring of 2024, continuing through the winter with its zenith in February 2025. Even as I tap these words out, the excitement amongst scientists and the staff at English Heritage, official custodians of Stonehenge, is reaching fever point as they announce a pop-up planetarium at Stonehenge and live streaming of this once-in-every eighteen-point six years event. A pop-up planetarium? Ironic really, as the ancients used Stonehenge itself as the arena of their own sky gazing planetarium, watching the heavenly bodies al fresco in all seasons and all weathers in real time and, of its time, Stonehenge was indeed extremely high tech.

This official hype was accompanied by a slew of media articles outlining 'new' discoveries and theories linking the Moon and Stone-henge, except they're not new at all and were first outlined in the early 1960's by two scientists, the urbane British born, US based astronomer Gerald Hawkins, arguably the father of Astroarchaeology, and amateur boffin C. A. 'Pete' Newham, a gas utilities executive from Northeast England. Independently of each other, these two very diverse scholars came to similar conclusions with Hawkins publishing his ideas on Stone-henge as a lunar calendar, and marker of solstices, equinoxes, and eclipses in prestigious Nature magazine in 1963. Newham published his, largely similar conclusions that same year in his excellent book *The Astronomical Significance of Stonehenge*, which was sold at the old Visitor Centre gift-shop for many years, but sadly no longer.

At the time many British archaeologists dismissed these theories, complete with their mathematical tabulations and diagrams, out of hand insisting the notoriously unpredictable weather of these islands would have made it impossible to make the necessary observations, and partic-ularly to make the alignments needed to hold ceremonies. This, in my view, demonstrated a completely arrogant, contemporary view of time and process, and a deep misunderstanding of the way Ancient Britons approached their religious enterprises in the quintessentially generational way I've already described. And the thousands of people I've seen congregate on miserable dawn mornings who still manage to give thanks for the Solstice, even one blindly observed through cloud and mizzle, gives the nonsense to those claims.

Sadly, a degree of personal animosity seems to have been directed at Hawkins, whether through jealousy or resentment at his fame in America I've no idea, but it's disappointing to see people recycling these sixty-year-old ideas without acknowledging Hawkins and Newham, who first came up with them. I don't include Prof. Darvill in this criticism as he added his own work to these lunar theories, was a couple of years ahead of the 2024 Lunar Standstill buzz, and fulsomely acknowledged his debt to Hawkins in the process. I think the Stonehenge blogger Simon Banton best summed-up the criticisms of the Stonehenge moon frenzy in a 2024 homage to forgotten Hawkins and Newham, cleverly entitled *Eclipse of the Moonmen.*

So much for things lunar but Stonehenge is also famously aligned with the passage of the sun, and I can give no better advice than to direct readers interested in the fine detail of this important, astronomical aspect of Stonehenge's 'reason for being,' to the Royal Society's website. Here they'll find a fantastic online pamphlet to download, describing the astronomical stuff in a clear and interesting way, and there's a link to it in the bibliography at the end of this book. Still, it's worth reprising the basics of the fascinating aspects of Solar Stonehenge and essentially it comes down to the temple being specifically and deliberately aligned along the angle of the Solstices, essentially placing hemispheres of the temple into shadow at the different Solstice sunsets and sunrises.

- One angle runs northeast to southwest from the Summer Solstice Sunrise, between Sarsen Stones 30 and 1 and then between Bluestone 15 and Sarsen Stone 16 to the Winter Solstice Sunset.

- The other runs northwest from the Summer Solstice Sunset and southeast to the Winter Solstice Sunrise between Sarsens 21 and 22, then 57 and 58 to Fallen Sarsen 8.
- Both lines intersect at the Altar Stone, in the centre of the complex stone circles and horseshoes, creating the signature 81degree angle of declination unique to the Stonehenge latitude.
- It's important to remember the Sarsens, which front these angles had their Solstitial faces polished by the ancients to make them distinctly white and glowing in the light of the Solstice sun.

These are important observations giving us material evidence the Neolithic farmers and the metalworkers of the Early Bronze Age had a complete understanding of the observable passage of the heavens and deliberately aligned their temple at Stonehenge, and elsewhere, to embrace those observations in stone. The question is just how did they achieve this alignment, how on earth did they calibrate the positions of their stones on such a large scale to track the heavenly bodies?

I'm about to show they had mathematically precise instruments with a stunning world provenance, enabling them to meticulously position the stones they'd chosen in order to make the observations which, presumably, were important both to the organisation of their society, the success of their agriculture and the canon of their religious observance.

16

THE GOLDEN
PROTRACTORS

I n this chapter I'm offering an exposition of what I believe to be the
most important Stonehenge discoveries to date bar none, revealing
the arcane knowledge of astronomy, mathematics and geometry
possessed by our Neolithic and Bronze Age ancestors at Stonehenge. I
believe they provide proof positive the temple was indeed a cosmic
tracking station, a solar clock, and a lunar observatory. I call it the Sacred
Geometry of Stonehenge, and its secrets are held within sets of precise,
linear inscriptions on three golden artefacts from three separate burials
within the orbit of Stonehenge.

For me, this story began three decades ago when I first learnt the
Solstice astronomy of Stonehenge is inscribed on the paper-thin gold of
the Bush Barrow Lozenge, excavated by the hand of young John Parker
in 1806, when he lifted the astonishing artefacts of the Stonehenge Giant
from the grave. Etched onto the lozenge by the ancient goldsmith are
exquisitely executed lines, which precisely describe the difference
between the angles of the sun at the Winter and Summer Solstices. It's
called an angle of declination and on the Bush Barrow Lozenge it's 81
degrees. More than that, the precise angle of 81 degrees is unique to the
latitude of Stonehenge and Stonehenge alone, demonstrating an
astounding degree of astronomical, mathematical and geographical
accuracy.

Later, I was to discover that same angle is also inscribed onto the gold on the base of the cone-shaped Upton Lovell Button, found buried alongside the high-status Amber Princess in the Golden Barrow. Again, it's marked with geometric precision onto the gold beneath the black, shale cone that holds the piece. I found the astronomical nature of these two artefacts, simultaneously exciting and exasperating as they demonstrate unequivocally the ancients had highly sophisticated mathematical and observational skills, but the information they provided only seemed to scratch at the surface of the story.

The source of most of my frustration was a third object known as the Clandon Barrow Lozenge, which seemed to have no discernible astronomical relevance despite its visual similarity to the Bush Barrow Lozenge. They are so alike that a casual glance they might be taken as golden twins, except more detailed examination reveals the Clandon Barrow Lozenge markings are based on decagons, while the Bush Barrow Lozenge has hexagonal patterns.

A little more battered and buckled from its four thousand years underground, the Clandon lozenge was found in the huge, trapezoid Clandon Barrow close to Dorchester, Dorset, together with some cremation remains, a bronze dagger, a shale mace-head decorated with gold studs (evidently a baton of office) and a high-status cup carved from solid amber.

For decades the geometry of the Clandon Barrow Lozenge was not decrypted and staff at the Dorset Museum in Dorchester where it's displayed, together with pretty much the entire archaeological establishment, have been uncertain and undecided about any astronomical purpose it might have, with expert opinion amounting to a resounding 'maybe.'

However, the two lozenges are so similar I long suspected there must have been some expression of the Sacred Geometry hidden within the intricately inscribed, geometric patterns of the Clandon lozenge as well as its Bush Barrow doppelganger. Their startling likeness is underscored by the fact they share an exact axial length of 155 mm along the Clandon Barrow Lozenge's short axis and the Bush Barrow Lozenge's long one. Surely, such a precise measurement can hardly be a coincidence.

I kept looking but found nothing to suggest any purpose other than the decorative and symbolic for the Clandon Barrow Lozenge, then enter stage-left American mathematician Ivy Jiang, assisted by her brother Eugene, who produced an academic paper in 2021 called *Lozenge Circumscribed Stonehenge*. With complex calculations they establish direct connections between the Bush Barrow Lozenge, the Upton Lovell Button and the Clandon Barrow Lozenge, all linked to the passage of the moon and sun, and the deliberate, astronomical alignment of Stonehenge.

THE SOLSTICE ANGLE INSCRIBED IN GOLD ON THE BUSH BARROW LOZENGE

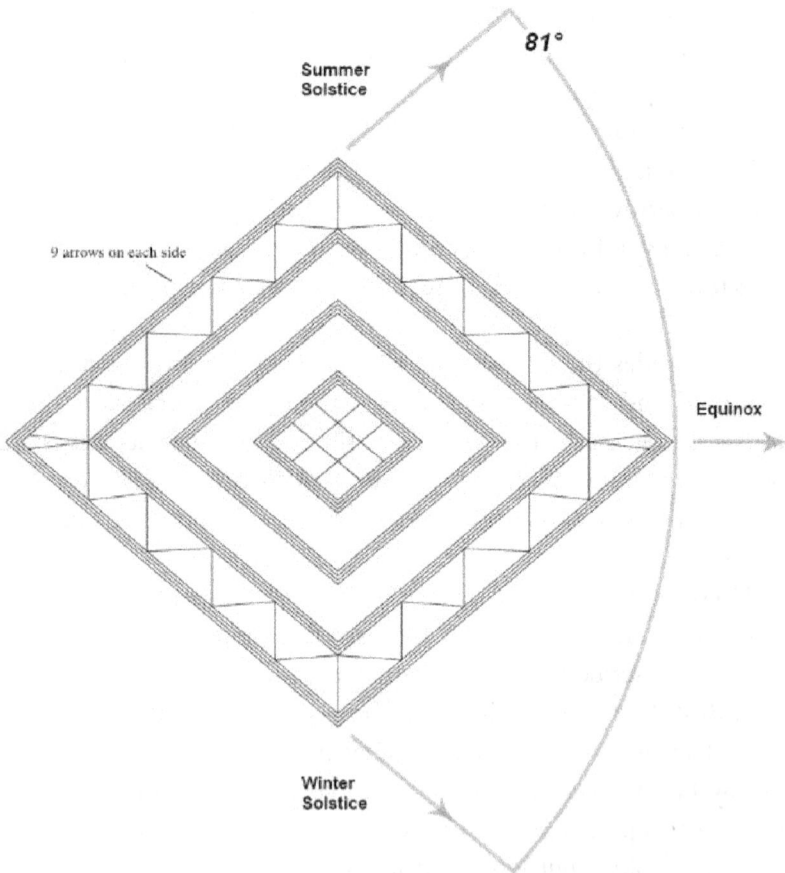

Summer Solstice

81°

9 arrows on each side

Equinox

Winter Solstice

The Solstitial angle encoded in the Bush Barrow Lozenge, which is only true at 51 degrees north, the exact Latitude of Stonehenge itself. Note the nine 'arrows' on each side matching the 36 inscribed around the base of the Upton Lovell Button reflecting the 360 degrees of first Sumerian, and now modern geometry.

At this point I'll attempt to navigate the Jiangs' maths and crystallise the findings from their paper as best I can, while recommending readers seeking more maths and further detail should read their paper, and a link to it can be found in the bibliography. Essentially, the Jiangs found that all three artefacts share a 'nested square pattern,' allowing a mathematician to transcribe the precise angles inscribed on their surfaces into a series of mathematically related, perfect circles. This designates each of them as a protractor, defined as *an instrument for laying down and measuring angles in drawing and plotting,* with protractors of varying degrees of sophistication, used as indispensable mathematical, surveying and architectural instruments to this day.

Having extrapolated the related circles from the 'nested square' decagons of the Clandon Barrow Lozenge, the Jiangs superimposed these circles onto a scale plan of Stonehenge, and in an astonishing revelation of prehistoric mathematical genius, found they perfectly circumscribe the 56 Aubrey Holes of the original outer circle, the two sets of thirty Y Holes and twenty-nine Z Holes, the Sarsen Circle, and the inner horseshoe of Trilithons. The Station Stone alignment at the heart of the henge is also reflected in the 41-degree solar and 49-degree lunar alignments on the lozenge patterns and, say the Jiangs, *"The real magic is the choice of latitude (that of Stonehenge) leading to this unique pair of complementary alignments."*

The Jiangs make the point this can only mean the non-circular expression of the 81degree geometry of Stonehenge, expressed in the angles etched onto the lozenges, must represent a tradition spanning across all the stages of construction of Stonehenge over nearly two millennia beginning with the Mesolithic selection of the site, through the first Aubrey Hole/Bluestone circle around 3000BC and the Sarsen Circles around 2500BC. The siblings also demonstrate mathematically that the patterns on the lozenges apply, incredibly, to the Woodhenge timber post array, raised at Durrington Walls two miles away around 2000BC.

They note the connection between the megalithic rings and the geometrical, nested patterns, together with the Solstitial significance of 81-degrees, was demonstrated in the gold lozenges around 1900-1700BC, at Woodhenge around 2500-1800BC, in the Sarsen Circle around 2700-2500BC and to the selection of the original Stonehenge site around 3100-3000BC. This represents a tradition practiced and taught, from the Neolithic to the Early Bronze Age, which suggests they are an expression of deliberate judgement, not luck or coincidence.

Ivy Jiang was left with one niggling problem she says gave her sleepless nights, and that was the scale used by the ancients to translate the mathematical knowledge enshrined in the lozenges into practical building use, in other words to protract them into 'stones on the ground.' Eventually, she found that if the circles nested within the Clandon Barrow Lozenge are scaled up exactly 1000 times, the outermost band circumscribes the Aubrey Holes, while the innermost band circumscribes the Sarsen Circle, giving a truly astonishing ratio of 1000:1.

The siblings also identify the Upton Lovell Button, the most recent in manufacture of the three, as a leap forward in design to the more modern form of a protractor, not ratio based as with the Bush Barrow and the Clandon Barrow Lozenges, but a polar style with thirty-six uniformly spaced zigzag or arrow marks, around the circumference of its base, representing tangible evidence of an astonishing technological advance.

Readers familiar with the modern, plastic full-circle 360-degree protractors used in schools and colleges will recognize the function of the 36 arrows around the circumference of the Upton Lovell Button. They signify 10-degree multiples when measured from the centre, or 5-degree multiples measured from the circumference. Increments of 5-degree multiples can be achieved with a single twist or pivot of the artefact and similarly, because of their shared length of 155mm, the Bush Barrow and Clandon Barrow Lozenges could have been used as one instrument if the Clandon Lozenge were laid over the Bush Barrow Lozenge then rotated.

The Jiangs characterise Stonehenge as *'a vacant astronomical observatory with all its original instruments scattered over time and place'* with three of them, the Bush Barrow Lozenge, Upton Lovell Button and Clandon Barrow Lozenge representing protractors and rulers, pre-dating the previously recognised, oldest known protractor from the tomb of an ancient Egyptian architect, known as Kha's Protractor (dated 1440 to 1350BC) by more than 700 years.

They also describe the two lozenges and the button in a remarkable Gen Z way, evoking digital and genomic analogies to suggest the portable Golden Protractors may have played the role of 'flash drives' or 'messenger RNA's' to carry and disseminate the measuring data around various communities and suggest, *"Stonehenge thus becomes a standard publisher for its surrounding area, effectively a prehistorical version of Greenwich Standard. Interestingly, Greenwich at Latitude 51. 5 degrees is within a 100 miles in distance and 0. 3 degrees in latitude from Stonehenge."*

So, in the Jiang model of Neolithic and Early Bronze Age architecture and astronomy Stonehenge represents a compass, not the moveable, magnetic type on a spindle used to establish a direction of travel, but one set in stone, a fixed point with particular headings on the horizon, to track the passage of the heavenly bodies. Crucially, Stonehenge can be used in concert with the Golden Protractors with the henge as the fixed point established by the ancestors to predict the direction of travel of the sun, the moon and the stars themselves.

There are other golden representations of the heavenly bodies in Britain and Ireland, but only the Golden Protractors bear the uncompromisingly accurate, carefully inscribed linear patterns endowing them with a portal-like mystery and aura. As the Jiangs' paper puts it, *"We suggest it is this angle-related practicality that had been fuelling such a long-lasting and regrettably long-forgotten STEM (Science, Technology, Engineering and Math) tradition."*

At this point, I'll ignore the well-rehearsed advice for authors and wilfully empty my locker of superlatives to describe the findings in the Jiang Paper as groundbreaking, transformative and simply jaw-dropping. The paper, which has been peer reviewed, becomes even more mind-boggling when I tell you that Ivy and her brother Eugene, wrote it when they were high school students at the Episcopal High School, Baton Rouge, Louisiana, USA, four-and-a-half thousand miles away from Stonehenge!

It seems the Jiangs may be unaware, at the time of my writing, that distinguished British mathematician Prof. David Gregg came to the same broad conclusions as theirs a decade earlier. They certainly don't cite Prof. Gregg's work among their sources so presumably they didn't know that his conclusions and their own are mutually validating. The more so as the professor came at the problem from the diametrically opposite direction, relying solely on measurements taken at the henge with no reference at all to the golden artefacts.

Using, in his own words, *'standard drawing instruments and a £20 engineering calculator'* Prof. Gregg, who is also an amateur astronomer, established the same geometric connections between the Aubrey Holes and the subsequent circles at the henge. And the professor declared his aim at the outset had been to rigorously test the proposition that built features of Stonehenge constructed over a millennium and more, are dimensionally related through formal geometry and scaling principles; an idea that's largely anathema to conventional archaeology.

Prof. Gregg outlined his important, ground-breaking mathematical relationships in his comprehensive 2014 book, *The Stonehenge Codes,* and they mirror those of the Jiang siblings. For convenience I've relied on a distillation of his conclusions made in a piece he wrote on the website World Mysteries.com where he observes: '*All the structures of Stonehenge, irrespective of supposed date in the building sequence, are dimensionally related via the geometry of regular polygons inscribed in the Aubrey Circle. The geometries of the heptagon, pentagon and square are prominent. e.g. A heptagon construction probably underlays the 56-hole Aubrey Circle and that construction also defines the much later Sarsen Circle and the even later Z and Y rings. The proposed heptagon construction also accurately encodes the site latitude.*'

In other words, Prof. Gregg had already discerned the same nested square arrangement as Ivy Jiang using his '*£20 engineering calculator,*' and like her proposes the entire structure of Stonehenge, in all its phases over multiple generations, was deliberately planned with advanced mathematical and astronomical knowledge. The professor also believes the site of the henge was deliberately positioned on its particular latitude, showing a knowledge of the whole-earth science of geodesy. Prof. Gregg then goes further to propose a captivating theory the latitude of Stonehenge was deliberately chosen to maximise the intensity of Solstitial shadows cast by the stones. It's a proposal that neatly fits with the English Heritage research showing the sarsen megaliths on Solstice alignments, were polished for visual effect, just as the Bluestones were buffed to shine like the stars of the night sky.

According to Prof. Gregg, the pentagonal and heptagonal properties of the dimensions involve functions of phi, the so-called Golden Section or Golden Ratio, which also happen to coincide with the ratios of key astronomical cycles, causing the professor to ponder whether the builders of Stonehenge were aware of them and *deliberately exploited these coincidences in their design.'*

He also found 'intriguing parallels' between Stonehenge and the Antikythera astronomical 'computer' from 200 BC Greece, with its dozens of bronze gears, and suggests similar tracking of heavenly bodies may have been achieved at Stonehenge, using fixed stones and 'rotating (human) priests', anticipating the discovery and purpose of the portable Golden Protractors.

Listing his other findings, the professor believes the 19 bluestones in the Stonehenge horseshoe may be linked to the 19 solar years of the moon's Metonic cycle, or the 19 eclipse years of the Saros cycle, while the 30 holes of the Y circle and the 29 in the Z ring within the henge could be the basis of a lunar calendar. He draws out a wonderful analogy in his final observation observing, *"the 'non-literate' megalith builders, were writing in stone."*

I find it thrilling that a high school student from the USA and a retired math professor from England and quite different generations, their investigations separated by a decade and four thousand miles, came to the same conclusions from quite different mathematical perspectives.

It's been suggested all three of the Golden Protractors may have been fashioned by the same master goldsmith. Who knows, perhaps the Upton Lovell Shaman had a hand in planishing and burnishing relatively small pieces of gold, rolled foil thin, then exquisitely inscribed with a series of near perfect lines, in precisely repeated hexagonal or decagonal patterns, framed within processions of notional concentric rings. If he did, the Shaman will have been responsible for crafting the first entirely accurate, astronomical observational instruments known to science and, if not him then, maybe his son or grandson because his timespan and those of the three Protractors coincide around 1900 to 1700 BC.

I may be stating the obvious, but an advanced knowledge of geometry is indispensable to plan and execute an architectural project deliberately aligned on the passage of heavenly bodies and placed precisely on a line of latitude which expresses the angles of the Solstices perfectly at that point. To do so needs protractors to conveniently record the geometry, and surveying instruments to implement the calculations on the ground.

Some fragments of wood and a few copper pins were found near the Bush Barrow Lozenge when it was excavated, and this led to speculation it had been mounted on a backing to equip it for the function of a surveyor's instrument, known as an alidade, placed flat on one of the stones to take astronomical sightings from the henge. These fragments have since been associated with the handle of one of the knives in the burial, but that doesn't discount the possibility the lozenge could well have been used for observations.

A protractor immediately transforms into an alidade when it's lined up on an object, earthbound or heavenly, through a simple sighting implement, which can be as rudimentary as a stick with a fork or split in it, or a string centred on a hanging weight, in other words a plumbline. In fact, the Upton Lovell Button has two fixings on the base, and is believed to have been a pendulate artefact, meant to hang around the Amber Princess's neck. I suspect this means it might just as easily have been used ceremonially, as the golden 'bob' or weight of a sighting plumbline used at great astronomical rites at Stonehenge.

It makes perfect sense to me that the Bush Barrow Lozenge, the Upton Lovell Button and the Clandon Barrow Lozenge would all have been used for surveying the heavens, if only on ceremonial occasions. Why wouldn't they have doubled-up as splendid badges of office and surveyor's instruments? Their manufacture in precious gold alone, would set them apart as sacred, and highly visible religious props in the hands of their owners at Solstice celebrations at the henge.

How then do the three Golden Protractors inform our visions of Stonehenge, how were they used in the years before they were buried with their exalted owners? I think the first thing to say is the secrets they held would have endowed their owners with great prestige and power so I'm going to say straight away, possession of the Bush Barrow Lozenge confirms the Giant from that grave as the 'King of Stonehenge' and highlights him as an obvious contender for the chief astronomer of the Stonehenge observatory. I can be forgiven then for being unashamedly delighted to see *the Crown Jewels of the King of Stonehenge,*' referenced a couple of times in the Jiangs' paper. It's a phrase I coined back in 2009, when helping to raise the profile of the Bush Barrow Collection while campaigning for a new, secure gallery to house those national treasures.

Certainly, ownership of the fabulous Upton Lovell Button places the Amber Princess right at the top of Stonehenge society, marking her out as a powerful high priestess, astronomer and seer, buried with the awe-inspiring regalia of the amber necklace. Similarly, the man buried with the Clandon Barrow Lozenge (the indications are it was a man) must have been a mighty ruler and the complete set of Stonehenge measurements held cryptically in his Golden Protractor, suggest he was an architect and an astronomer too.

Clandon is on the chalk hills close to the Dorset coast, but the fifty-mile distance from Stonehenge doesn't faze me at all as these people were seasoned travellers, and I'm reminded of the 18th and 19th Century Bishops of Salisbury, whose own famous Cathedral 'temple' was close to Stonehenge, but they had their summer residence at Lulworth on the Dorset coast, not far at all from Clandon. I don't think it's an accident that down the millennia, the wealthy and powerful have always found the best locations to enjoy.

The fact a scale of 1000-to-1 is contained within the geometry of the Clandon Barrow Lozenge is remarkable indeed and sets me to consider the exclusivity of these Golden Protractors. Why would they bury and lose, such fantastic expressions of their technology if other versions were not available? Gold is famously incorruptible of course, and more Golden Protractors may still be out there waiting to be found, while others may have been melted down and repurposed in the centuries that followed, perhaps when the Iron Age Celts arrived, and their mathematical and religious significance had long since been forgotten.

IVY JIANG'S GOLDEN PROTRACTOR SUPERIMPOSED OVER STONEHENGE

1:1000

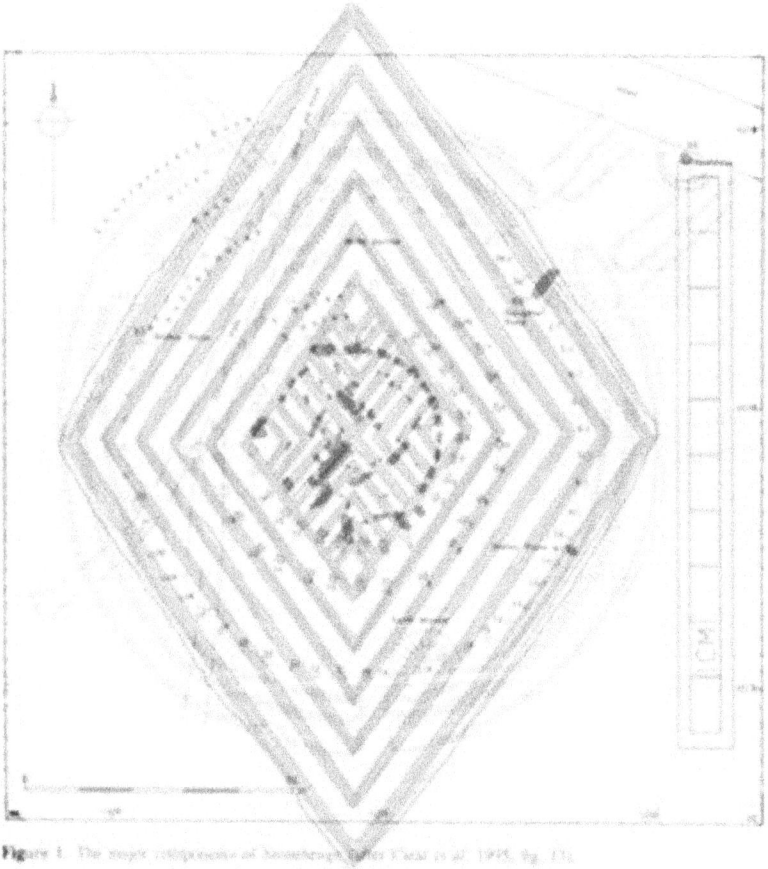

Figure 1. The aerial interpretation of Stonehenge (after Field et al. 1995, fig. 13).

This diagram by Ivy Jiang graphically sums up her Golden Protractor theory. She superimposes a diagram of the Clandon Barrow Lozenge over an existing graphic of Stonehenge (Cleal et al. 1995) showing how the successive circles of construction at the henge fall into line with the components of the lozenge on a scale of 1:1000, predicted by her nested square mathematics.

It also occurred to me that carefully plotting the astronomical measurements they wanted to record on these three artefacts would have meant using some sort of existing set-square instrument to mark-off the angles on the gold leaf used in all three. Surely then, after burying the golden Lozenges with their exalted owners, they must have kept spares, maybe duplicates with the sacred angles inscribed on less valuable but corruptible copper, rather than rare and expensive gold. Needless to say, I wouldn't mind the cheaper version at all, and sometimes I imagine there's one lying on Salisbury Plain, crusted with Verdigris, for me to find, although I wouldn't be at all envious if Ivy Jiang found it first as that would certainly square the circle.

The thrilling truth is these three Golden Protractors mark Stonehenge as a distinct culture, inextricably linked with the Neolithic Star Stone cult of the Bluestones from Preseli, and the moon-tracking folk of the Scottish Recumbent Stone Circles who may well have donated the Altar Stone for the temple. The Golden Protractors are unique and precious artefacts, which describe an incredibly important and precise mathematical link between Stonehenge, the Sun and the Moon representing an unsurpassed trilogy of ancient wisdom as well as a quantum leap in the development of mathematics and astronomy; unique as the first known protractors in the world.

For me, the Golden Protractors also represent tangible evidence of the generational commitment of the ancients, enabling them to execute and sustain great concepts down the centuries. Possession of such knowledge in the concrete form represented by the Protractors, would have glued together the centuries-long, time lapse of such generational efforts, in perfect accord with Ivy Jiang's description of the Golden Protractors as 'messenger RNA.' We heard Prof. Gregg declare our ancient ancestors recorded their astronomical secrets by 'writing them in stone' and now, thanks to Ivy Jiang, we have the thrilling idea they also wrote them in gold.

THE CLANDON BARROW LOZENGE

This photograph, courtesy Austin Kinsley of Silent Earth, shows the intricate and precise linear inscriptions on the gold leaf, and while it's very similar in appearance to the Bush Barrow Lozenge the two are mathematically distinct.

17

THE GLASTONBURY
FACTOR

For many years I lived in a cottage that stood on the banks of the
River Kennet, my kitchen window just thirty feet from the gin
clear stream that rises six miles away, west of the great Avebury henge.
The Kennet is a bourne, Anglo-Saxon for a river that bursts from the
chalk when it's charged by winter rainfall, and New Age adherents
believe it's a river fused with mystical power, endowed by its passage
from Avebury itself, past Silbury Hill where it forms a winter lake, then
brimmed by the Swallow Head spring below the West Kennet Long
Barrow before flowing on towards the Thames, sixty miles away.

I make no bones about it, the Kennet fed my soul for the dozen or so
years I inhabited its riverbank, a place of otters and voles, cuckoo calls,
soaring kites and dazzling kingfishers. Steaming with Arthurian mystery
in winter, summer saw it burst into life, and I would sit on my riverside
bench and lose myself as I watched the whorls, hypnotically spooling
down the surface of the stream.

The science of fluid dynamics explains these small vortices, concentric rings of water thrown up by a disturbance to the flow; perhaps by a
rock or a branch trapped on the riverbed below. Fluid dynamics is one
thing but as I watched the lazy spools gyrating down the Kennet I'd be
reminded of the cup and ring marks of the Neolithic and the Triskele
symbols of the Iron Age Celts. Somehow, I felt they were connected.

What did these constantly repeated whirling motifs represent to
Neolithic people? Symbols obviously, but symbols of what? My own

belief is they are the Neolithic version of the double-looped infinity icon used in modern mathematics; sometimes referred to as the lemniscate curves. Why not? We know those people were mathematically literate and cosmically inquisitive, why wouldn't they too, be insatiably curious about the vastness of creation? Wouldn't they want to fuse infinity into some easily recognised, tangible, shorthand form as we do?

I think they did, but trying my best to avoid venturing into the realms of what is sometimes described as 'hippy hogwash' I'm going to delve deeper into the eternal truths I believe are hidden within the story of Stonehenge. It would be cowardly not to go slightly off-piste away from the largely factual, or at least evidential, into the realms of the sibylline and mystical, so I'm going to take the plunge and describe my take on it all.

What's clear is Neolithic and Early Bronze Age people, carved those spirals, circles and cup and ring marks, into significant stones at great sites like Newgrange in Ireland and Barclodiad-y-Gawres on Mon/Anglesey, to name only two of many. They're also a recurring motif on the most exquisitely carved decorative mace heads, some of which have been found at Stonehenge, but I believe they may have spilled over into the way the ancients 'decorated' the landscape with their monuments too.

That's because I see the Greater Stonehenge area itself as a place of rings, circles and spheres; concentric and sacred. They dominate its construction, with two circles described by gigantic sarsen megaliths, two more by elegant arcs of Bluestones: all four bounded by the giant rings of an outer ditch and bank, encircling the monument. Scores more rings are haphazardly scattered across the landscape for miles around the monument, in the shape of burial barrows broadcast over the landscape in great sweeps by our ancestors.

The Long Barrows and chambered passage-tombs of the early Neolithic aren't so prevalent in the ritual landscape of Stonehenge, as they were largely abandoned in favour of a frenzy of round barrow and disc barrow construction that continued into the Early Bronze Age. We see these in apparently random clusters at The Cursus, Lake Barrows, Wilsford Barrows, Lake Downs and of course Normanton Downs where Bush Barrow itself was positioned on the Solstitial Axis.

Twenty-first century technology has identified dozens more rings in the shape of long-buried Henge Pits, which ellipse around the great henge at Durrington Walls revealing the truly epic architecture of Greater Stonehenge. These huge pits, at least thirty feet in diameter and sixteen feet deep, must surely have been designed and marked out on the ground before the Durrington people began the backbreaking task of digging them out.

Truly, Stonehenge is a place of rings, elliptical and eccentric, a place of multiple loci from the ornamental, through the astronomical to the architectural, and we can only guess at the religious imperatives that compelled the Neolithic people of Britain, perhaps instinctively rather than by design, to construct interlinked structural hoops of so many kinds on the chalk downs of Salisbury Plain. And knowing the pinpoint precision, which the Golden Protractors endowed on the construction of Stonehenge itself, I've been set to wondering if the same care went into the design and lay-out the spectacular ritual landscape that surrounds the henge for miles around. The question I pose is this... was there some overarching plan to the way the Greater Stonehenge landscape has been laid out in the complex patterns we see on the ground today?

I'm not the first to point out that Neolithic architecture, on the grand landscape scale, seems to have had a blueprint the ancients worked too. It was first raised by one of the founding fathers of archaeology, the 18th Century Antiquarian William Stukeley. He visited Avebury four times, sometimes accompanied by a couple of antiquarian artists, and while plotting on paper the various Neolithic sacred works in the area, Stukeley discerned the shape of a dragon on the page. At the heart of Stukeley's dragon is the Avebury henge itself, and in the two magnificent avenues of standing stones, west to Beckhampton and east to the small henge called The Sanctuary, he saw the coils of a dragon's tail, enfolding Silbury Hill and the West Kennet Long Barrow. To the north lies Hackpen Hill, an ancient name, which translates as Dragons Head, giving further weight to his hypothesis.

But does Stukeley's perception of a Neolithic dragon, inscribed onto the landscape around Avebury, make any sense? It's certainly a powerful and evocative image, but is it likely the ancients could have pulled off such a feat of geodesy? Well, recent discoveries in Saudi Arabia might help us imagine how such an outline could have been delineated on the ground by the ancients. There, in the Arabian Desert, nine-thousand-year-old 'aerial maps' have been found, carved into stone slabs showing the exact outline of large-scale animal traps. We know they do because the archaeological remains of those ancient structures, designed for ambushing herding animals, are still preserved in the dry desert air. The 'maps' found nearby were described in the science journal Plos One in May 2023, as *extremely precise depictions* of landscape-scaled hunting traps, incorporating 13 feet-deep killing pits, in the Saudi Arabian desert, which are known as 'kites' because of their distinctive shape.

Evidently, our Stone Age ancestors were capable of envisaging and executing monumental structures on a huge scale across complex topographies, and they were able to map them too, which brings me to the remarkable Cochno Stone in Scotland, halfway between Glasgow and Dunbarton. It's a natural, flat panel of sandstone, the side of a bus in size and inscribed with a veritable frenzy of Europe's finest cup and ring marks, spirals, linear rectangles and diffusing rays. For good measure two, four-toed feet are represented on the panel, and the whole piece eloquently describes the Neolithic preoccupation with the swirls of infinity and enigmatic rock carvings. The story of Cochno should be uplifting but, sadly, it's rather depressing as the Stone has barely seen the light of day since it was first revealed and documented in 1887. Cochno didn't become famous until 1937 when archaeologist Ludovic MacLellan Mann visited the site with a small team and decided the petroglyphs should be painted to accentuate them, helping him to demonstrate his theories of their astronomical meaning. Not best practice by today's standards, but photographs of the results, mostly white, with some blue and red highlights, are spectacularly vivid. However, as time passed Mann's calculated act of vandalism paled compared to the extensive graffiti damage perpetrated on the Neolithic panel by 20th Century vandals. It was decided they should be reburied to protect them and that's been the disappointing state-of-play ever since, with brief interludes for further examination and a digital mapping in 2018. What, if anything then, does the Concho Stone portray? Were the carvings the result of some Neolithic rapture by religious zealots, or does the panel commit their oral history to 'writing'? Those four-toed feet go some way to supporting the theory it may be a hieroglyph tableau, depicting some long-forgotten saga, or maybe they were just graffiti too. Personally, I'm more convinced by the argument the Cochno Stone may be a cartographic representation of long-lost sacred sites in that area of Scotland. Maybe there was the dash of a saga thrown into the mix too, and don't forget sacred sites might include natural features such as rocky tors, springs, streams, lochs or even the liminal spaces of bogs; all difficult to discern through the medium of five-thousand-year hindsight.

Like most of us, I've never had the opportunity to see this wonder, and probably never will except in photographs, but I've often been struck by the passing similarity between the Cochno panel and aerial photographs I've seen of the Greater Stonehenge landscape. Recently, looking at a map representing the proliferation of religious features around Stonehenge I thought it looked very Cochno-like, with the shape of the Cursus and the Avenue uncannily similar to the stretched-out rectangles marked on the Cochno Stone. I'm not the first to suspect the Concho Stone may be some arcane form of map or projection, as Cochno advocate Alexander McCullum, acknowledges it may mark other sites in the Neolithic world of the Clyde Valley. Equally it might be a portal representing, death and rebirth, in his words 'a tomb or a womb,' perhaps permutations of all of three.

Nothing enigmatic at all, about the 4000-year-old Saint-Belec slate in northwest France, which was excavated a hundred years ago then forgotten until 2014 when researchers analysed the markings on the slate and found they represented the positions of local megaliths, springs and river systems across an area of six hundred and thirty square kilometres. The slate cartography has already led archaeologists to new finds, offering clear evidence the ancients understood cartography, albeit expressed differently to modern map makers. Utterly remarkable! Maybe then, the ancients were accustomed to working to a plan and thought out the macro-view of the Stonehenge landscape too, just as they certainly planned the micro-detail of the Henge itself with the help of the Clandon Barrow Golden Protractor. And isn't it unlikely that in an environment so obviously controlled as that of Stonehenge, not just anyone would be allowed to come along and throw-up a barrow. I suggest you'd have to consult the Neolithic version of a cemetery superintendent, probably a high priest, for permission and then be told where to cut the first sod for your burial mound or maybe there'd be a council of the elders, and the positioning of sacred architecture would be resolved in the circle of light around the hearth fire.

All these thoughts are, of course, entirely speculative although there's nothing wrong with thinking outside the box. Wouldn't it be wonderful though if someone could break the code and read the Concho Stone, and from that extrapolate some ideas of what might have been happening with the development and planning of Stonehenge.

Perhaps AI could be deployed to read the Concho runes before it turns its robotic intellect to the destruction of our kind but, in the meantime, I have an unwavering belief the repeated motif of circles, cup and ring marks, triskele and the layout of barrows, are an expression of the quantum nature of an ancient creed. Like the swirling rings inscribed on the ceremonial mace-heads found in graves nearby, these monumental impressions on the Stonehenge landscape must surely be expressions of infinity, as their spirals vanish into the whirlpool of the cosmos so unforgettably portrayed by Da Vinci in his famous illustration of human proportions we call the Vitruvian Man. No accident then that in the 17th and 18th Century great men like architects Inigo Jones and John Webb the Elder, and the Antiquarian William Stukeley strongly disagreed about the purpose of Stonehenge, whilst all agreeing it was constructed on 'Vitruvian principles.'

There's yet another enigmatic construction at Stonehenge, revealed by archaeology in the enlightening days of the Stonehenge Riverside Project around 2009, and I'm drawn to memories of a conversation I had on the slope that lifts away to the west of Stonehenge, on a brisk, dry day in 2008. At the time I was freelancing for the Mail on Sunday and through my passionate interest in archaeology I was at the site to write a piece on yet more of the Riverside Project's discoveries.

I'd taken my youngest son Morgan along with me (I think it was one of those school, 'go to work with a parent' days) and I was chatting to the agreeable Josh Pollard, then doctor, since Professor of archaeology at Southampton University. He was talking me through his dig, which was delineating the post holes of an extraordinary, twenty-foot-high timber palisade that once snaked for a couple of miles along the western perimeter of Stonehenge. It was a massive structure, but it evidently wasn't defensive, nor could it have been for agriculture or hunting, said Dr Pollard. Naturally enough I asked what he thought its purpose might have been, and I'll never forget his answer as he shrugged and said, "Well, Michael Eavis, who runs the Glastonbury Festival not so far from here, might have some insights into why you'd build a wall around a festival site. Maybe you should ask him."

Josh Pollard was, of course, referring to the five miles long, virtually unclimbable, security fence around the famous annual festival on the Eavis farm at Pilton. The barrier is there to ensure those who haven't paid or aren't in the know, don't get in. Josh was implying the Stonehenge palisade was all about exclusivity and elitism and it's no surprise to me it was dated to the later phases of the temple, at a time when metal workers and their sumptuous gold jewellery arrived on these islands. With gold comes an inevitable self and societal awareness of wealth and status.

That may have been the motivation for building the Stonehenge palisade, to keep the common folk away from exclusive ceremonies and celebrations. They weren't able to glimpse what went on, inside the perimeter as the fence was constructed of solid, abutting tree trunks and ran between two points where the topography naturally shielded a good view of Stonehenge from the east. What they sought to hide from sight was probably a stupendous piece of religious showmanship with many of the aspects of a modern music festival; all-consuming sensory stimulation around a Bluestone sound and light show, big personalities strutting their stuff, and the almost addictive feeling of oneness perceived within an audience.

The same elements of modern showmanship then; only the technology would have been different. The approach of the Winter Solstice must have been a deeply anxious time as the fateful day of its nadir became one of nail-biting observation, and solar astronomy became a religious preoccupation. Who knows then what the panoply of their gods may have represented, or what the nature of the litanies performed at Stonehenge might have been?

18

LOST STONES:
FULL CIRCLE

W inston Churchill once famously called the confusion at the start
of WWII as 'a riddle wrapped in a mystery inside an enigma'
which, I'm sure, is equally applicable to many facets of the Stonehenge
story that are difficult to explain or simply impossible to unravel. One of
the great unsolved conundrums of Stonehenge revolves around the
whereabouts of the majority of the Bluestones brought from Preseli.
Around eighty of the precious slabs of dolerite and rhyolite were shipped
to Stonehenge to erect the first simple circle on the site, represented by
the fifty-six Aubrey Holes and another twenty-four erected at the end of
the processional route of The Avenue at Bluehenge, on the banks of the
River Avon at West Amesbury.

The Bluehenge stones are thought to have been removed from the
riverbank around 2500BC for a reconfiguration of Stonehenge on the
Plain above, to create the outer Bluestone ring and the inner horseshoe,
but only twenty-nine are still in situ at the monument. I believe I know
the location of two undamaged Bluestones, re-purposed in the area, but as
that location isn't public I don't intend to point it out here for the benefit
of souvenir hunters. Another two are said to have been used in the
construction of a mill 'hatch' or overspill, on the stream at Elston close to
Stonehenge. The whereabouts of the rest of the Bluestones, brought so
far at such great community effort, remain a mystery except for a local
legend, which may point to the location of some of them at least.

And that's where famous Red Lion Inn, a coaching hostelry in the centre of Salisbury, enters the story. It was originally built in the 13th Century to lodge the master masons and draughtsmen working on the construction of the magnificent, then new, Cathedral nearby. Work began in 1220 when the Diocese fell out with the military, with whom they previously shared a hilltop eyrie at Old Sarum. The Masons' lodging house eventually morphed into the White Bear Inn as the 'new' City of Salisbury grew around it, before it was renamed the Red Lion, which still welcomes guests today, nearly a thousand years after its foundations were laid by the cathedral masons.

Intriguingly, a persistent legend has it that when the masons arrived at the site where the Cathedral now stands, a pristine Stone Circle stood in in the maze of water meadows at the confluence of the Avon and its sister chalk streams. It's said the stonemasons, never slow to source good material, simply demolished that circle to build the foundations of their lodgings and, who knows, they may have taken some of the standing stones to underpin the first courses of the Cathedral itself. If the legend is true it's not beyond the realms of possibility the Water Meadow Circle of legend may have been constructed with the Bluestones missing from Stonehenge ten miles away.

I know Phil Harding of Time Team fame carried out an archaeological assessment of the Red Lion Inn quite recently, but I have no idea whether he's aware of the legend and doubt very much he was on the lookout for broken-up Preseli dolerites. I do know that dolerite and rhyolite have a luminescent property and can be identified under ultraviolet beams as they emit a particular colour signature. Somewhere inside my febrile imagination, I see scientists scanning the basement stonework of the Red Lion, and the Cathedral itself to see the lost Star Stones of Preseli twinkling back at them. What a dream come true, that would be!

There are countless other Stonehenge mysteries waiting to be solved as the world of archaeology grapples with the mountain of information revealed by Prof. Vince Gaffney's recent lidar surveys of the ritual landscape around the monument. What does that massive orb of deep pits circling Durrington Walls represent, does it have some astronomical significance? Who knows, but I've no doubt there'll be more revelations in the months and years to come.

At least one pressing Stonehenge conundrum has been solved with north-east Scotland sensationally revealed as the source of the Altar Stone, which now lies broken at the heart of the temple, I've already expressed my belief the exceptional, northern powerbase represented by the Ness of Brodgar on Orkney, was dialled into the rest of these islands through blood ties, trade, diplomacy and a shared religion. I suspect temple stones were individually famous 'characters' in the litho-centric culture of the time, and I can imagine the Altar Stone being famous in its own right, before it was sent as an impressive gift to grace the new temple at Stonehenge. It's illuminating to realise the Altar Stone came from an area famed for its recumbent stone circles, one stone laid flat with two flankers like bookends, used to track the phases of the moon in particular. It wouldn't surprise me if the Altar Stone had featured in a famous recumbent circle in Scotland, before coming south to be laid flat in its Stonehenge setting too. That would explain the situation it's found in today and it would suggest the Altar Stone was always laid flat and didn't topple, instead the stones above cracked it when they fell onto the Altar Stone.

As far as the Altar Stone's transportation, maybe as far as 600 miles south to Stonehenge, is concerned the choice is simple, by land or by sea. No doubt the stone could have been sailed south along the North Sea coast, around to the Thames Estuary and up the Thames to its tributary, the Kennet, which gives access to Salisbury Plain. But I believe it's more plausible the Altar Stone was dragged south on a Barnabas Sled, and it occurs to me that a well-trodden path already existed, one followed by the drovers who brought Scottish cattle to Durrington Walls for the Solstice feasts.

Right up until the arrival of steam trains in the Industrial Revolution four thousand years later, drovers were moving cattle along the same route southwards to the lucrative markets of London and the south. Cattle on the hoof moved along this route at ten to twelve miles per day, suggesting the Altar Stone would have taken two months to arrive at Stonehenge by this means; perhaps towed along by cattle destined for the roasting spit and Durrington.

While we wait to hear more about the Altar Stone I'm sure the discoveries at Waun Mawn are just the tip of a Preseli archaeological iceberg, and more work will be done in those wonderful mountains. I'd love to see some enterprising team carry out a lidar survey of the estuary at Newport, focussing on the ancient harbour close to the Hen Castell, the Old Castle. I have a strong hunch there's a Neolithic hard waiting to be found somewhere close-by on the banks of the Nyfir. However, an obvious archaeological 'first' would be an investigation at the twenty-one Aubrey Holes at Stonehenge, which have never been excavated. Who knows what secrets they hold? It's a fair bet they may contain cremations buried in leather satchels, which may yield more links to Preseli and perhaps to Scotland and other, as yet undreamt-of geographies.

These would be fantastic projects for archaeology's up and coming personalities and then there's Bush Barrow. Surely, it's long overdue a visit by archaeology as nearly two centuries have passed since the Parkers, father and son, sank a shaft through its centre. The bones of the Stonehenge Giant lie there waiting to tell us his secrets, together with thousands of microscopic gold pins, and who knows what else waiting to be retrieved from the grave.

When Cunnington excavated Bush Barrow, he took the wonderful artefacts away, leaving the skeleton in the ground, with only the thousands of discarded, golden hilt-pins, left to accompany him into the afterlife. The presence of another skeleton below, was referenced in the dig journal and, who knows, that may well be the Stonehenge Giant's parent or grandparent.

Two skeletons then wait to be excavated, and I'd love to see a modern, technology-based investigation that might give us the answers to a whole host of questions. How did he die? Who was buried beneath him, and were they related? Was the giant a match for any of the cremation burials in Aubrey Hole VII? Does he have the tiniest trace of Preseli isotopes, or maybe some signatures from the North of Scotland linking him to the Altar Stone?

I'm fully aware that projects in and around Stonehenge require a mountain of paperwork to gain consent, but I know the renowned archaeologist Julian Richards has an ambition to see a dig at Bush

Barrow again, so I hope new research to delve into the Recoverable Past of our greatest monument begins sooner rather than later.

Rumours abound that a piece of the Upton Lovell Shaman's skeleton, perhaps that of the woman buried with him, has been found at the back of a drawer in some university archive or other and is currently being analysed. I really hope so, and I'm waiting with bated breath to discover if that's true. The strontium analysis alone of either of those remains, the Giant, the Shaman or his woman, would answer so many questions. Where did they come from, were they local or continental types like the Amesbury Archer? Had they been to Preseli, showing that long link between the two locations survived into the Early Bronze Age? Who knows, strontium analysis might tell us the Giant and his people came from Scotland with the Altar Stone.

The Stonehenge story I've tried to tell is one of the conjunction of time and place, unique artefacts and inspirational geology, but most of all it's a story of people, the story of the bold and innovative cultures who took over the tenancy of our most iconic monument during the four thousand years it served as the major centre of religion in Britain's prehistory.

On these pages we've met the Mesolithic hunter gatherers who stumbled across the Talon Marks of the Gods, aligned with the Solstice at Stonehenge. We've seen how Neolithic farmers arrived with dynastic connections to Preseli, which saw the geologically unique Bluestones conveyed to Stonehenge in the greatest logistic feat of British prehistory.

Sparkling like stars with mineral pins and cauda, the Bluestones must have evoked the great wheel of the universe in the minds of our ancestors, and they could be chimed to send celestial notes to the heavens. No wonder when they eventually crossed from the continent, the Beaker Folk, those metal workers of the Early Bronze Age, kept the Bluestones at the heart of Stonehenge while they developed their own, increasingly sophisticated phases of the temple.

Against this truly epic background, I've tried to inform the long life of Stonehenge within the context of a series of snapshots of the people discovered by archaeological excavations and, more recently brought to life by advanced isotope and genome science. It's difficult to comprehend

this five-thousand-year-plus story as anything but a series of disassociated human dioramas, yet I hope I've been able to gather the lives of the
Stonehenge players in a more cohesive way on these pages, bringing to
life some of the people who created such a place of splendour.

Along the way we've met some of the other players, ancient and
modern, in the Stonehenge drama. They're a diverse lot, ranging from
Antiquarians like Stukeley, Colt-Hoare and Cunnington to the inestimable trowel wielding John Parker. Charles Darwin, Halley of Comet
fame and Christopher Wren too, not forgetting modern archaeologists
like the two Mikes, Pitts and Parker-Pearson, together with the Wainwright and Darvill duo, Professors Josh Pollard and Vince Gaffney, and
the font of knowledge that is David Dawson of the Wiltshire Museum.

We've also seen the power of myth and oral history emerging as a
credible source in the study of prehistory, and one potent legend of
Stonehenge comes from the geologist William Judd in his 1913 Wiltshire
Magazine article about the monument, mentioned earlier in the book.
Judd isn't able to point directly at Preseli as the place of origin, that's a
mystery that would be solved a little later, but Judd had this to say... *The
old traditions (locally) concerning Stonehenge, that it consisted of a circle of 'bluestones,' which had acquired a certain sanctity in a distant locality and had been
transported from the original home of the tribe when it emigrated or was driven to
Salisbury Plain, or that it was a trophy of war, the larger monoliths being afterwards erected around the primitive, sacred stone circle.*

This concept of 'sanctity in a distant location' being referred to anec-
dotally in the Salisbury area, so close to Stonehenge, is spine-tingling.
The question is, just where did Judd hear these 'traditions' in the Salisbury area? They are incredibly prescient and accurate, and this account
also differs significantly from the Geoffrey of Monmouth legend, being
far more detailed and measured. I'd give my eye teeth to know where
Judd heard these traditions repeated as, on his own word, this mythology
is sourced in Wiltshire not Wales making it a remarkable fragment of
Tribal Memory in the Stonehenge scheme of things.

No surprise then, I champion the cause of a closer study of these
cultural vectors and urge historians to view the world's legends with
more positivity, seeking whatever truths are locked within them, rather

than dismissing them as primitive gobbledygook. That process has already begun but perhaps a new, formal branch of historical study might be appropriate, let's call it 'Lectofabology' the 'Reading of Fables,' teaching students to unravel legends that might be truth-bearing fragments rather than illogical figments of the imagination.

Writing this book has filled me with humility and unalloyed admiration for the way our ancestors approached their great works of astronomical observation and architectural endeavour with a generational commitment that is truly awe inspiring. They handed on the torch of inquiry and the flame of dedication with unwavering trust and confidence, not just for one or two generations, but through hundreds and sometimes more than a thousand years.

Descendants followed ancestors with the clan vision, watching the heavens and making their calculations with a humbling level of perseverance. Men like the Winterbourne Chieftain, the architects of Calanais in the Western Isles and the golden mathematicians of Stonehenge itself, who went about their work with an unwavering faith in the ambitions of their ancestors, and unquestioning trust in the resolve of the generations to come, to complete the vision: a life enhancing philosophy hard to comprehend in a 21st Century culture of instant gratification.

So many mysteries then, and some explanations too, but also an understanding there was a singular Stonehenge Culture able to accurately read the passage of the heavens, a people who were not in any sense superstitious savages, but a mathematically literate, quantum culture, who understood some of the deeper Fibonacci secrets of the universe and, it seems, may have expressed them on a landscape scale too, mapping out their architectural vision then executing it on the ground.

Emerging from the disparate streams of this narrative we have the compelling and ground-breaking story of the three Golden Protractors, revealed through the inspired mathematics and single-minded determination of Ivy Jiang. Those surveying instruments show Stonehenge to be a carefully planned solar and lunar observatory, with the Clandon Barrow Lozenge holding the precise measurements of the successive, concentric circles of the monument, giving credence to the notion the whole of the Greater Stonehenge complex, stretching for miles around the temple, was indeed an intentionally planned masterpiece of ritual landscape, mathematical genius and astronomical wisdom.

In my next and final chapter, I'm going to propose my own theory as to the origins of this fabulous font of astronomical and mathematical knowledge. I believe it came from a very long way away, indeed; some three thousand miles to the east.

19

STONEHENGE &
THE GATE OF SOULS

For a couple of years after reading Ivy Jiang's analysis, I puzzled and head-scratched over the nature of the math and astronomy inscribed on the gold of the exceptional Upton Lovell Button and the Bush Barrow and Clandon Barrow lozenges. The niggling question was where and how the New Stone Age and Early Bronze Age people who built Stonehenge came by such advanced empirical thinking. Eventually, I've come to my own, completely new theory about the provenance of the Stonehenge culture that created the temple, and I believe my theory may fundamentally change our view of British prehistory.

I arrived at my ideas simply by following the clues etched onto the Golden Protractors, revealed by Ivy Jiang, and exploring the nature of the thirty-six, equally spaced 'arrows' around the base of the Upton Lovell cone with its multiples of 10 and 5 degrees acknowledged and noted in her paper by Ivy. Interestingly, Ivy Jiang implies the sum value of the arrow markings are a total of 360 degrees but doesn't directly say so, although it's clear the Upton Lovell Button does have a 'dial' of 360 degrees represented on its base. Indeed, the Bush Barrow Lozenge reflects this same geometry as there are nine arrows inscribed on each of its four sides expressing 360 degrees within its heptagon and we have to ask ourselves whether this relationship can be coincidental.

But if you forget the math itself for a moment to consider its cultural provenance instead and look into the origins of the seemingly arbitrary division of circles into 360 degrees the links begin to tumble out and the circle is squared so to speak. Most of us have little or no idea about the origin of the 360 split, while the standard math teachers' explanation for the division says it was formalised around 200BC by the Greek mathematician and astronomer Hipparchus of Rhodes. However, the division of thirty-six, implied spaces of 10 degrees each on the Upton Lovell Button, was executed by a goldsmith on these islands some 1800 years earlier than Hipparchus, and I believe the thrilling solution to this cultural equation lies in the fact Hipparchus himself was relying almost exclusively on the ancient astronomical knowledge and math of the Sumerians, a civilisation first recorded in the explosion of farming, science and society in the Middle East.

In plain language Hipparchus pinched the 360-degree idea from the Sumerians, and made it his own, which leaves us with the question of just who were these inventive, and technologically advanced Sumerians. They first emerged in the mountainous southern corner of modern Turkey called Anatolia, some 3000 miles from Stonehenge, where they created the stunning, proto-civilisation represented by the 11,000-year-old stone temple of Gobleki Tepe and the first, recognisable city of Catalhoyuk. These evidently dynamic and resourceful people then colonised the lands to the south-east where they developed the earliest known agriculture in Mesopotamia on the deltas of the Tigris and Euphrates rivers, a region famously known to history as the Fertile Crescent.

Eventually, the Sumerian empire stretched across to modern Lebanon, Syria and part of Iran, but the epicentre of this cultural cauldron remained in Anatolia, and this was where the explosive, westward expansion Neolithic farming began. People with the Sumerian knowledge of grain cultivation who needed more land to cultivate, gathered on the migratory launch-pad of the Steppes of Asia Minor to the north of Anatolia, then began to colonise and farm pretty much the whole of Europe.

Agriculture wasn't the only Sumerian gift to mankind, as they also left a legacy of sophisticated astronomy and mathematics, notably with the formulation of the 360-day calendar from their observations of the cycle of the sun and moon. From this they extrapolated the 360 degrees dividing a circle, which represented the wheel of the heavens in their culture and then, in line with their sexagesimal, sixty-based system of maths, they bequeathed us the 60 second minute and the 60-minute hour, and all this was a very long time ago, perhaps as early as 6000BC. Neither should we forget the Sumerians formulated the world's first trigonometric table inscribed on a clay tablet known as Plimpton 322, currently held by Columbia University, New York Along the way the Sumerians also gifted us the wheel and the first organised cities before they were succeeded in the region by the Babylonians.

In the 18th Century the famous British astronomer Edmond Halley dubbed the Sumerian/Babylonian astronomical table the Saros Cycle from the Babylonian word *saru* meaning 360. The Saros Cycle relied on thousands of years astronomical observation, showing the extraordinary longevity of heavenly surveillance and star gazing in our deep past, and had already been in use for many centuries when it was referenced in a famous Sumerian poem, the Epic of Gilgamesh around 2000 BC.

Key to my theory about the Sacred Geometry of Stonehenge is the westward migration of Sumerian peoples and Sumerian ideas and in 2013 a genomic study carried out by the Natural History Museum and University College London, confirmed the Anatolian links to the Neolithic people who eventually migrated some three thousand miles to Britain. It was the descendants of these Sumerian migrants who swept away the Mesolithic hunter gatherer bands, like the Blick Mead folk, and eventually built Stonehenge, together with hundreds of other stone monuments across the British landscape.

A famous example of this Anatolian/Sumerian exodus is Otzi the Iceman, the Chalcolithic wanderer whose frozen remains were found on a mountain pass straddling Italy and Austria. Half-way to Britain, Otzi is symbolic of this link between the Sumerians and the western migration over the Alps to colonize the entire north-west of Europe, and research by the Max Planck Institute for Evolutionary Anthropology in 2023, found that only 8% of Otzi's DNA is European, while the other 92% is Anatolian farmer.

Another individual from that Neolithic/Early Bronze Age transition is the Amesbury Archer, whose home was in the Alps too, and while none of his DNA could be retrieved some was taken from his Companion buried nearby, and that has given us another genomic link, showing his family origins were on the Steppes of Asia Minor, that giant marshalling yard for the new metal working culture from Anatolia where folk gathered before the westward migration across Europe.

Otzi and the Amesbury Companion provide us with an undeniable genomic link across the great divide between Europe and ancient Sumeria, and there can be little doubt these migrants from Sumerian Anatolia, brought their knowledge of the heavens with them. Genetics provide us with a circumstantial case for the cultural osmosis of Sumerian astronomy along the length of the Neolithic exodus from Anatolia, and it's my contention the thirty-six arrows inscribed on the Upton Lovell Button and the Bush Barrow Lozenge are concrete proof Sumerian mathematics were brought to the British Isles through the two waves of Neolithic and then Bronze Age migration.

The three Golden Protractors from Stonehenge are not the only pieces of tangible evidence to back my theory Sumerian astronomy was the driving force behind the purpose and construction of Stonehenge. Exhibit Four is the world famous Nebra Sky Disc which, together with the two lozenges and golden button, draws the whole story together.

The Sky Disc was dug up by illegal metal detectorists in 1999 on the Mittelburg Hill, standing at the centre of a vast ritual landscape west of Leipzig, Germany; four hundred miles north of the Alpine pass where Otzi was found. Without detailing the criminal machinations of the case, the two thieves were caught trying to sell the Disc but were given reduced sentences after agreeing to lead archaeologists to the exact spot where they'd looted the artefact.

You don't need to understand its purpose to recognise the Sky Disc is an utterly beautiful object, a twelve-inch bronze disc with a blue-green Verdigris hue, elevated to the realms of the magical by representations of the heavens set in gold on its face. There are depictions of the sun, the moon, the passage of the Solstices, and the group of stars known as the Seven Sisters of the Pleiades; all superbly crafted around 1800 to 1600BC. It's said to be *the oldest concrete representation of astronomical phenomena, known anywhere in the world* and in 2013 it was deservedly added to the UNESCO register of the 'Memory of the World.'

The depth of astronomical knowledge gilded onto the disc is truly awe-inspiring, and its roots are undeniably in the Sumerian astronomical tradition. The makers understood the stars of the Seven Sisters are one pillar of a Sumerian cosmological portal known as the Golden Gate of the Ecliptic in the constellation of Taurus. This stellar gateway is called an asterism, where all the planets of the solar system, the sun itself and our moon too, pass along an elliptical line close to the Golden Gate, which the ancients represented as a heavenly path to the home of the Gods, sometimes known as the Gate of Souls.

The Golden Gate of the Ecliptic was first observed by the Sumerians, and they wove it into their culture and religion depicting it as one of their primary deities, a turtle god called Enki and the eventual destination of their souls after death. Once again, I propose this shows the influence of Sumerian astronomy on the Neolithic and Early Bronze Age of Northern Europe was huge, tangible and represented in one of the most feted and beautiful icons of our prehistory.

In itself the Sky Disc gifts us a vision of Europe's distant past and the beliefs and motivations of the people who inhabited the northern margins of the continent but that's still hundreds of miles away from Stonehenge, so where's the connection you may ask. Well, there are indeed absolutely tangible and spine-tingling connections between the Nebra Sky Disc and Stonehenge, drawn from a world of Tolkien-like myth, where long-ago miners panned for gold from an otherwise unremarkable Cornish creek, and incredibly it's this Cornish gold that provides a direct link between the Nebra Sky Disc and the Golden Protractors of Stonehenge.

Thrillingly, all four artefacts, the Sky Disc and the three Golden Protractors, were made with gold panned from the Carnon River in Cornwall, close to a place where the Fal River becomes estuarine at the modern Devoran Bridge on the road between Truro and Falmouth, a place I know well. Carnon River gold was the by-product of the nascent tin mining industry in the area, where deposits of the mineral cassiterite outcropped in the valley and were extracted by a technique known as tin-streaming.

Hardy men and women worked the river in fair weather and foul, using antler picks and wooden shovels, together with the hydraulic power of diverted, rushing water, to separate the heavy cassiterite, known as 'black tin,' from the lighter sediments in the deposits. More scenes from Erebor a couple of miles away at a place called Tremough, as foundry workers laboured over a round-house furnace to create flat ingots of tin about a foot square, from the egg-sized nodules of black tin. But those long-ago metal workers were also patiently harvesting the dust and small nuggets of gold revealed by the tin-streaming process on the Carnon River. Here, archaeologists found a deer antler pick, with a date matching the Sky Disc, and to emphatically seal the connection, the tin used to create the bronze for the 12-inch Nebra disc, as well as its gold decoration, also came from the Carnon River workings.

It's a humbling thought that enough Carnon Gold was accumulated through this laborious process to create a host of the most spectacular Bronze age golden artefacts across the Islands of Britain and Ireland, quite apart from the Sky Disc and the Golden Protractors. A stunning example is found in the gold-wire pins of the Bush Barrow knife hilt, and the most recent assay of the pins by Dr. Chris Standish of Southampton University through analysis of lead isotopes, show them to be 9 per cent silver, 0.48 per cent copper, and 0.0006 per cent tin. The rest is gold from Carnon and 'indistinguishable' from the precious metal used in a number of articles found in Ireland and Southern England, including many of the signature, crescent-moon shaped lunula. The same gold from Carnon too in examples of sheet goldwork like those found at the Knowes of Trotty on the Orkney Isles, and the Knockane Plaque in County Cork, Ireland.

This single source for so many golden artefacts leads to the obvious conjecture there was a stock of Carnon Gold securely held somewhere for trade, which was then drawn upon when high status Bronze Age men and women wanted to express their rank and wealth in the incorruptible, precious metal. Who this gold dealer was will never be known, perhaps the gold was stashed near Carnon itself, maybe it was held in Ireland or Wales. Who knows, what's left of the Carnon Gold is still waiting to be discovered, a pristine cache buried somewhere, literally the crock of gold at the end of an archaeological rainbow.

It's difficult to believe the communities, cultures, call them what you will, using precisely the same precious materials, in the same time frame, to create the Nebra Sky Disc and the Golden Protractors weren't communicating, at least at a priestly level. Surely, they must have been talking about the quality of gold and tin they were trading, and it's hard to believe they wouldn't' have discussed the transcendent wonders of the Golden Gate and the Seven Sisters of the Pleiades they were mapping in Cornish gold on their Cornish alloy Sky Disc. And surely, they would have been excitedly discussing the ambitious new phases of the state-of-the-art, astronomical temple and observatory at Stonehenge.

I suggest our Neolithic ancestors and then their Bronze Age successors, whose distant origins were in modern Anatolia, brought Sumerian astronomy with them as they moved inexorably across Europe until they arrived on the Islands of Britain. This offers a credible explanation for the advanced geometry and astronomy incorporated within the Nebra Sky Disc and the Golden Protractors, exemplified by the thirty-six 'arrows' of the Upton Lovell Button and the Bush Barrow Lozenge. I believe they are all inspired representations of the Sumerian calendar, compass and astronomical knowledge and I believe the same math gave us the 'nested squares' of the Stonehenge architecture.

Indeed, another ethereal link to the Sumerian/Anatolian tradition, may lies within the design of the Upton Lovell Button, which may have been a bracelet ornament; an idea proposed by modern Antiquarian Martin Doutré, resting on the similarity of the Upton Lovell Button to high status Sumerian, Babylonian and Assyrian bracelets. On the base of the Upton Lovell Button are two neatly incised holes, through which the ends of gold cords or twists can be threaded, allowing it to be worn on the arm or wrist. Typically, these cords were decorated with flowers, long tail hairs or feathers and sometimes with amber beads like those found loose in the Golden Grave and, of course, the two piercings in its base would allow the Upton Lovell Button to be used as the bob in a ceremonial plumb line.

THE UPTON LOVELL BUTTON

Note the finely executed arrows around the base of the stunning and unique Upton Lovell Button. There are thirty-six of them in all, making the Button and the related Bush Barrow Lozenge, the first known representations of the 360 degrees of a circle after the Sumerian 'planispheres' imprinted onto clay tablets with the sun as the centre of the circle.

(With grateful thanks to the Wiltshire Museum..)

If my contention is correct, and our ancestors did import Sumerian astronomical knowledge there are other implications and, as Prof. Gregg possets, it's likely the Stonehenge astronomers were able to predict both lunar standstills and solar eclipses through the methodology of the Saros Cycle; still in use today, and so reliable it features on the NASA website. I suspect the Stonehenge people could indeed predict those heart-stopping moments when the sun 'goes out' and still I have to pinch myself when I realise the priests of Stonehenge were arguably using precisely the same astronomy to predict eclipses of the sun and the moon as that used to this day by NASA.

What's certain is the evidence of the Golden Protractors and Nebra Sky Disc blows apart the accepted wisdom that our ancient forbears at Stonehenge, and other great dynastic monuments, didn't possess writing and therefore could not, and did not record their astronomical knowledge for posterity. In fact, they recorded their knowledge of the sun's passage and the moon's cycles precisely and in a way completely intelligible to 21st Century minds through the timeless language of mathematics. They did so diagrammatically and with great panache and stunning artistry in the form of the three Golden Protractors created some seven hundred years before the Ancient Egyptians achieved the same triumph of technology.

The Nebra Sky Disc and the Golden Protractors then are archaeological flash-drives and iconic cultural 'progeny' sharing the same DNA of Cornish gold and Sumerian math and astronomy. They give us the spine-tingling vision of a chain of ideas, fizzing with the electricity of ancient knowledge along the length of the Neolithic and Bronze Age migrations from Asia Minor, over the Alps and across Europe to our island home. In reality the Bush Barrow Lozenge, the Upton Lovell Button, and the Clandon Barrow Lozenge are quadruplets with the Nebra Sky Disc, all four sharing the same birth gold and all four should be part of the same conversation.

I contend the celestial wisdom of the Sumerians did arrive here in Britain with the first farmers, where it coalesced at the great temple on Salisbury Plain forging a connection between Stonehenge and the Cradle of Civilisation in Asia Minor. More than that, an understanding of the significance of these remarkable golden artefacts has transformative implications for our comprehension of the true majesty of the Stonehenge temple.

The three Golden Protractors are undoubtedly Britain's greatest, unsung prehistoric treasures, holding the Sacred Geometry of Stonehenge in coded form, and acknowledging this must surely exercise a paradigm shift on our view of Britain's pre-history and it's Pan-Continental nature, whilst recognising, the absolute, religious primacy of Stonehenge at its zenith. Little wonder then Stonehenge established itself as one of the paramount places of worship in the world of Bronze Age Europe, a cultural magnet attracting pilgrims from as far away as the Alps, and still a cultural magnet to this day.

In the meantime, my dreams are inhabited by Presli star-stone quarrymen, Cornish estuarine gold panners and bold Lithonauts who sailed Bluestone flotillas down moonbeams on the metronomic tide of the Bristol Channel. Visions too of great ceremonies at Stonehenge when torch-bearing priests passed among the mighty Trilithons, illuminating the ghostly white of the sarsen megaliths and lighting-up the star-scapes held within the Preseli stones.

And, in my mind's eye, I see the Stonehenge Giant striding to the Solstitial axis at the centre of the henge, gold-hilted knife at his waist, the regal sceptre crooked in his arm, while a priestess, draped in a shawl of dazzling amber attends on him. Nearby, a shaman and his enchantress evoke the gods of old, gone now beyond recall, until the Giant lays his Golden Protractor flat on the Altar Stone to take a ritual bearing on the sun. I can almost feel the electricity of it, and the groaning weight of anticipation before the Giant shows where the sun will rise once more, and the Star Stones start to chime as the great wheel of the universe turns again.

Imaginations and daydreams perhaps, and it matters not whether the players in my mind were synchronous for surely they were all in that sacred space at one time or another, and I suspect my oneiric 21st Century visions may not be so far off the mark, and oh, what a banquet for the senses it all would have been.

The End

GLOSSARY OF TERMS

Mesolithic: Literally the Middle Stone Age which, in Britain represents the final phase of hunter-gather culture and lasted here from around 10,000BC to 4300BC when farming people arrived on our shores after migrating from the Fertile Crescent of Asia, across Central Europe and the Iberian Peninsula.

Neolithic: The New Stone Age with a more sophisticated use of stone tools, particularly smaller microliths but more significantly the advent of systematic agriculture with fixed allotments of cereals and vegetables, together with herds of domesticated animals. It replaced the long era of hunting and foraging. The 'Neolithisation' of Northern Europe is believed to have been achieved by a rapid genocide of Mesolithic, hunter-gatherer peoples.

Chalcolithic: Also known as the Copper Age, it defines the time of transition from exclusively stone technology to the introduction of a metalworking culture. It's a relatively short period because the hardening of copper into bronze through the addition of tin was discovered quite quickly. It overlaps the Neolithic era and in Britain, like most such technological advances it took about 1000 years to cross the Channel from Europe.

Early Bronze Age: This is a much-debated time phase and seems to have been a melange of existing Neolithic culture and metal working technology of the Bell Beaker Folk who arrived her around 2500BC. It is characterised by the use of harder, bronze tools and the emergence of sumptuous gold jewellery and decorative items.

The Bronze Age: Around 1200BC the cross-fertilisation with the Neolithic was over and the culture was dominated by metal with huge copper mines developed in places like the Great Orme in North Wales. It was wealthy and vibrant time until there was a sudden, unexplained collapse in the bronze economy around 900BC. Climate change, invasion and revolution have been posseted as reasons for this decline. The Bronze Age was eclipsed by the arrival of much more durable iron with the Celtic influx around 700BC, establishing the Iron Age, beyond the scope of this book.

NEOLITHIC STONE ARCHITECTURE

Standing Stones: This largely speaks for itself and covers all stone structures erected by mankind. The architecturally different, man-made structures below all come under the general heading of Standing Stones.

Menhir: A large, solitary stone placed upright in the ground by prehistoric people with great symbolism. A menhir is synonymous with a Standing Stone.

Megalith: A large stone that's been used to build any prehistoric, sacred structure, whether standing alone or with other stones in a circle or a more complex structure such as a cromlech.

Cromlech: According to the Cambridge Dictionary it's *'an ancient group of stones consisting of one large, flat stone supported by several vertical ones.'* Some of these structures were once covered in rubble and earth making them the framework of a chambered tomb, others were not covered and were courtyard tombs where funeral remains were brought for reverence but not interred.

Dolmen: The Breton name for a cromlech, now in general use in Britain.

Quoit: The Cornish specific word for a dolmen, named after a medieval game.

Coetan: The Welsh word for a quoit, sometimes used to name dolmen in Wales as in Cornwall.

Trilithon: Two large, vertical stones or orthostats, which support a third stone set horizontally across the top and known as a lintel. In Britain this refers uniquely to the trilithons at Stonehenge.

Sarsen: Hard, silcrete rocks found in 'streams' on the surface across a large area of Southern England, particularly concentrated around the Marlborough Downs where they were sourced for the megalithic architecture of the World Heritage stone circles of Stonehenge and Avebury.

Bluestone: Intrusive, volcanic stone, consisting of dolerite and rhyolite, found in the rocky outcrops of the Preseli Mountains of Pembrokeshire, where they were sourced and carried 150 miles or more to Stonehenge.

OTHER PREHISTORIC STRUCTURES

Cursus: Cursuses are Neolithic and the earliest, truly monumental structures on these islands dating to around 3400BC. They consist of two, roughly parallel linear ditches with the accompanying trench, up to 100 yards wide, and stretch across the landscape anywhere from fifty yards to six miles in length. So named by the Antiquarian Stukeley, who mistook them for Roman horse racing courses, nearly sixty have been spotted in the UK through aerial surveys. The most notable cursus still visible, is close to Stonehenge.

Barrows: These are large, earthen mounds thrown up as graves for the internment of corpses or placing of cremation remains. Barrows come in various shapes with descriptives like Bell, Disc, Pond or Saucer Barrow. They were raised in profusion all over Britain around 3000BC and there was a particular explosion of Barrow building around Stonehenge.

Tumulus: Another name for a Barrow.

Cairn: This is the name given to a Barrow in the Celtic countries of Wales, Ireland and Scotland.

Tump: Another regional name for a Barrow, particularly in the West Country and Southeast Wales.

Henge: The technical, archaeological definition of a henge is a circular or oval enclosure defined by an outside ditch and bank. The earthwork bank is always outside the ditch meaning it cannot be a defensive structure but a symbolically sacred one. They may or may not enclose a stone circle and there are around one hundred twenty surviving henges in Britain with many more destroyed by agriculture.

Hard: A hard is a prehistoric landing place or wharf for ancient boats, often associated with the Neolithic and Bronze Age. Most usually constructed of wooden planking and hurdles, sometimes located on the outer edges of marshes and estuaries, occasionally connected to the mainland by causeways and bridges.

Acknowledgments

This book reflects my love of our Neolithic and Bronze Age past, ignited and informed by the alchemy of Stonehenge, the signature monument of those times. Consequently, there is a host of people I owe a debt of friendship and shared enthusiasm, but sadly too many to name all of them here.

However, there are a few whose help has been crucial to my endeavours, notably Mike Pitts, archaeologist, editor and writer, who has been a friend for many years and patiently explained many things archaeological over mugs of tea in the kitchen of his Wiltshire home. Hugely knowledgeable, I count him as my mentor in those early days of my fascination with the past. Another great guide has been David Dawson, Director of the Wiltshire Museum, whose knowledge, love and custodianship of the finest artefacts from the British Neolithic and Bronze Age is unsurpassed.

I've stood on the shoulders of many Stonehenge specialists who have my particular admiration, including Mike Parker-Pearson, the Darvill and Wainwright duo (Tim & Geoffrey), Josh Pollard, Julian Richards, Jacquie McKinley and Vince Gaffney. I've also been inspired by the archaeological writings of Francis Pryor. Between them they've magnified our knowledge of the monument, and I also recognise the tireless work of an army of dedicated backroom specialists who analyse the finds of archaeology. In combination, they have done so much to inform and illuminate the world of Stonehenge.

The Antiquarians, people like Aubrey, Stukeley, William Cunnington and Sir Richard Colt-Hoare are owed a debt of thanks for raising their eyes to Neolithic and Bronze Age horizons and opening ours, but it's the life of the illiterate, young farm labourer and first, true field archaeologist John Parker that most humbles and inspires me.

This book and prehistory in general are infinitely enhanced by the revelations made through the mathematical genius of the Jiang siblings and the equally impressive Stonehenge computations of Prof. David Gregg with his £20 engineering calculator, and I humbly acknowledge their keystone contribution to the ideas in this book.

Huge thanks, of course, to one of my oldest boyhood friends Captain Peter Binding of Trinity House and Barry Island, whose encyclopaedic knowledge of the Bristol Channel opened my eyes to the potential of the tide as nature's gigantic conveyor belt. I believe his contribution is pivotal to the Stonehenge transportation debate.

I must also thank Hefin Wyn of Cymdeithas Waldo - the Waldo Williams Society - for his reflections, and Waldo's niece Eluned Richards who kindly gave permission to use a stanza from her uncle's wonderful poem 'Cofio' – 'Remembrance' in a translation by David Sutton. Waldo is emblematic of the wonderful people of Preseli and their stand against the military who, but for them, would have obliterated sacred Preseli and cauterised our vision of Stonehenge forever.

Speaking of Preseli people, five star thanks to my friends Ed and Lou Sykes of the wonderful Llys Meddyg hotel and restaurant in Newport, Pembrokeshire who've hosted Stephanie and me on our forays around Preseli over the past decade. Diolch! Thank you!

During the writing process I was helped with advice and pithy critiques from my eldest son Harry, a publisher by profession, and my trusted friend Mike Ghent who read drafts and offered enthusiastic and insightful comment. Thanks are also due to Alyssa Larkin of Three Pools Publishing for her sterling work and production of the marvellous cover of the book.

Lastly, undying thanks to my partner and life's love Dr Stephanie Shelburne who has been a constant source of support and Native knowledge, and wholeheartedly shares my passion for stone circles, henges, barrows, menhirs, dolmens, sacred springs and the spirits that abide within them.

BIBLIOGRAPHY

ADDLEY, ESTHER. Transporting the bluestones of Stonehenge. Theguardian.com. Tuesday, February 19. 2019.

ALLEN, M, Chan, Cleal, French, Marshall, Pollard, Richards, Ruggles, Robinson, Rylatt, Thomas,, Welham & Parker-Pearson, Stonehenge's avenue and Bluestonehenge 10.15184/aqy.2016.98

BURLEY, PAUL D. Station Stones of Stonehenge - Megaliths with Sacred Intent. University of Minnesota. March 2012.

CHAMBERS: Myths and Mysteries. Anthology.

HISTORIC ENGLAND RESEARCH RECORDS. Monument Number 219856. Stonehenge Car Park Post Holes.

NICHOLAS, CLEMENT. PAILLER, YVAN. An Early 3D-Map of a Territory? The Bronze Age Carved Slab from Saint- Bélec, Leuhan, (Brittany, France) Oxford Journal of Archaeology. November 2021.

COTSWOLD ARCHAEOLOGY, Timeline: Neolithic henge at Vaynor farm, Carmarthenshire, Report. 29th April 2021.

CRASSARD RÉMY. THE OLDEST PLANS TO SCALE OF HUMANMADE MEGA-STRUCTURES PLOS ONE. Published: May 17, 2023

CRELLIN, RACHEL J, Materials in movement: gold and stone in process in the Upton Lovell G2a burial. Antiquity, Cambridge University Press. 16 December 2022. Rachel J. Crellin, Christina Tsoraki, Christopher D, Standish. Richard B Pearce. Huw Barton. Sarah Morriss. Oliver J. T. Harris.

CURRENT ARCHAEOLOGY MAGAZINE. October 10. 2016. Rethinking Durrington Walls: a long-lost monument revealed.

DARVILL, TIMOTHY. Stonehenge excavations 2008. September 2009. The Antiquaries Journal. 89(212):1-19 Timothy Darvill. Geoffrey Wainwright. DOI:10.1017/S0003581509000002X

DARVILL, TIMOTHY. Beyond Stonehenge: Carn Menyn Quarry and the origin and date of bluestone extraction in the Preseli Hills of south-west Wales Timothy Darvill & Geoffrey Wainwright. Antiquity 88 (2014) 1099-1114. http://antiquity.ac.uk/ant/o88/anto881099.htm

DARVILL TIMOTHY. Stonehenge: The Biography of a Landscape. Timothy Darvill. History Press. ISBN 10:0752436414.

DARVILL, TIMOTHY, Stonehenge 'No Place for the Dead, Phys.Org magazine. November 16th, 2006. DAVIS, R M, Selected Spring Sites in South-West England. University of Worcester, Published Online.

Darvill T. Keeping time at Stonehenge. *Antiquity.* 2022;96(386):319-335. doi:10.15184/aqy.2022.5

DEVEREUX, PAUL & WOZENCROFT, JON. Stone Age Eyes and Ears: A Visual and Acoustic Pilot Study of Carn Menyn and Environs, Preseli, Wales. Time and Mind · March 2014 DOI: 10.1080/1751696X.2013.860278

DUNKLEY, MARK. Travelling by water: A chronology of prehistoric boat archaeology/mobility in England. English Heritage

EVANS, J. A. Bronze Age childhood migration of individuals near Stonehenge, revealed by strontium and oxygen isotope tooth enamel analysis. J. A. Evans, C. A. Chenery, A. P. Fitzpatrick. Archaeometry. Volume 48. Issue 2. May 2006.

Quaternary Research. 2022; Edvardsson R, Patterson WP, Bárðarson H, Timsic S, Ólafsdóttir GÁ. Change in Atlantic cod migrations and adaptability of early land-based fishers to severe climate variation in the North Atlantic. 108:81-91. doi:10.1017/qua.2018.147

EVIRILL, PAUL. The Parkers Of Heytesbury: Archaeological Pioneers. September 2010. The Antiquarians Journal. 90 (28):441-453. Paul Evirill. The University of Winchester.

FITZPATRICK, A. P. The Amesbury Archer and the Boscombe Bowmen. Bell Beaker burials at Boscombe Down, Amesbury, Wiltshire

GARROW, DUNCAN. The World of Stonehenge. Duncan Garrow and Neil Wilkin. British Museum Publication. (in conjunction with eponymous 2021 exhibition) ISBN: 978-0-7141-2349-3

GREGG, DAVID P. The Stonehenge Code: A New Light on Ancient Science. Green Mann Books. 2014.

HISTORIC ENGLAND RESEARCH RECORDS, Coneybury Anomaly. Hob Uid: 855972

JIANG, IVY & EUGENE, Lozenge Circumscribed Stonehenge (July 2, 2021). Available at SSRN: https://ssrn.com/abstract=3909535 or http://dx.doi.org/10.2139/ssrn.3909535

LEWIS-WILLIAMS, DAVID. Inside the Neolithic Mind. David Lewis-Williams. David Pearce. Thames and Hudson. ISBN: 0-500-05138-0

LILLIE, MALCOLM. Prehistoric seafaring: Bronze Age sewn plank sea craft from the Humber Estuary, England, UK and their role in an island economy. University of Hull

LUND UNIVERSITY, Phys.Org. February 12, 2024. Scandinavia's first farmers slaughtered the hunter-gatherer population, DNA analysis suggests.

MARTORANO, MARILYN. Archeological Assessment of Lithophones of Great Sand Dunes Park and Preserve and the San Luis Valley, Colorado. Historical Colorado. State Historical Fund.

MCKIE, ROBIN. Stone Age Rope Weaving. theguardian.com Tuesday, 04 August. 2020.

MCLELLAN MANN, LUDOVIC, The art of the Cochno Stone. The Urban Prehistorian. May 1, 2018.

MONMOUTH, GEOFFREY OF. The History of the Kings of Britain. Penguin Classics. ISBN 13. 9780140441703

PRYOR, FRANCIS, Britain B C. Harper Collins. 2004.

PRYOR, FRANCIS, Scenes From Prehistoric Life. Head of Zeus Publishing. 2021

SOUDEN, DAVID. Stonehenge: Mysteries of the Stones and Landscape. English Heritage. TOLSTOY, NICOLAI. The Mysteries of Stonehenge, Amberley Publishing.

PARKER-PEARSON, MIKE et al. The original Stonehenge? A dismantled stone circle in the Preseli Hills of west Wales. Antiquities. Cambridge University Press. Online. 12 February 2021. Mike Parker Pearson, Josh Pollard. Colin Richards Kate Welham. Richard Bevins. Rob Ixer.

PARKER-PEARSON, MIKE. Stonehenge: Making Sense of a Prehistoric Mystery.

JACQUES, DAVID, PHILLIPS, TOM et al. Mesolithic settlement near Stonehenge: excavations at Blick Mead, Vespasian's Camp, Amesbury. Wiltshire Archaeological and Natural History Magazine. Vol 107. (2014) P7 - 27

LANDSCAPE & MONUMENTALITY. The Boles Barrow Bluestone. Posted March 18, 2018. No author cited.

MORRISSON, Tessa. *The International Journal of Critical Cultural Studies.* Volume 11. 2014.

NATIONAL LIBRARY OF MEDICINE Brace S, Diekmann Y, Booth TJ, et al. Ancient genomes indicate population replacement in Early Neolithic Britain [published correction appears in Nat Ecol Evol. 2019 May. 2019;3(5):765-771. doi:10.1038/s41559-019-0871-9

PARKER-PEARSON, MIKE et al Reconstructing extraction techniques at Stonehenge's bluestone megalith quarries in the Preseli hills of west Wales. December 2022. Journal of Archaeological Science Reports 46(31):103697. Mike Parker-Pearson. Richard Bevins. Nick Pearce. Robert Ixer.

PARKER-PEARSON, MIKE Archaeology and legend: investigating Stonehenge.. 30th December 2021. (electronic) Archaeology International. UCL Press.

PARKER-PEARSON, MIKE. Materializing Stonehenge: The Stonehenge Riverside Project and New Discoveries. Journal of Material. Volume 11. Issue 1 – 2. Mike Parker-Pearson. Josh Pollard. Umberto Albarella. https://doi.org/10.1177/1359183506063024

Pearson M. P, Chamberlain A, Jay M, et al. Who was buried at Stonehenge? *Antiquity*. 2009;83(319):23-39. doi:10.1017/S0003598X00098069

PARKER-PEARSON M, Pollard J, Richards C, et al. How Waun Mawn stone circle was designed and built, and when the Bluestones arrived at Stonehenge: a response to Darvill. doi:10.15184/aqy.2022.13

PEARSON M. P, Pollard J, Richards C, et al. Megalith quarries for Stonehenge's bluestones. 2019;93(367):45-62. doi:10.15184/aqy.2018.111

PARKER PEARSON, M, Pullen, R, Robinson, D, and Teather, A. Stonehenge for the Ancestors. Sidestone Press

PEARSON, M. P. (2013). Researching Stonehenge: Theories Past and Present. Archaeology International, 16(1). https://doi.org/10.5334/ai.1601

PITTS, MIKE. Hengeworld. Arrow Books. ISBN 978-0-099-27857-7

PITTS, MIKE. How to Build Stonehenge. Thames & Hudson. ISBN 978-0500024195

POLLARD, COLIN JOSHUA Welham, Kate Thomas, Julian, Richards, Parker Pearson, Mike. Craig Rhos-y-Felin. A Welsh bluestone megalith quarry for Stonehenge. Published by Council for British Archaeology, 2015 ISBN 13: 9781909990029

PRYOR, FRANCIS. Britain BC. Harper Perennial. ISBN 0-00-712693-x *Proceedings of the Prehistoric Society*

ROYAL ASTRONOMICAL SOCIETY. Stonehenge and Ancient Astronomy. http://ras.ac.uk/sites/default/files/2018-06/Stonehenge.LowRes.pdf

SARSENS. ORG. Musings and bookmarks about Stonehenge and related stuff. Saturday 24 November 2012 Stonehenge Periglacial Stripes

SOUDEN, DAVID Stonehenge: Mysteries of the Stones and Landscape. Collins & Brown. English Heritage. ISBN 1-85585-291- B

THOM, ALEXANDER. Cracking the Stonehenge Code. Alexander Thom. Robin Heath. Bluestone Press. ISBN: 978-0-9526151-4

UCAL, ASUDE. The harmonic healing houses of Turkey, The Psychologist. February 2021.

UNITED STATES FOREST SERVICE. Medicine Wheel/Medicine Mountain National Historic Landmark.

ROWLEY-CONWY P, Gron K J, Fernandez-Dominguez E, et al. A Meeting in the Forest: Hunters and Farmers at the Coneybury 'Anomaly', Wiltshire. *Antiquity*. 2022;96(390):1530-1537. . 2018; 84:111-144. *Antiquity* doi:10.1017/ppr.2018.15

VAN DE NOORT, ROBERT. (2009). Ch. 11: Exploring the Ritual of Travel in Prehistoric Europe: The Bronze Age Sewn-Plank Boats in Context. In Bronze Age Connections: Cultural Contact in Prehistoric Europe (pp. 159-175). Oxford: Oxbow Books.

WILLIS, CHRISTIE, Marshall, Peter, McKinley, Jacqueline, Pitts, Mike, Pollard, Joshua, Richards, Colin, Richards, Julian. Thomas, Julian. Welham, Kate. The dead of Stonehenge: Bioarchaeology. Published online by Cambridge University Press: 06 April 2016

WILLIS, CHRISTINA CATHERINE. Stonehenge and Middle to Late Neolithic cremation rites in mainland Britain (*c.*3500–2500 BC). Thesis submitted for the degree of Doctor of Philosophy University College London Institute of Archaeology 2019

WILLIS C, Marshall P, McKinley J, et al. *Antiquity*. 2016;90(350):337-356. The dead of Stonehenge. doi:10.15184/aqy.2016.26

About the Author

Alun Rees was born and raised on the Bristol Channel coast in Wales and enjoyed a long career in journalism as a staff correspondent for the Daily Mail, Daily Express and Mail on Sunday covering wars, disasters and major crimes. His awards include UK Campaigning Journalist of the Year. Alun is author of two military non-fiction best sellers and an historical non-fiction, *The Book of Sticks: Ancient and Modern*. He has lived near Stonehenge in Wiltshire for 45 years sharing time in the US with his American partner, and he's proud father of three adult children, respectively a publisher, an author and a soldier.

www.ingramcontent.com/pod-product-compliance
Lightning Source LLC
Chambersburg PA
CBHW062136040426
42335CB00038B/1162